Modernising British Local Government

John College

Also by John Stewart
The Nature of British Local Government
Management in the Public Domain

Modernising British Local Government

An Assessment of Labour's Reform Programme

JOHN STEWART

palgrave
macmillan

First published 2003 by
PALGRAVE MACMILLAN
Houndmills, Basingstoke, Hampshire RG21 6XS and
175 Fifth Avenue, New York, N.Y. 10010
Companies and representatives throughout the world

PALGRAVE MACMILLAN is the global academic imprint of the Palgrave
Macmillan division of St. Martin's Press, LLC and of Palgrave Macmillan Ltd.
Macmillan® is a registered trademark in the United States, the United Kingdom
and other countries. Palgrave is a registered trademark in the European
Union and other countries.

ISBN 0–333–96464–0 hardback
ISBN 0–333–96465–9 paperback

This book is printed on paper suitable for recycling and made from fully
managed and sustained forest sources.

A catalogue record for this book is available from the British Library.

A catalog record for this book is available from the Library of Congress.

10   9   8   7   6   5   4   3   2   1
12   11   10   09   08   07   06   05   04   03

Printed in China

Contents

List of Tables and Figures

Tables

Figures

Acknowledgements

As in all my books I have built my understanding of local government on work with and visits to local authorities and many discussions with councillors and officers. Academic colleagues have helped to strengthen that understanding and I would particularly mention Michael Clarke, George Jones, Steve Leach, Chris Skelcher and Stephanie Snape. My wife Theresa has been an important guide in the world of local government drawing on her experience as councillor, leader and lord mayor of Birmingham.

JOHN STEWART

1 Introduction: The Modernisation Programme

The modernisation programme and beyond

The Labour government elected in 1997 set out a programme 'to modernise' local government as part of a wider ambition to 'modernise' Britain for a new century. The government launched its modernisation programme in a series of consultation papers, firmed up in *Modern Local Government: In Touch with the People* (DETR, 1998a).

The government set out its concept of a successful 'modern council fit for the 21st century':

> Successful councils' priorities are to lead their local communities. They organise and support partnerships to develop a vision for their locality, and to contribute to achieving it. They strive for continuous improvement in the delivery of local services. They are committed to best value. They involve and respond to local people and local interests. Their relationship with local businesses and other local interests is strong and effective. There is trust between them and their local people. It is these councils, in partnership with Government and others, which are able to make real improvements to the quality of people's lives. (DETR, 1998a, p. 12)

To build this modern council, the modernisation programme, as set out in *Modern Local Government*, stressed three themes:

- community leadership or the role of local authorities working with their partners and with local people in meeting economic, social and environmental needs;
- democratic renewal building a new and active relationship between local authorities and their citizens; and

1

● improving performance in meeting needs and in providing services.

The main themes of the modernisation programme were legislated for in the Local Government Acts of 1999 and 2000. Community leadership was given expression through the powers of well-being and the duty to undertake community planning, described in Chapter 2. The main emphasis on democratic renewal was given to the new political structures described in Chapters 4 and 5. Improving performance was supported by the best value regime, described in Chapter 7.

The government's commitment to the modernisation programme was renewed by the 2001 White Paper, *Strong Local Leadership: Quality Public Services* (DTLR, 2001a). It initiated further changes directed at improving performance, including the comprehensive performance assessment described in Chapter 8. Proposals on local government finance were included in Modern Local Government, but were not covered by legislation until after *Strong Local Leadership* and the introduction of the Local Government Bill in 2002.

The government's analysis

The newly elected Labour government was committed to strengthening local government. The Labour Party had set out in its policy statement on local government (Renewing Democracy, Rebuilding Communities) a commitment to 'revitalise local government' and 'increase councils' power to act on behalf of local people' (Labour Party, 1995a, p. 2). Its 1997 manifesto said, 'Local decision-making should be less constrained by central government and also more accountable to local people' (Labour Party, 1997, p. 34).

The Labour Party had become increasingly committed to decentralisation in the period of the preceding Conservative government. That government had been responsible for a reduction in the role of local government, direct control over the expenditure of individual authorities and intervention in their workings through the requirement to submit many of their activities to competitive tendering. The Labour Party's commitment to decentralisation was in part because as the opposition it had attacked these measures as centralisation. In part, it was because Labour controlled or shared power in the majority of authorities. But beyond these considerations, there was an appreciation of the dangers of concentration of power caused by the removal of responsibilities from local people and their elected representatives.

While committed to building up the role of local authorities and giving them greater freedom to act, the government was at the same time deeply suspicious of local government, including many Labour-controlled authorities. The government proclaimed itself as New Labour, claiming to reject ideology in favour of a more pragmatic approach – 'What matters is what works' – and a process of modernisation. Many Labour-controlled authorities were seen as Old Labour in attitude and approach, accepting reluctantly, if at all, the policies of New Labour.

The government regarded many councils, of all forms of political control, as entrenched in an inward-looking culture. The government considered local authorities as too little changed in response to the needs of a changing society. Local councils were seen as seeking the restoration of the role and ways of working of local government as it had been before the Conservative government. The local authorities of the past were seen as enclosed organisations that focused on the producer rather than on the public or on partners who could work with them and that culture was seen by the government as still dominant in local government. That traditional culture was described in *Modern Local Government*:

> Too often within a council the members and officers take the paternalistic view that it is for them to decide what services are to be provided, on the basis of what suits the council as a service provider. The interests of the public come a poor second best. The culture is still one where more spending and more taxation are seen as the simple solution rather than exploring how to get more out of the available resources.
>
> In addition where the relationship between a council and its essential local partners – local businesses, voluntary organisations and other public sector bodies – is neither strong nor effective, that council cannot hope to lead its community

successively. Worse, such an inward looking culture can open
the door to corruption and wrongdoing.

Too often people are indifferent about local democracy, paralleling, and probably reflecting, this culture of inwardness.
(DETR, 1998a, p. 14)

The government considered that some authorities – a limited
few – had changed and modernised. There were excellent
authorities. 'Local government at its best is brilliant and cannot
be bettered' (Blair, 1998, p. 7). A few authorities were characterised as failing. The vast majority of authorities were seen as
neither excellent nor failing, but set in the traditional culture.
Modern Local Government summed it up. 'Overall, the picture is
one where the best councils are excellent, many councils need to
drive up their performance standards, and a few councils have
failed badly in key local services such as education and personal
social services' (DETR, 1998a, p. 13).

The dilemma for the government was how to reconcile
the stated commitment to strong local government with a deep
suspicion of many actual local authorities. The answer to the
dilemma was the modernisation programme presented by the
prime minister in terms that show both the commitment to local
government and the suspicion:

I want the message to local government to be loud and clear.

A changing role is part of your heritage. The people's needs
require you to change again so that you can play your part in
helping to modernise Britain and, in partnership with others,
deliver the policies on which this government was elected.

If you accept this challenge, you will not find us wanting,
You can look forward to an enhanced role and new powers.
Your contribution will be recognised. Your status enhanced.

If you are unwilling or unable to work to the modern
agenda then the government will have to look to other partners
to take on your role. (Blair, 1998, p. 22)

In effect, the government said, 'we will strengthen local authorities, but not as they are or as they have been, but only when
and if they have modernised and councils dominated by the
traditional culture have been replaced by councils "fit for the

21st century"'. The modernisation programme was designed to bring about the required change but the warning was there that if local authorities failed to change they would not merely not be given an enhanced role and new powers, but they could lose even their existing role and powers. The assumptions about the dominance of the traditional culture and the general suspicion of local authorities reflected in the quotation would be major factors in how the modernisation programme was implemented, giving rise to many of the problems identified later in the book

The views about the dominant culture and the judgements on authorities were based on assumptions rather than on analysis. While many would accept that there were weaknesses in the dominant culture, there were also strengths. Those concerned to bring about change should identify the strengths as well as the weaknesses, so that the former can be maintained, while overcoming the latter.

The book's approach

The book is based on the view that effective local government is necessary for the good government of society. The national system of government faces the problems of a complex and changing society. In responding to these problems, the hard truth has to be learnt that all ideas, all knowledge and all understanding do not lie in the corridors of Whitehall or even in Downing Street. The problems faced in society demand a learning system of government and effective local government is critical to building such a system. Effective local government has a value in its own right as a means of meeting the diversity of needs and aspirations, of relating national policies to local circumstances and of stimulating innovation and initiative at local level. Local government also adds value to the overall system of government, creating a capacity for diversity within the overall system of government. From the diversity both of response and of initiative by effective local government, learning within the overall system of government is enabled and enhanced.

Effective local government requires a significant scope for local choice, with local authorities able to respond to their particular problems, to take account of local conditions, but also to allow and stimulate initiative and innovation, building diversity within the system of government. Local government is, however, set within a national system of government that ensures the necessary uniformities of a national society. In any system of government a balance has to be achieved between necessary uniformity and desirable diversity. The right point of balance can be and is disputed. It is easier to identify imbalance than to identify the optimum point of balance. The book is based on the view that the limitation on the powers and resources of local authorities and continuing processes of centralisation, culminating in policies of the Conservative government from 1979 to 1997, had created imbalance in the overall system of government with a weakened local government and a limited capacity for diversity. This view leads to support for the three main themes of the modernisation programme, not so much because of the assumed need for change in the traditional culture, but because they contained the promise of building effective local government with a enhanced scope for local choice based on strong local democracy.

The book will analyse whether the modernisation programme and developments beyond can build that effective local government. The book takes as its starting point a model of the requirements of effective local government. Effective local government has a wide-ranging concern for the well-being of its area, with sufficient powers to give expression to that concern. It has significant scope for local choice, creating a capacity for diversity within the overall system of government. It seeks high and improving standards of performance. Its role and the scope for local choice are based on strong local democracy, enabling the active involvement of communities and citizens in the process of local government and grounded in strong local accountability. The system of local government finance supports that local choice and local accountability.

The book analyses the strengths and weaknesses of the modernisation programme against these requirements for effective local government. The three themes of the programme had potential for effective local government and are its main strengths. Community leadership could widen the role of local government, and enhance the scope for local choice. Democratic renewal could strengthen the basis of local government through an active relationship between the local authority and its citizens, legitimating local choice and the capacity for diversity. The commitment to improving performance is a necessary condition of effective local government in action. The main weaknesses lie in certain of the means used to give expression to the themes, in the way the programme was implemented and in limitations placed on the scope of the programme, which neglected central–local relations and the need for radical change in local government finance.

Against this background, the book describes the modernisation programme along with later developments both within the programme and beyond it. Where the programme developed out of or in reaction to past practice, that will be described so that the changes can be understood in context. As already indicated, the main themes of the government's modernisation programme are discussed in Chapters 2 to 9. Chapter 2 covers community leadership, Chapters 3 to 6 democratic renewal and related topics, and Chapters 7 to 9 aspects of improving performance. Chapter 10 deals with the structure of local government, left largely untouched by the modernisation programme but raised for the future by proposals for regional government. Chapter 11 presents central–local relations as still requiring modernisation, while Chapter 12 deals with the related topic of local government finance.

The main legislation on the modernisation programme described in this book applies to England and Wales, although on occasion, as set out later in the book, the Welsh Assembly has used its powers over secondary legislation to draw up regulations that modify the approach. The Scottish Parliament has introduced its own legislation, also described later. While following some of the main principles of the modernisation programme, the Scottish Parliament and Executive have adopted a more flexible approach over aspects of the programme.

In the Conclusion of the book an overall assessment will be made of the programme, judged by its impact in building effective local government. Strengths and weaknesses will be identified and proposals developed for building effective local government as a key element in a learning government for a learning society.

2 The Challenge of Community Leadership

Community leadership is one of the three main themes of the modernisation programme. It develops a role for local government based on a concern of local authorities for the well-being of the community that encompasses, but goes beyond, the services provided. That role has the potential to build local authorities better able to respond to the needs and aspirations of their community and if fully developed can provide a strong foundation for effective local government.

Enshrining in law

The government stated it would 'enshrine in law the role of the council as the elected leader of their local community with a responsibility for the well-being and sustainable development of its area' (DETR, 1998a, p. 80). It carried out this commitment through the Local Government Act 2000, giving all local authorities in England and Wales powers:

To achieve any one or more of the following objects

(a) the promotion or improvement of the economic well-being of their area,
(b) the promotion or improvement of the social well-being of their area, and
(c) the promotion or improvement of the environnmental well-being of their area. (s. 2.1)

These are commonly called the powers of community well-being. The same Act also laid a duty on local authorities 'to prepare

8

a strategy . . . for promoting or improving the economic, social and environmental well-being of their area and contributing to the achievement of sustainable development in the United Kingdom' (s. 4.1), which is widely described as the duty to undertake community planning. Similar provisions have been introduced by the Local Government in Scotland Act 2003.

It is difficult to overestimate the significance of these changes. There have been two different concepts of the role of local government:

> Local authorities are responsible for the provision of a series of services, many of them required by national legislation. Yet local authorities are also political institutions constituted by local elections with a capacity for local choice and local voice. Within the parameters set by these conditions, different emphases can be given to the role of local government. Local authorities can be seen as agencies for the delivery of a service . . . They can, however, be seen as political institutions constituted for local self-government with a concern for their area that extends beyond the services provided. (Stewart, 2000a, p. 26).

At different periods and in different areas, one or other concept has tended to dominate. In the late nineteenth century, the wider concept grew in importance as Joseph Chamberlain in Birmingham and other leaders in urban areas marked out a role for local government in meeting the challenges of industrialisation, using private Acts in Parliament to extend their powers (Hennock, 1973). Over time, as the responsibilities for the provision of major national services were laid upon local authorities, they came to be seen more as agencies for the provision of services in accordance with national legislation.

The concept of the role of local authorities as a political institution with a wide-ranging concern for the community and a capacity for local choice and local voice was never completely lost. The local authority as the elected council was expected to take the lead where major problems faced the area. When major disasters struck, the local authority played a leading role over and above its statutory requirements. Faced with serious economic problems and growing unemployment, local authorities developed a role in economic development, for which the

Conservative government eventually gave them specific powers, even if only in order the better to control their activities. Local authorities campaigned against the closure of local hospitals and local stations. Yet these were particular and spasmodic initiatives. The local authority was not organised to undertake the role of community leadership on a continuing basis. The authority's role was seen, almost wholly, as an agency for the provision of services. In that role local authorities came to see themselves as self-sufficient, employing all the staff required for the delivery of the services, without any need for partnerships with other organisations, except in clearly defined activities.

In much of Europe there is a different concept of the role of local government. Local authorities are first and foremost communities governing themselves. They have the power of general competence or the power to act on behalf of their communities beyond the powers given by specific legislation. That power is not an add-on to other powers, but derives from the concept of local government; local authorities as communities governing themselves naturally have the right to act on behalf of local communities, except where it is specifically barred by law. As Philip Blair, an official of the Council of Europe, wrote, the power of general competence

> bolsters the conception of the municipality as a general political authority that acts in its own right to foster the welfare of its inhabitants and confronts whatever problems arise in the local community. It encourages the citizen to see in the local authority not one agency among many for carrying out administrative tasks, but the corporate manifestation of the local community (*collectivité locale*) which is the first resort in the case of difficulty. (Blair, 1991, p. 51)

This concept of local government has important consequences. The identity of the local authority comes from the community and not from the services provided. This concept has implications in Europe for the size of local authorities, with many being much smaller than in the United Kingdom, being built on felt communities. There are implications too for the means of service provision, with a greater readiness to work with and through other authorities and other organisations. It must not be assumed, however, that the concept of local government as community leadership is opposed to local authorities' role in service provision. Community government is a wider and more embracing concept. The role means that authorities have a concern for community well-being that extends beyond the services provided but those services remain important means for securing that well-being.

There have always been advocates of the role of local government as community leadership. Committees of inquiry into local government have stressed the role. The Bains Report asserted, 'Local government is not, in our view, limited to the narrow provision of a series of services to the local community, though we do not intend in any way to suggest that these services are not important. It has within its power the overall economic, cultural and social well-being of that community and for this reason its decisions impinge with increasing frequency upon the individual lives of its citizens' (Bains, 1972, p. 6). The role was not recognised in legislation beyond the powers given by section 137 of the Local Government Act 1972 (as later amended by the Local Government and Housing Act 1989) which enabled authorities to spend a limited amount of money that 'in their opinion is in the interests of and will bring direct benefit to their area or any part of it or all or some of its inhabitants'. These were the powers used to build the role of local authorities in economic development. But an explicit statutory base was lacking for the role of community leadership, even though local authorities were increasingly developing that role. Community leadership should not be seen as a role imposed by central government on reluctant local authorities, but as an aspiration by local authorities. The role has been developed as a response to issues faced by the system of community governance, by which is meant the complex processes through which local communities are governed.

The rationale for community leadership

Some see the development of community leadership by local authorities to be a response to the reduction of their role in service provision, as basic services have been transferred to appointed boards, as transfers have taken place of housing stock and residential homes or as local authorities contracted out the delivery of particular services under the impact of the Conservative government's legislation on compulsory competitive tendering. At the same time, financial cutback and constraint have made local authorities search for other resources, seeking partners who can bring those resources to bear on community problems. Many of the area-based initiatives launched by both the Conservative and Labour governments required bids showing evidence of partnership working. These developments challenged the assumption of the self-sufficient authority or the authority that assumed it could itself discharge all its responsibilities through its own organisation and with its own resources.

These reasons for the focus on community leadership reflect the weakening of local government. There are more positive and more important reasons. Recognition of the challenges faced by local communities led authorities to develop a new role or to rediscover a former role. Local authorities became aware that many of the most pressing, but also the most difficult issues – the so called wicked issues – could not be resolved by any single organisation. These issues include, but are not limited to:

● the environmental issue and the hope for sustainable development;
● crime and disorder and the hope for safer communities;
● discrimination and the hope for a fairer society; and
● social exclusion and the hope for more meaningful lives.

The word 'wicked' was first used about 'problems' which were contrasted with 'tamed problems' (Rittel and Webber, 1973). Tamed problems were problems well-understood to which the response was clear and for which responsibility could normally be securely placed within a single organisation. Even where more than one organisation was required to deliver the response, those requirements could be clearly specified for each organisation concerned. Wicked issues are issues imperfectly understood, whose causes are not clear and to which the response has to be worked out in uncertainty. 'Wicked' is being used as a mathematician or a crossword puzzle addict might use it to describe a difficult or even intractable problem.

Many organisations can be involved in wicked issues since the response and hence which organisations are involved cannot be predetermined. Wicked issues are cross-cutting issues which cannot be treated in the same way as tamed issues where the response required from each organisation is clear and for which each can be given a defined responsibility. With wicked issues the response has to be worked out and evaluated, adapting and modifying as learning proceeds. Interaction between organisations is a necessary part of the learning process.

Many towns and cities have faced and face major economic change, as do rural areas. Towns based on shipbuilding, mining, textiles and steel have seen their industries collapse. Many towns have seen their shopping centres decline as out-of-town shopping centres developed. New technology both threatens and gives opportunities. Areas in strategic locations face overheated pressure on their environment and on their social and physical infrastructure. Rural areas face challenges to agriculture and to the industries built around it. Economic change brings social problems, as the costs of economic change are not borne evenly by different groups in society. The infrastructure and the local environment formed by past necessities are challenged by both economic and social change.

Each town, each city and each rural area has to find new opportunities and new roles. These differ from area to area, as each has its own heritage, its own present condition and its own possibilities for the future. Some towns and cities aspire to play an international role, others to be regional centres. Some see their future as cultural centres, while others find opportunities given by new technology. Some seek to revive the town centre. Others balance economic growth with conservation of the environment that attracts it. National policy can set a framework in which urban and rural futures can be worked out, but central government cannot itself work out the future for each area. The future has to be worked out at local level. Nor can the local authority work out the future alone. It requires many public agencies, the private and voluntary sectors and local communities to take action, but also to learn and to adapt as experience develops.

The wicked issues and urban and rural transformations are faced by a fragmented structure of community governance in which responsibility is divided between many different public or quasi-public agencies. There has been no more misleading phrase than 'unitary authorities' to describe single-tier local authorities. If one asks 'who governs?' in the area of a unitary authority, the answer will include the local authority, but also the strategic health authority, the health trusts, the primary care groups or trusts, the boards of governors of sixth form colleges and further and higher education institutions, the Learning and Skills Council, the police authority, Connexions, joint boards for services such as fire and public transport and the housing associations that play an increasing role in social housing; all this without mentioning the many agencies of central government playing a vital role in the life of an area. Together these organisations deploy more resources than the so-called unitary authorities. Wicked issues and urban and rural transformations require a response from many or all of them.

The structure is not described as fragmented because it is split into different organisations. Any organisation or any system of government will be differentiated, but any organisation or system of government has to have a capacity for integration. The system of government is fragmented because it is highly differentiated without a requisite capacity for integration. Community leadership by local authorities should enable the necessary integration to respond to community problems. Community leadership brings together partners in the public sector and in the private and voluntary sectors for that response. Community leadership rests upon the local authority as the elected body, but also as a multi-functional body with responsibility for the 'multi-valued choice' (Vickers, 1972), differing from single-purpose organisations with necessarily more limited perspectives.

The government argued:

Councils are the organisations best place [*sic*] to take a comprehensive overview of the needs and priorities of their local areas and communities and lead the work to meet those needs and priorities in the round.

Modern Britain faces a number of key challenges at the end of the twentieth century. Concerted action at local and national level is needed to address issues such as sustainable development, social exclusion, crime, education and training.

Councils are at the centre of local public service and local action to tackle these difficult issues. They have a wide range of diverse responsibilities which contribute to all aspects of their local communities, bring them into day to day contact with local people and which in many cases require them to work in partnership with others successfully.

So councils are ideally placed to work with government, their communities and the wide range of public, private and voluntary sector bodies who operate at local level and who need to come together if these challenges are to be successfully addressed. (DETR, 1998a, p. 79)

There is another theme in community leadership – the involvement of the diverse communities and of the people who constitute them. The word 'community' can mislead, if it is taken to mean that in any area there is one community, rather than many communities. There are communities of place, but also communities of interest, concern and background. The map of communities is marked out by bonds of cooperation, but also by lines of conflict and competition. Community leadership has to respond to the diversity within the area and not assume a false consensus or seek to impose a uniformity of approach.

The need for an authority to get close to the communities within and to its citizens should be a driving force in community leadership. Community leadership is meaningless if it is not based on communities and citizens, first because the problems and issues identified by that leadership must be those felt and known within communities. Second, many of the most difficult issues faced can only be resolved if people change their way of life and patterns of behaviour. Third, and perhaps the most important, community leadership in response to problems faced requires the capacity for innovation and initiative that lie within communities and with citizens. Community leadership should aim to release that initiative and innovation. The need to involve communities and citizens is important for community leadership as well as for the general work of authorities and is explored in the next chapter.

The powers of well-being

Community leadership has been 'enshrined in law' by the new powers of well-being. The powers are wide-ranging and go far to meet the aspirations of those who sought powers of general competence for local government. Some have been disappointed that the legislation has not abolished the doctrine of *ultra vires* that a local authority cannot act beyond its powers. What the legislation has done, however, is extend those powers so that they approach the powers of general competence in most European countries.

The government's guidance states:

> The breadth of the power is such that councils can regard it as a 'power of the first resort'. Rather than searching for a specific power elsewhere in statute in order to take particular action, councils can instead look to the well-being power in the first instance and ask themselves:
>
> ● Is the proposed action likely to promote or improve the well-being in our area? . . .
> ● Is the primary purpose of the action to raise money? . . .
> ● Is it explicitly prohibited on the face of other legislation? . . .
> ● Are there any explicit limitations and restrictions on the face of other legislation?
>
> If the answer to the first question is 'Yes' and the answer to the next two questions 'No', then a council can proceed to the fourth question, i.e. any restriction or limitation that may apply by virtue of being spelt out on the face of other legislation. (DETR, 2000a, pp. 2–3)

This extract highlights both the potential and the limitations of the power, for the Act both gives the power and places limits on its use. In addition, it gives the Secretary of State powers to impose further limits, although there is no present intention to use those powers. Limitations are not necessarily to be objected to. The powers of general competence in Europe are not unlimited. Such powers cannot override national laws. A local authority cannot use the power of general competence to escape from a statutory constraint. The similar limitation on the power of well-being is reasonable, provided it is interpreted by the courts as covering only explicit limitations on the face of the legislation.

The most serious limitation was the apparent prohibition on raising money. While it would certainly be acceptable to deny authorities the right to use the power to raise new taxes that should require specific legislation, the limitation appears to prevent a local authority charging for a service to cover costs.

There was, however, uncertainty as to the government's intentions. The guidance suggests a more limited restriction in the question 'Is the primary purpose of the action to raise money?' The Local Government Bill introduced in 2002 has clarified the position, giving authorities a power to charge for discretionary services including those provided under the powers of well-being.

The power does not permit a local authority to prescribe regulations. The government argues that 'the power should be used to take positive action that promotes community well-being' and that 'it is usual to require specific provision for such regulatory rules . . . Local authorities should, therefore, continue to rely on their existing range of powers to create by-laws' (DETR, 2001a, p. 14). A by-law is a law covering the area of the authority, made by it under powers given by statute. The use of these powers is, however, subject to confirmation by government ministers. Central government departments draw up models for by-laws and confirmation is unlikely to be given to by-laws that depart substantially from the models or are innovations outside the topics covered by the models. The government's approach to by-laws restricts the ability of local authorities to promote the well-being of their area. Recognition of the role of local authorities in community leadership should lead to a greater readiness by central government to confirm by-laws to resolve local issues, even if they do not conform to the model by-laws.

The new powers of well-being are instruments to be used in support of community leadership. Local authorities have to extend their thinking if they are to be fully used. Existing thinking inevitably tends to be constrained by existing activities, themselves based on existing powers. When local authorities in the past have been asked how they would use new powers, they have had few suggestions to put forward, leading past governments to argue that such powers were unnecessary. Local authorities were answering the question in terms of present rather than future activities. The new power has to be interpreted in the light of the role of community leadership. The Local Government Association publication, *Powerpack*, contains useful suggestions on the use of the power – removing graffiti from privately owned buildings; pooling funds to carry out regeneration; providing new services to schools (LGA, 2000a) – but even these are related to existing activities.

Full use of the new power requires new thinking beyond objectives set by existing activities and responsibilities. The use of the power should be related to the needs and aspirations of communities over and above existing activities and objectives. The development of community strategies should stimulate the new thinking required. The powers are a contribution that local authorities bring to the achievement of these strategies and to their role in community leadership.

Community planning

The role of community leadership is also enshrined in law by the duty to prepare community strategies. Unusually, but wisely, the government has said it does not intend to specify the content of these strategies in detail. Guidance has been issued covering general principles, although at times the guidance goes into a degree of detail that seems to belie the intention. Community planning should:

- engage and involve local communities;
- involve active participation of councillors;
- be prepared and implemented by a broad 'local strategic partnership' through which the local authority can work with other local bodies; and
- be based on a proper assessment of needs and the availability of resources. (DETR, 2000a, p. 7)

The guidance sets out stages in the development and implementation of the strategies:

- establishing a vision;
- resource and activity analysis;
- establishing priorities;
- establishing an action plan;
- delivering community priorities;
- coordinating and rationalising local activity;
- monitoring systems;
- measuring progress; and
- reviewing and modifying the strategies. (DETR, 2000a, pp. 22–9)

The process of community planning should not start with a vision as the guidance suggests. Visions should not spring anew, but should be based on an understanding of needs, problems and opportunities. Building a shared understanding of the issues faced by local communities should be the starting point in developing a local strategic partnership. That shared understanding can ensure the authority and its partners act against a common background in their separate activities.

There is a danger that the visual emphasis implied by the word 'vision' will concentrate attention on physical development, to the neglect of social issues. More dangerous still is the assumption that a vision for ten or twenty years ahead can or should be foreseen, since it makes no allowance for the changes that will take place in the future or the uncertainties that lie in the present. A vision drawn up twenty years ago would not have taken account of the growth of the Internet or the extent of globalisation. The danger is that visions are more often based on the assumptions of the present rather than on those of the future. Such visions can lead to actions that close off options by steps taken to achieve a future that can prove to be unattainable, or if attainable irrelevant to the needs of the future. The one thing that can be said with certainty about the vision for an area in the year 2020 is that the area will not be like that in 2020. The guidance states that the vision must include 'some explicit outcome targets' (DETR, 2000a, p. 22). If they are achieved twenty years ahead, it could mean that other more relevant, but unforeseen, outcomes have been neglected.

A sense of direction probably conveys better what is required than a vision, which suggests a fixed end state. A sense of direction requires looking ahead, but allows for uncertainty and does not assume that fixed end state. Yet the word 'vision' cannot now be avoided; it is too firmly embedded in the discourse of both central and local government. So, reluctantly, I will use the word in the discussion of community planning that follows. Emphasis on the dangers should nurture awareness that visions can blind, if they give an impression of certainty rather than being regarded as working hypotheses that require continuing modification over time.

In some of the early developments in community planning (Rogers, 1998) the emphasis was on needs and opportunities, visions and priorities for action. There was little or no reference to resources, yet resources provide the means by which community strategies will be achieved. Unless community strategies lead to change in the use of resources, they will have no real impact. Changes in or better use of resources provide the cutting edge for community strategies. If in a shire area, county, district and health authorities and the voluntary sector consider together the financial resources used for the care of the elderly, it is almost certain that better ways will be found of using those resources than if each organisation considers its use of resources separately.

Resource analysis is a key instrument for community planning. Resource analysis should cover not just financial resources, but also staff and their skills, property, information and powers and activities. As the guidance states:

> Councils and their partners should carry out an analysis of their own expenditure, staffing, and skills in relation to the priorities and objectives identified by the strategy. The deployment of both revenue and capital resources should be examined to determine whether, considered jointly, they are being used in the most effective and sustainable way. The aim should be to establish where there are gaps, overlaps or contradictions in resource use. (DETR, 2000a, pp. 22–3)

Unless resources are pooled, each organisation still has to make its own decisions on resource use, but those decisions can be informed by the resource analysis carried out for community planning.

A community strategy should be selective when it focuses on action. If a community strategy seeks to be comprehensive, it will become not a means to action, but a barrier to action. If everything is strategic, then nothing is strategic. The community strategy should set agreed priorities for action. That is not easy; in reaching agreement the temptation is to add to priorities so that all are satisfied. But unless the number of priorities is limited, effort will be dispersed and the strategy will be ineffective. Once priorities are agreed then action plans should be prepared. These action plans should indicate where responsibility for the action lies and which organisations should play the lead role for each priority.

Community planning should not be a fixed process ending with the adoption of the community strategy. Community planning should be a continuing learning process, sensing changing problems and opportunities, monitoring actions and outcomes, reviewing priorities and gaining a new sense of direction, or a new or modified 'vision'.

Issues to be faced

The leadership role

The statutory responsibility for preparing the community strategy is placed on the local authority. Unfortunately no statutory responsibility for cooperating in community planning has been placed on other public bodies in England and Wales, although it has been in Scotland. A local authority would be unwise to assume that its statutory responsibility means it must take the lead on every issue in community planning. The local authority should be the catalyst and stimulus for community planning, ensuring that the process is shared. In pursuing particular priorities and implementing an action plan, it will often be appropriate for other organisations to take the lead where they have the most to contribute. It will not be easy for a local authority to achieve the right balance in the leadership role. The local authority has the statutory responsibility for initiating the process, building a local strategic partnership, seeing that the community strategy is prepared and ensuring the vitality of the process, yet this has to be done in a way that creates ownership of the process by its partners.

Local strategic partnerships

The government regards forming a local strategic partnership (LSP) as a necessary first step in building the process of community planning, although LSPs are not specifically referred to in the legislation which merely states that 'in preparing or modifying their community strategy, a local authority . . . must consult and seek the participation of such persons as they consider appropriate' (Local Government Act 2000, s. 4.3). The guidance on LSPs describes them as 'a single body that brings together at a local level the different parts of the public sector as well as the private, business, community and voluntary sectors, so that different initiatives, programmes and services support each other and work together' (DETR, 2001b, p. 15). The concept emerged in the development of the government's policies on social exclusion and has been adopted in the guidance on community planning. Local strategic partnerships have also been given responsibility for delivering a local neighbourhood renewal strategy, reflecting the origin of the concept.

There is an ambiguity in the role of LSPs. The guidance puts them at the centre of the community planning process (DETR, 2001b, p. 30) but the statutory responsibility for the process rests upon the local authority. The government regards local authorities as having 'a particular responsibility towards LSPs'. They should be 'the prime movers in instigating LSPs' although the local authority need not chair the LSP. *Strong Local Leadership* makes clear that whoever chairs, the local authority retains responsibility for the effective working of the LSP: 'This is a key part of every councils' [*sic*] responsibility as community leaders' (DTLR, 2001a, pp. 18–19).

The guidance recognises the growth in the number of partnerships at local level, as government initiatives have required their formation. The growth of partnerships can almost be described as the latest form of fragmentation as different organisations join together to form another organisation. There are complaints from the private and voluntary sectors of partnership overload. One role for LSPs, as an overarching partnership, is to review the multiplicity of partnerships.

Partnerships to consider wide-ranging community issues had already been constituted in a number of authorities well before the election of the Labour government, providing a basis for LSPs. The Liverpool Partnership Group was created in the early 1990s as a result of Liverpool's urban programme and regeneration. The Leeds Initiative began in 1990 as a partnership between the council and the chamber of commerce, focused on economic development, the city centre and promoting Leeds as a European city, but gradually widening, both in scope and membership (LGA, 2001b).

The government argues that 'The membership and size of a local strategic partnership should reflect both its aims and the breadth of issues that might fall within its scope' (DETR, 2000a, p. 11). The number of organisations that are included in LSPs varies. The guidance on LSPs, while recognising that membership can and should vary with local circumstance, nevertheless suggests that public sector members of LSPs could include:

- local authorities (including social services and education);
- health authorities and other members of the health community;
- the police;
- the probation service;
- drug action teams;
- the fire service;
- education (at all levels, including higher and further education);
- local Learning and Skills Councils and the new Connexions service;
- the Employment Service and the Benefits Agency;
- the Small Business Service;
- legal services or other members of community legal service partnerships;
- housing providers (including registered social landlords);
- culture, sporting, historic environment and tourism agencies;
- the Environment Agency;
- the Highways Agency;
- passenger transport executives. (DETR, 2001b, pp. 55–6)

With regard to the private sector, the guidance advises that 'engaging with the business community means working with representative groups, but also going beyond them' (p. 57). The community and voluntary sectors should also be involved, recognising that these sectors 'are diverse with differences in the nature, scale and support needs of groups' (p. 58).

The size and complexity of the list poses problems for LSPs. In Bournemouth the partnership included 94 organisations. Others included fewer, but still a significant number. In Croydon there were twenty organisations in the partnership, and the intention was to include more, reflecting the aim of including as many interests as possible (LGA, 2001b).

Even with these numbers there is a danger of an LSP being an 'exclusive clan' (Osborne, 2000, p. 45). A representative organisation such as a council for voluntary service may not represent all relevant bodies. Mutual dependency between the local authority and the representative organisation may be a barrier to wider representation, since the representative body could consider itself undermined if separate places were given on the LSP to bodies within its scope but outside its membership.

With large numbers an LSP can become a mass meeting, rather than a partnership in which all are fully involved in drawing up the strategy and equally committed to it. The public sector organisations can dominate by numbers and by resources. Almost inevitably there will be an inner and an outer group, which may be given recognition in an executive or working group reporting to the full LSP. The danger is that the LSP then becomes a talking shop or a meeting to rubber-stamp conclusions reached elsewhere. Yet in preparing the community strategy it is inevitable that the local authority with other key actors will play the leading role. If disillusion is to be avoided, much will depend on the way other partners are involved in the work of LSPs and on the style adopted by the local authority and other members of any inner group.

Problems of LSPs as partnerships

An effective LSP is not easily achieved. A variety of organisations with different interests and with different degrees of commitment to the process have to be brought together. Each organisation has its own structure, its own responsibilities, its own way of working, its own culture and its own system of accountability. An investment of time and space is needed to build up understanding of each other's organisation and interests, and of the process of community planning. LSPs require an equal investment in sustaining them as in building them up. There are problems in securing a continuing commitment to the process of community planning as it develops over time. There are issues of how the partnership is accountable, whether directly or through the accountability of the partners. If the latter, then different accountabilities have to be reconciled. LSPs, far from clarifying accountability, can confuse it, reflecting a general problem for partnerships. Partnerships can weaken accountability, enabling organisations to pass responsibility to the partnership, which is itself not clearly accountable and often less visible than the separate organisations that constitute it.

A special responsibility, although not the sole responsibility, rests upon the local authority in building and in sustaining the process. Local authorities will need skills in the management of cooperation that do not always come readily to authorities whose management experience has been built around direct control of services. A local authority has to learn new ways of working in LSPs and in partnerships generally. The approaches used in organisational hierarchies or in the management of contracts are not appropriate for LSPs. The management of cooperation requires attention to the workings and the interests of the partners, but those involved in partnerships have also to pay attention to their own organisational base. Otherwise those who have to implement what is agreed in partnerships can feel remote from the process. The management of cooperation brings its own challenge to management development. Local authorities could at times require the combined skills of:

● contact people to open up relations;
● mappers of conflict and consensus;
● interpreters who can read and speak the languages of other organisations;
● consensus builders;
● builders of relationships;
● networkers who sustain and develop multiple contacts;
● project managers who can guide action;
● inter-organisational understanding in reading other organisations;
● the management of influence; and
● listeners who hear the unfamiliar and unexpected.

Partnerships are rarely equal partnerships. As partnerships develop over time, it becomes clear some partners have more influence and more power. As Newman says:

The discourse of partnership speaks of equality, shared values and high trust creating an illusory unity, which masks fundamental differences of power and resources and directs attention away from the need to engage with the gritty political realities of divergent interests and conflicting goals. Naïve or optimistic views of partnership focus on what the partners have in common and ignore power differences and inequalities.

The history of relations between the voluntary and statutory services is littered with examples of the difficulties resulting from power inequalities. (Newman, 2001, p. 117)

The guidelines make no reference to power, or to the possibility of conflict. They can be regarded as giving expression to Newman's 'naïve or optimistic views'. The guidance on LSPs specifies six criteria for accrediting them for the neighbourhood renewal fund discussed later:

- they are effective, representative, and capable of playing a key strategic role;
- they actively involve all the key players, including the public, private, community and voluntary sectors;
- they have established genuine common local priorities and targets and agreed actions and milestones leading to demonstrable improvements against measurable baselines;
- members have aligned their performance management systems, criteria and processes to that of the LSP;
- they reduce, not add to, the 'bureaucratic burden'; and
- they build on best practice from successful partnerships, by drawing on experiences of regional structures, and national agencies. (DETR, 2001b, p. 51)

If it were as simple as that! If the accreditation procedures were rigorously applied, none would be accredited. The world is a little more complex than the guidance suggests.

Local authorities face issues about power, about conflicts of interest and about the difficulties of building partnerships. Local authorities have to be ready to work with the imperfect rather than to expect partnerships of perfection. They will be most effective if they realise that the management of cooperation also involves the management of conflict, of misunderstanding and of inertia, and that their own behaviour can cause these problems.

County, district or both

The guidance on community strategies stresses 'it is especially important for . . . different tiers of authority to work together to establish a joint approach to the preparation of community strategies . . . Unless the county and districts work together, the process of preparing community strategies is likely to lead to considerable duplication, conflicting priorities and "consultation/partnership fatigue". Such an approach will quickly lose credibility in the eyes of local partners and the public.' The focus should be on the processes by which the strategies are prepared as much as on the product. 'Separate community strategies will only be effective if the strategies themselves and the processes by which they are prepared, are complementary' (DETR, 2000a, p. 19).

The guidance suggests '"nesting" district level strategies within a broader vision and framework established at county level' (DETR, 2000a, p. 19). The phraseology of nesting *within* a county framework suggests, perhaps unintentionally, a county-dominant approach. An alternative to such a top-down approach would be a bottom-up approach carrying out the basic work at district level with the county involved as a partner. Neither a top-down nor a bottom-up approach is adequate, since each could lead to the neglect of important perspectives. In Devon as in other counties attempts have been made to achieve a balance. It was planned there should be a county and eight district LSPs. The emphasis is being placed on nesting strategies together rather than nesting within. 'The process will develop organically and the issues covered by each strategy will be those best covered at each "level"' (LGA, 2001b, p. 21). The guidance also suggests as an alternative 'a series of joint strategies for parts of counties based on agreed geographic communities' (DETR, 2000a, p. 19).

Community involvement

There is a tension in community planning between macro and micro approaches – between the local strategic partnership and community involvement. Authorities that develop the former without the latter can turn community planning into negotiation between bureaucratic empires. Authorities that develop the latter without the former face the frustration of discussion without necessary action. Equal emphasis should be given to both the macro and the micro approach.

Community representatives on a partnership do not secure community involvement. The representatives of public and private sector organisations can dominate numerically and practically. A few community representatives cannot speak adequately for the complexity of communities – the range of communities of

place, interest and background is too great. Community planning should reach out directly to communities and citizens.
Approaches to community involvement and public participation
will be discussed in the next chapter. These approaches can be
linked to LSPs by involving the partners in their development.

Community planning requires analysis at the macro level, setting a framework of possibilities, and also at the micro level,
where understanding can be built of the needs and aspirations of
communities. Recognition of communities of place, interest,
background and concern highlights the reality that community
leadership is not set within a homogeneous community.
Communities do not necessarily share the same interests, have
the same needs or make the same demands. Interests, needs and
demands can conflict.

Community leadership must accept the reality of difference
within. Where there is conflict the task must be to seek to reconcile differences and, if that is not possible, to balance differing
interests, objectives and demands. The task calls for political
judgement, but judgement informed by the diversity within.
Approaches to conflict resolution and consensus building by
differing groups can be important in community planning.
Reconciling, balancing and judging underlie the authority's role
in community leadership. These are tasks often required, but too
rarely recognised.

Neighbourhood management and neighbourhood renewal

In its early formulation of the modernisation programme the
government paid little attention to the neighbourhoods within
authorities, although *Modern Local Government* did recognise the
need 'to consult and engage with local communities' (DETR,
1998a, p. 39). There was, however, little further said and no reference to the need for structures and processes at area or neighbourhood level. The draft legislation on political structures
contained no provision for area committees and would have
meant their removal in authorities such as South Somerset,
although under pressure the draft legislation was revised to
allow for area committees with some executive powers.

Since then the government has developed policies for neighbourhood renewal and management as a response for areas of

social exclusion. These policies reinforce the bottom-up approach to community planning, but highlight the tensions between macro and micro approaches. The national strategy for neighbourhood renewal was set out in *A New Commitment to Neighbourhood Renewal* (Cabinet Office, 2001). The government identified the problem of 'hundreds of neighbourhoods' which have seen 'their basic quality of life become increasingly detached from the rest of society' and many of which 'have been stuck in a cycle of decline' (ibid., p. 7). The government's 'long-term goals' are for all the poorest neighbourhoods 'to have lower workless-ness; less crime; better health; better skills; and better housing and better physical environment', and 'to narrow the gap on these measures between the most deprived neighbourhoods and the rest of the country' (ibid., p. 25).

Local strategic partnerships developed as a concept for neighbourhood renewal have been adopted for community strategies. In doing so, LSPs may have become less effective for neighbourhood renewal. Work on community strategies may dominate, limiting work on neighbourhood renewal, focused as it is on particular deprived neighbourhoods. The way ahead is for the authority-wide partnership to enable neighbourhood partnerships to carry forward neighbourhood action plans.

The government also proposed the development of neighbourhood management: 'Neighbourhood managers can help focus services on residents' priorities and customer needs by making service level agreements; running local services; managing a devolved budget; and/or putting pressure on higher tiers of Government' (Cabinet Office, 2001, p. 51). It is not clear how the neighbourhood manager gets leverage on higher-tier organisations. They could be employed by a neighbourhood partnership or by the LSP, but much remains to be worked out, as with the relationship between neighbourhood management and community planning. In practice it will have to be worked out area by area in facing the tension between macro and micro approaches.

New powers to relax requirements

Section 5.1 of the Local Government Act 2000 gives powers to the Secretary of State 'to amend, repeal, revoke or disapply' any enactment that in his opinion 'prevents or obstructs' the use of the powers of well-being. The powers of the Secretary of State can be used to overcome problems that arise because the powers of well-being cannot be used to overcome limitations in existing legislation. Similar powers have been given by legislation on best value and on regulatory reform. These provisions echo the experience of the free commune experiments in Scandinavia, which enabled local authorities to apply for exemption from existing statutory constraints (Baldersheim and Stahlberg, 1994).

The government has also been given powers by section 6 of the Act to abrogate requirements on authorities to prepare plans or programmes that have been made unnecessary by the development of community strategies. Local authorities have to work out the relationship between the community strategies and other required plans. The government recognised the problem: 'A community strategy should provide a practical context for informing and linking other service – or theme – specific plans, including those already prepared with local partners. In reviewing or drawing up such plans, authorities should consider with their partners the extent to which the plans can and do contribute to the priorities in the community strategy' (DETR, 2000a, p. 25).

Challenges for central government

The government has enshrined in law local authorities' role in community leadership, but has not fully faced up to its implications for its own ways of working. After an uncertain start, central government departments are beginning to consider the implications of community strategies for their own requirements for plans. The Department of Health consultation paper *On Tackling Health Inequalities* states that their requirements should 'fit with local community strategies' and emphasises the role of LSPs (DOH, 2001).

If community planning is to achieve its full potential, it must have the wholehearted support of the partners at local level, despite other public bodies not having any statutory requirement to be involved. Most public sector partners will cooperate, but a task outside their statutory requirements can be seen as peripheral. There is a responsibility on central government, having willed the end, to ensure the means, by central departments making clear the importance of involvement in community planning to organisations and agencies within their remit. The government has recognised this need in *Strong Local Leadership*. While ruling out the need for a statutory requirement, it intends to use other means, such as budgetary mechanisms and performance management processes, 'to encourage engagement with LSPs' (DTLR, 2001a, p. 19), and hence with community planning. In Scotland, however, a duty has been laid on the main public bodies at local level, including health boards and joint police boards, 'to participate in community planning' (Local Government in Scotland Act 2003, s. 16.1), placing community planning on a firmer basis.

The unresolved issue is how central government responds to the community strategies developed by individual authorities, since these will have implications for government policies and practice. Local priorities may differ from national priorities. National policies may not fit local circumstances. Central government will not be prepared to abandon its own priorities or totally reverse its policies. The issue remains whether central government is prepared and organised to learn from community strategies, to consider its response and modify its policies, at least in application. Separate departmental responses will not be enough, because then only departmental considerations would apply, whereas the point of community strategies is their preparation on a cross-organisational basis, reflecting community needs.

Community strategies can provide a rich source of learning for central government. In the quest for joined-up government, community strategies can provide part of the answer. If central government is to realise the potential of community planning for its own learning and for the development of policies, it has to consider them on a cross-departmental basis that takes account of the community perspective on which they are prepared. This requires a readiness to take account of local circumstances as well as of departmental priorities. Dialogue is required between authorities with their LSPs and central government. Dialogue is developing on the local public service agreements described in Chapter 8, but as will be emphasised there, they do not provide for as wide a discussion as dialogue on community strategies would make possible.

The changes required from central government are fundamental and are not likely to be easily achieved. Yet unless they
are achieved, community strategies will be limited in scope.
Community leadership will be restricted unless there is space for
it to be exercised beyond the limits set by the separate departments of central government. The response of central government is a question overhanging the future of community
planning.

Conclusion

The legislation enshrines in law the role of local authorities in
community leadership. This role goes beyond the narrower concept of local authorities as merely agents for the delivery of
a series of services – the role that had become embedded in their
organisational structures and procedures. Although the role in
community leadership is wider than a role based solely on service
responsibilities, it is a mistake to assume that service responsibilities are now almost irrelevant, as has been suggested by Filkin
and his colleagues: 'Our localism rejects the dominant view of
local councils as primarily producers of services and replaces it
with a new conception of their role as community leaders' (Filkin
et al., 2001b, p. 11).

The role of local authorities in community leadership should
not replace the role of local authorities in service provision, but
should encompass and deepen it. The services are important in
their own right, but are also key instruments for community
leadership. The confusion in thinking is shown when, correctly
stating that opinion polls show people are most concerned with
the issues of crime, jobs and health, Filkin and his colleagues conclude that none of these come from the 'traditional "services" of
local government' (2001b, p. 14). Yet those services have much
to contribute to these and other community issues, as joined-up
government must recognise.

Responsibilities for services make local authorities active
participants in community governance. It confirms their leading role, as their services are amongst the most important in
the complex of organisations making up the system of community government. Local authorities without any responsibility for social services, transportation, leisure or education

could hardly claim to be major actors in the promotion of social, economic and environmental well-being. Far from lessening local authorities' responsibilities, community leadership would justify an extension of responsibilities into other major areas of community well-being, of which health is a clear example.

Responsibilities for services are a means of learning. They bring the authority into direct contact with its citizens in many different ways. A local authority touches its area at a myriad of points. In a major town, the authority has responsibilities for the education of its children, confronts pressing social issues, and has built and sustains the urban infrastructure and the many activities on which urban life depends, as well as being a, if not the, major employer. The challenge of community leadership for local authorities is to learn from its many contacts and to use that learning in partnership with others.

Community leadership turns on the ability of local authorities to influence their partners and that requires levers. If local authorities lost responsibility for services, they would lose important levers of influence for community leadership. Without significant service responsibilities a local authority could be seen as a mere talking shop and not the significant actor it remains today. Raising the issue of local authority responsibility for services is a distraction from the difficult issues faced by authorities in giving practical meaning to community leadership.

Local authorities have to develop a capacity to think beyond existing activities if the new powers of well-being are to fulfil their promise. Community planning can provide the stimulus to that thinking. The development of community planning will not be easy. There are difficult problems that have been described earlier. The temptations are many. Local authorities could assume total responsibility for preparing the community strategy, merely seeking ratification from their partners which they might obtain, but without any real commitment. Community planning could focus on the partners at the macro level, neglecting any community involvement beyond the superficial. The process could focus on the vision without the hard appraisal of resources which can give community planning a cutting edge. These temptations can be avoided if certain principles of community planning are maintained:

- Community planning sets key directions leading to the effective use of resources.
- Selectivity is required rather than comprehensiveness and that involves hard choices.
- Partnerships have to be worked for both at the outset and on a continuing basis.
- A community involves many communities with differing interests and aspirations.
- Community planning requires shared learning throughout its processes.

For local authorities the most important lesson is that community leadership cannot be imposed. The style of leadership cannot be based on presumed authority. Community leadership has to be built through the relationship with its partners and the communities within.

The powers of community well-being and the duty to undertake community planning recognise the role of local government in community leadership, one of the main themes of the modernisation programme. While there are problems that have to be overcome by local authorities in realising the full potential of community leadership, the main limitation of the government's approach has been the failure to appreciate the significance of the development of community leadership for its own workings. Community planning, reflecting as it can the needs and aspirations of different areas and backed by the powers of community well-being and aspirations, can enhance the scope for local choice, creating a greater capacity for learning within the whole system of government. Unless the machinery of central government can respond on a joined-up basis to joined-up government at local level, then the potential of community planning will not be fully realised. To make that response the need has to be recognised although the barriers created by departmental cultures and ways of working may prevent that recognition. Nevertheless the steps taken to 'enshrine in law' the role of local authorities in community leadership are important in the development of effective local government and constitute a main strength of the modernisation programme.

3 Democratic Renewal for Local Government

Democratic renewal is the second main theme of the modernisation programme. Local government is based on local democracy and the strength of local government depends therefore on the strength of local democracy. Yet the current state of local democracy provides an uncertain base for local government and any programme to build effective local government must focus on building up its base in local democracy, making democratic renewal a potential strength of the modernisation programme.

Low turnouts

The government argued that low turnouts meant that 'Too often local people are indifferent about local democracy' (DETR, 1998a, p. 14), showing the need for democratic renewal, quoting in support the turnout in local elections compared with other countries in the European Union (see Figure 3.1).

The government pointed out that since these figures were produced turnout had fallen further. In May 1998, 'Scarcely more than a third of electors voted in London, compared with a turnout of more than 40% at each of the previous three London Borough elections' (DETR, 1998a, p. 14).

Low and falling turnouts are not found in local government alone. There is a wider problem with falling turnouts in parliamentary by-elections, European elections and the 2001 general election. Despite this general trend there is and has long been a problem of low turnout in local elections in the United Kingdom. There has not been a golden age of turnouts, disappointing although that is for those who argue that low turnouts are due to increasing centralisation. Indeed, during the period of the Conservative government, turnout tended to increase slightly as

Figure 3.1 *Average turnout in local elections in the European Union*

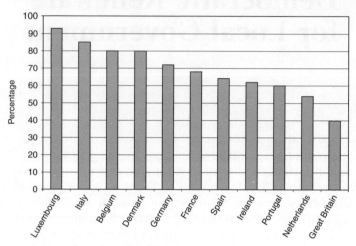

Source: Data from Rallings *et al.*, 1996

the powers of local government declined, possibly due to local government being a subject of controversy in national politics.

The Labour government suggested that low turnouts reflected the culture of inwardness: 'Too often within a council the members and officers take the paternalistic view that it is for them to decide what services are to be provided, on the basis of what suits the council as a service provider. The interests of the public are a poor second best' (DETR, 1998a, p. 14). Whether this generalisation is justified or not, the government was right in regarding low turnout as a symptom rather than the problem itself. This chapter argues that low turnouts should be regarded as a symptom of weakness in local democracy, as low turnouts generally are symptoms of a general weakness in democracy in the United Kingdom.

Modern Local Government contained two chapters on democratic renewal entitled 'Improving Local Democracy' and 'A Bigger Say for Local People', with the first focusing on political structures: 'New political structures will help councils to engage with their communities more effectively. Local people will be encouraged to take greater interest in their council's affairs' (DETR, 1998a, p. 38). No evidence was brought forward to support this argument and it is hard to see why new political structures, which have aroused little public interest, were regarded as such an important contribution to democratic renewal.

The government recognised, however, that more was required for democratic renewal than political structures:

> New structures alone will not bring about renewal of local democracy which is necessary if councils are to be confident that they are reflecting the priorities and wishes of the people they serve. That can only come about if there is higher participation in local elections and close and regular contact between a council and local people between elections. This cannot happen if local people are not interested or feel that the council, or their views about it, are irrelevant. (DETR, 1998a, p. 38).

The government stressed that authorities should involve people as citizens in local affairs, although it has failed to recognise there was an equal, if more difficult, issue of involving citizens in national affairs. Whilst the government's White Paper *Modernising Government* (Cabinet Office, 1999) recognises the need for responsive services, there is not the same recognition of the need for democratic renewal at national level as there is in its policies for local government.

The government's policies

Despite the government's recognition that democratic renewal involves more than new political structures, its emphasis in legislation, guidance and ministerial speeches has been on those structures. Inevitably, as a result, local authorities have focused their attention on political structures, driven by the imperatives of legislation. This chapter focuses on the wider issues of democratic renewal, leaving political structures to the succeeding chapters.

The government did set out three main proposals for democratic renewal, apart from political structures:

- more frequent elections;
- help for councils to develop their arrangements for participation and consultation; and
- developments in electoral procedures.

More frequent elections

The government in its consultation paper on democratic renewal proposed annual elections, arguing they would 'significantly improve accountability' (DETR, 1998b, p. 13). This proposal aroused strong opposition from those authorities (counties, London boroughs, most shire districts and some unitary authorities) which had all-out elections every four years. It was seen as unproblematic by those authorities (metropolitan districts and the remaining shire districts and unitary authorities) which were used to annual elections, except in the fallow years when county elections are or were held.

The government modified its proposals. In *Modern Local Government* it proposed that in counties and all shire districts there would be elections by halves, arranged so that in a four-year period there would be elections every year, two for the county and two for the district. It still proposed that there should be annual elections in London boroughs and unitary authorities, as in metropolitan districts, with a fallow year which could be used for mayoral or other elections.

The changes were still opposed by those authorities whose electoral cycle would be changed. Each authority saw its existing system as the only satisfactory system. Objections by the London boroughs that the change would create instability and continuous electioneering were seen as unrealistic in metropolitan districts where the political activity was welcomed and gradual change in the composition of the council seen as an advantage. The opposition was strong enough for the government not to proceed with the proposals in its first term. It kept the issue open for the future by taking powers in section 86 of the Local Government Act 2000 to alter the frequency of elections.

Strong Local Leadership states that the government is asking the Electoral Commission to propose options to simplify the complex patterns of elections in different authorities. The government indicates a possible change in its position on annual elections, arguing that the present arrangements in some authorities can 'lessen the immediate impact of voters' behaviour on council control' (DTLR, 2001a, p. 16). The meaning is not completely clear, but it would suggest opposition to annual elections which only involve part of the council and need not affect council control, even when opposition parties have won a majority of the seats at stake. The call for annual elections, the last unmet demand of the chartists in the nineteenth century, may no longer appeal to ministers, even though they would certainly not have regarded local annual elections as a precedent for national elections!

Has there been help for councils?

The government did little on its proposal to give 'help for councils to develop their arrangements for participation and consultation' (DETR, 1998a, p. 38). It commissioned and published research on local government's use of different forms of public participation (Lowndes *et al.*, 1998a). It also published guidance based on this research (Lowndes *et al.*, 1998b). Beyond that, there is probably relatively little that central government can or should do to help local authorities develop their approach to public participation and consultation. It can play a role in spreading knowledge of practice, but this was happening anyway through the Local Government Association and the Local Government Management Board (LGA/LGMB, 1998) and other organisations and individuals (see, for example, New Economics Foundation, 2000; Stewart, 1995, 1996, 1997, 1999).

Government can legislate requiring public participation and has done so on many occasions, and the modernisation programme has brought its own batch of requirements for consultation. Section 5.5 of the Local Government Act 1999 includes requirements to consult on best value. The government has made consultation obligatory on new political structures (Local Government Act 2000, s. 25.2). The legislation on community strategies requires authorities to 'seek the participation of such persons as they consider appropriate' (Local Government Act 2000, s. 4.3a), and the guidance says, 'The involvement of local people is central to the effective development and implementation of community strategies, and key to change in the longer term' (DETR, 2000a, p. 16).

The Select Committee on Public Administration was unable to find a 'map' setting out all the obligations to consult. It recommended that 'the multiplicity of individual statutory obligations to consult should be replaced by providing one framework' (Select Committee on Public Administration, 2001, p. xvi). It is doubtful whether statutory requirements to consult are useful, since enforced consultation is rarely effective. As the Select Committee said, 'The worst reason for consulting would be just because it is required or has become routine' (ibid.).

The government has done relatively little on providing the promised help for councils, perhaps because it recognises that it would be inappropriate nationally to make suggestions about the most appropriate forms of consultation to fit local circumstances. There would be something presumptuous in central government, itself so inexperienced in public involvement, prescribing forms of consultation, or even giving such guidance, although that has not prevented such guidance on other matters, such as local political structures, in which it has as little experience.

In *Modern Local Government*, the government proposed legislation to confirm the powers of local authorities to hold referendums. There was uncertainty over this, although a number of authorities have held referendums on their budgets and other matters. The government has included this provision in the Local Government Bill introduced in 2002.

Electoral procedures

The government has taken powers to allow experiments in electoral procedures, designed to make voting easier. It is remarkable how little has changed in electoral procedure since the secret ballot replaced the open hustings in the nineteenth century. The notices put up outside council offices read and look like the notices of over a hundred years ago, for the simple reason that they are the same. The stubby pencils tied to a piece of string – still the almost universal instruments for voting in polling stations – may well date from the same period. At last, change is being considered.

The experiments allowed by the legislation were first tried in 2000 and again in 2002. Weekend voting and changes in voting hours were tried in some authorities. New technology was introduced. Few of the experiments made a significant difference to turnout, except the introduction of easier postal voting and, in particular, of universal postal voting, although those who used the other innovations welcomed them. In 2000 universal postal voting led to 50 per cent increases in voting in most of the authorities concerned and up to 100 per cent where no declaration of identity was required (LGA, 2000b). In 2002 the

Electoral Commission's conclusion was that 'Postal voting has undoubtedly proved to be a success in terms of improving electoral turnout' (Electoral Commission, 2002, p. 6). The introduction of postal voting generally is a possible outcome from the experiments, although issues have been raised about the dangers of abuse of the process. Even general postal voting could leave local government turnout relatively low by European standards. Changes in voting methods that make voting easier have a value in their own right, but do not resolve the need for democratic renewal, since they leave untouched the relationship between government and the public.

The government dismissed one other possibility: – change in the method of election as opposed to the method of voting. It rejected any consideration of proportional representation, using the argument that 'it does not view changes to the voting system as a panacea for the current weaknesses in local government. Local government modernisation is more fundamental than simply changing how people cast their vote. The Government favours a wider and more radical reform programme' (DETR, 1998a, p. 43). This argument assumed that there was a necessary choice between an electoral system based on proportional representation and the modernisation programme as a whole, but the issue was surely whether proportional representation should have been part of the modernisation programme, not whether it should have been an alternative to it.

Proportional representation could not have been a panacea on its own, but neither would any other element of the modernisation programme be on its own, although some advocates of elected mayors presented them as such. Proportional representation cannot be ruled out as a possibility for the future. It is an anachronism that the Scottish Parliament, the Welsh Assembly and the London Assembly are elected by proportional representation, but not Scottish and Welsh local authorities or the London boroughs. It is possible that proportional representation will be introduced for Scottish local authorities by the Scottish Parliament as it has the power to do.

A limited approach

The main conclusion of this analysis of the government's approach to democratic renewal must be that it has done relatively little on this theme, apart from legislation on political structures whose impact on democratic renewal is uncertain. The emphasis on political structures has been a distraction for local authorities from the main issues facing democratic renewal. Democratic renewal can only be developed at local level, although central government can encourage such renewal. In order to do so effectively, it must recognise that the understanding of what is required is much greater at local level than at national level. Indeed, there are lessons to be learnt from local authorities by central government for its own working. Its approach to consultation too often follows past routines: the Green Paper; the standard list of consultees; the checklist for responses; the favoured group for discussion. There has been far more innovation in consultation by local authorities than by central government.

Weaknesses in local democracy

Much requires to be done to build a vibrant local democracy. The turnout figures should be seen as symptoms of weaknesses in local democracy as recent national turnouts should be seen as symptoms of problems at national level. Four factors in that weakness are put forward in this chapter:

- a limited conception of the role of local government;
- a limited electoral base;
- a limited conception of representative democracy; and
- a limited concept of citizenship.

A limited conception of the role of local government

Chapter 2 argued that local government in the United Kingdom had come to be seen as an agency for the delivery of a series of mainly national services. Seen in that way, the need for local democracy can seem limited. In so far as there is scope for local choice and local voice, the case remains, but it is a weaker case than one based on a conception of local government as communities governing themselves – a dominant conception in many European countries, where turnout is consistently higher.

In these European countries, local government is not, as it has too readily been seen in the United Kingdom, a mere creature of statute. Local government, although not its political form, can be written into the constitution. In Germany, for example, 'the constitution guarantees communes the right to regulate on their own responsibility all the affairs of the community within the limits set by the law' (Norton, 1994, p. 243).

The limited conception of local government in the United Kingdom has probably affected attitudes towards local democracy. It was argued in Chapter 2 that the government's measures were designed to establish the role of local authorities in community leadership with a wide-ranging concern for community well-being and with powers to match, bringing local authorities close to the European conception of local government. This change provides a fuller basis for local democracy and could over time change public attitudes, but there remain uncertainties as to how local authorities respond to this role and whether they realise the opportunities created. There are even greater uncertainties as to whether central government will allow space for the role to develop.

A limited electoral base

Local government is based on representative democracy, yet the representative base of local government is numerically weak in the United Kingdom. There are a little over 20,000 councillors with each councillor representing, on average, 2,600 people. This means that the potential of local government is not fully realised. Local government makes possible a density of representation that is impracticable for national government and in most other European countries there are significantly more councillors in relation to their population. In France about 1 per cent of the electorate are councillors! Table 3.1 shows the figures for countries in the European Union.

The differences are due to the size of local authorities in the United Kingdom compared with other countries in Europe. Lower-tier and unitary authorities are on average ten times larger in population than their equivalents in Europe (these calculations do not include parish councils since they do not have the substantial powers held by communes in Europe, some of which have more power than our shire districts).

Table 3.1 *Local government representation in the European Union*

	Number of inhabitants per councilor
Austria	209
Belgium	811
Denmark	1,115
Finland	410
France	118
Germany	350
Greece	1,075
Ireland	2,336
Italy	608
Netherlands	1,555
Portugal	1,131
Spain	610
Sweden	256
United Kingdom	2,603

Source: Wilson and Game, 2002, p. 247.

Local government in the United Kingdom lacks the density of representation that should be its strength. Local authorities cannot achieve the closeness of contact common in Europe, where many more people are involved on councils and many more people are therefore in contact with councillors in their normal way of life. These differences could be a significant factor in explaining the low turnouts in the United Kingdom.

The limited number of councillors has an impact on the condition of democracy, limiting the civic education nurtured by experience as an elected representative. Mill saw that experience as one of his arguments for local government, stressing 'the importance of that portion of the operation of free institutions which may be called the public education of the citizens', and regarded local government as 'the chief instrument' for this purpose (Mill, 1904, p. 266).

Another weakness in the basis of representation has already been discussed. The electoral system means that the council's composition does not adequately reflect the range of political views found in the electorate. The issue is more acute in local government than in national elections. The relative homogeneity of some local authority electorates results in an even greater imbalance than in national elections. There are authorities where one party dominates on an almost permanent basis, with some councils such as Newham having had no opposition at all at certain times.

In many countries in Europe, local authorities are elected by a system of proportional representation, avoiding the extreme results possible in the British system. Advocates argue that proportional representation is one reason for the higher turnouts in Europe.

A limited concept of representative democracy

Local democracy, like national democracy, has too often been based on an attenuated concept of representative democracy. The representative role has been seen not merely as dependent on elections but as consisting of elections and little more, apart from dealing with constituents' cases and sometimes not even that. This view reflects a passive concept of representation, reflecting Schumpeter's view of representative democracy. Schumpeter argued that any other view was unrealistic and undesirable because the citizen 'is a member of an unworkable committee, the committee of the whole nation, and that is why he devotes less discipline on mastering a political problem than he expends on mastering a game of bridge' (Schumpeter, 1950, p. 200). Schumpeter did consider citizen involvement could be a little, but only a little, greater at local level as 'more within the reach of the citizen's mind' (p. 259). The passive concept considers representative democracy opposed to participatory democracy. Beyond the election, there is only the politics of protest. While the right to protest is important, it reflects a negative approach to local democracy, if it is the main expression of democracy beyond elections.

An active concept of representative democracy is opposed to the passive concept. The active concept sees the involvement of citizens as necessary for the full development of representative democracy. The active role is expressed in a continuing relationship between representative and represented. Far from representative democracy and participatory democracy being opposed to each other, the former requires the latter. Otherwise, how does the representative know what to re-present?

Direct democracy could, if practical, be an alternative to representative democracy and therefore could be argued to be opposed to it. Town meetings and referendums are examples of direct democracy, with decisions taken directly by the citizens. They are found in Switzerland and parts of the United States, and, to a limited extent, in parish meetings in the United Kingdom. Town meetings in areas with large populations are either impractical or are meetings of the few. Referendums can only cover a fraction of the decisions to be made. Direct democracy cannot replace representative democracy generally, although there is a place for referendums on specific issues and for parish meetings at a very local level.

Participatory democracy does not replace representative democracy but informs it. Participatory democracy does not mean that the representative has to follow the views expressed. If citizens, both those directly and indirectly involved with an issue, spoke with one voice, it would be an unusual elected representative who did not follow their views. On most issues, the public does not speak with one voice, but with differing voices. Citizens have different interests, needs, aims and demands. Those who oppose free access of cars to city centres are balanced by those who defend it. On this issue, as on many others, the councillor has to seek to reconcile differing views. If that cannot be achieved the councillor has to balance views and, in the final resort, to judge them. Such judgement should depend on hearing the diversity of views. An active concept of representative democracy should underlie policies for democratic renewal.

A limited concept of citizenship

The citizen has been regarded as an elector and little more than an elector, except, as already discussed, a protester or a complainant. These are occasional roles, reflecting the passive concept of representative democracy. There has recently been a tendency to redefine the citizen as customer. This tendency was seen in the Citizen's Charter, which focused on users of services and not on the citizen as an active participant in the process of government. The first annual report on the Citizen's Charter emphasised that it 'sees public services through the eyes of those who use them' (Prime Minister and Chancellor of the Duchy of Lancaster, 1992). To narrow the scope of citizenship to the role of customer is to limit citizen involvement. I am no longer a 'customer' of schools, but as a citizen I have views about schools and a claim to have them listened to.

The alternative to the passive citizen or the citizen as customer is the citizen as a participant in government. This conception involves a rediscovery of the importance of deliberation
amongst citizens, between citizens and representatives and
amongst representatives. Miller has described the deliberative
ideal as starting

> from the premise that political preferences will conflict and
> that the purpose of democratic institutions must be to resolve
> this conflict. But it envisages this occurring through an open
> and uncoerced discussion of the issue at stake with the aim of
> arriving at an agreed judgment. The process of reaching a
> decision will also be a process whereby initial preferences are
> transformed to take account of the views of others. That is,
> the need to reach an agreement forces each participant to
> put forward proposals under the rubric of general principles
> or policy considerations that others could accept. (Miller,
> 1992, p. 75)

Fishkin has argued that deliberation is a necessary condition
for a fully realised democracy: 'Without deliberation, democratic choices are not exercised in a meaningful way. If the
preferences that determine the results of democratic procedures are unreflective or ignorant, then they lose their claim to
political authority over us. Deliberation is necessary if the
claims of democracy are not to be delegitimated' (Fishkin,
1991, p. 29).

The argument for deliberation challenges the conduct of those
representative institutions where deliberation is constrained by
the excesses of party discipline. 'The opposition made good
points, but there was nothing we could do about it because the
line had been agreed in the group beforehand' has been too
often heard in local authorities.

Public apathy challenged

Many in local government see an emphasis on citizen participation and on deliberation as unrealistic. Past attempts to involve
citizens are quoted, showing the public's lack of interest in being
involved in public meetings, never mind deliberation. 'We've

tried all that, but the public are apathetic, so there is nothing we can do about it' is endlessly repeated. It is strange reasoning. If the public is apathetic, it could be equally argued as a reason for doing something. The managing director who was told that the public was apathetic about the products of his or her firm – or in other words that sales were low – would not say that the public is always apathetic so there is nothing we can do about it. Design, price, service and marketing would all be looked at to correct the position.

There are reasons for public apathy. Some of the methods used to involve the public have almost been designed to stifle public interest. The form of public meeting too often follows the sterile practices of the past. The platform is set apart from the audience; the visual aids may not work; presentations go on too long, inciting an angry response from the audience or alternatively a lack of response. Whereas in training courses, care will be taken in local authorities to design approaches to encourage participation by those attending, public meetings can be arranged without any such consideration. If a public meeting has about a hundred people present, then at the very least, one would expect time and space to be provided for small groups to discuss the issues with councillors or officers, or, dare one say, to allow time for deliberation. There is a need for innovation in democratic practice. It is remarkable that while there have been major innovations in management and in policy, there has until recently been virtually no innovation in democratic practice.

Attitudes are important. Unless public involvement and deliberation are valued by those within a local authority, the process is likely to lead to frustration on the road to apathy. Without a positive attitude, the processes used will be set up to suit the requirements of the organisation rather than the requirements of the public. The presentation, procedures and premises used will reflect the organisation's, not the public's, convenience. What the public says will not be heard or will be regarded as trivial if it does not fit the organisation's perspective. When meetings are held to discuss problems on housing estates, 'dogs' are almost certain to be raised as an issue. Dogs do not come very high in the hierarchies of local authorities. There is not even an assistant director (dogs) so 'nothing new was raised' or 'only minor points were made'. Worse still, if the authority rejects the views expressed, there will be no response giving the reasons to the public concerned. The views just disappear into the black box called the local authority. Members of the public are not being treated as citizens, involved as of right in the process of government.

Too often the public are not told of the conditions underlying the process of consultation. If consultation is on neighbourhood improvements, it is critical that at the outset the authority makes clear the resources available. Citizens can challenge the amount, but they need to know the authority's position before they put forward proposals, rather than finding out long after they have put forward their views that there are not sufficient resources available – a sure-fire way to create frustration and apathy. In this and in many other ways local authorities themselves create the apathy used as an excuse for inaction.

Innovation in democratic practice

There *has* been innovation in democratic practice in recent years, particularly in methods designed to enable deliberation. Citizens' juries are probably the best-known of these approaches, but there are now a variety of similar approaches designed to seek out the informed and considered views of citizens.

These approaches can be distinguished from public opinion surveys, which seek out immediate responses to predetermined questions about which those surveyed may not even have thought before being asked. At the time of local government reorganisation, surveys were held to find out public views on the structure of local government. The surveys found a mixture of views, but on one question the vast majority were agreed. They knew little or very little about the issue. To ask people whether they are in favour of elected mayors, without any explanation of what that involves or without hearing the issue discussed, is hardly a guide to informed opinion. Local referendums taken after campaigns in which the issues were discussed have had different results from those suggested by the surveys. On many but not all issues, public opinion surveys have a role to play, but they are not necessarily a guide to informed and considered opinion. The distinction between off-the-cuff responses and views formed after deliberation is close to Yankelovich's distinction between mass opinion tested in surveys and public judgement. Public judgements are formed when 'people have struggled with the issue, thought about it in their own terms, and formed a judgment they are willing to stand by' (Yankelovich, 1991, p. 42).

Most approaches to citizen deliberation have three features in common. They are based on random selection or more often a structured sample designed to represent the make-up of the population. Participants hear evidence on the issue before them. They question the evidence and discuss it among themselves, taking time for reflection – in other words they deliberate.

Citizens' juries are based on these features. They normally consist of up to 25 people, who spend three or four days considering an issue posed by an authority before reaching their conclusions. A facilitator guides the process. Local authorities have normally chosen an issue on which they are uncertain how to proceed. In Lewisham a jury considered the drugs issue; in Hertfordshire it was waste disposal. The authority does not undertake to follow the jury's views, but does undertake to take them seriously and to give a considered response. Although not statistically representative, these juries are a representative group of citizens considering an issue of public importance (Hall and Stewart, 1996). The time and cost involved limit the extent to which citizens' juries can be used by authorities, but all issues do not need the same commitment of time, and hence of cost. A variety of approaches have been developed, using the same principles of representation, evidence and discussion, but without the same time commitment (Stewart, 1999).

These developments have shown the potential of citizenship, unrealised in traditional approaches to public involvement. First, the readiness of many people to take part in these approaches has been an unexpected bonus. Many who have never taken part in public affairs and would never respond to a general invitation do respond to a personal invitation coupled with an explanation of the commitment involved. Second, authorities are impressed with the reports produced and by the way the participants deal with witnesses and take part in discussion. Third, and perhaps most important, the majority of participants come to appreciate the difficulty of many of the issues faced by authorities, but find the experience rewarding and are ready to be further involved if the opportunity occurs. Involvement breeds involvement if the experience is rewarding.

Other innovations in democratic practice focus on deliberation, not between representative citizens, but between stakeholders.

Characteristically these bring together for a weekend a wide range of stakeholders, numbering up to three hundred or more. The process is sometimes called visioning, particularly when considering the future of an area. These conferences work in a variety of forms using the whole conference, stakeholder groups and mixed groups. Different techniques are used to present issues, to explore views and work on responses. Approaches include future search, system alignment and open technology (Stewart, 1996, 1997, 1999).

Future search sets the issue in context, reviewing the past and exploring the present, before seeking common ground in the future. While differences are recognised, they are not allowed to become barriers, being set aside for future discussion. The focus is on what is agreed as forming a basis for action plans. Future search, like other approaches, enables deliberation between those concerned with an issue (Weisbrod and Janoff, 1995).

The methods used differ from those used for citizen deliberation, with less emphasis on evidence, because stakeholders and their knowledge are there in the conference taking part in the process. Stakeholder deliberation can also be used in conflict situations, such as environmental disputes over new development. Those involved are brought together in ways designed to ensure discussion instead of confrontation.

Further innovations in democratic practice include:

- new forms of public meeting, enabling discussion;
- community forums through which authorities reach out to diverse communities, recognising there are communities of interest and background as well as communities of place;
- teledemocracy which, as time passes, will come to play an increasing role;
- local referendums, which at their best can encourage public discussions on issues;
- standing citizen panels, normally used for surveys, but also used for deliberation;
- public scrutiny of services, village appraisal or environmental assessments by citizens; and
- issues forums based on existing organisations, libraries or membership groups that meet together to discuss selected public issues.

Most of these approaches enable deliberation, contrasting with the passive role of the citizen exemplified by the public opinion survey and even the vote, critical though it is to local democracy.

The DETR research into public participation in local government concluded that 'all modes of public participation are on the increase . . . Even traditional modes of participation such as public meetings and question and answer sessions are being more widely used than previously' (Lowndes *et al.*, 2001a, p. 210). The research found a significant level of innovation and a significant number of local authorities using deliberative mechanisms. The researchers concluded: 'far from being a focus on a few fashionable innovations, the participation agenda has encouraged local authorities to renew their acquaintance with traditional forms of participation as well as to experiment with alternatives' (ibid). The distinction between traditional and innovatory methods can mislead, since it does not allow for innovation in traditional forms, such as public meetings. The conclusions are clear. There has been a general increase both in public participation and in innovation. This increase can in part be ascribed to the modernisation programme, but mainly represents trends that were present even before the modernisation programme was launched.

The research rejected the view that the public is 'universally apathetic' (Lowndes *et al.*, 2001b, p. 454). It identified deterrents to participation which could be overcome by the development of local authority strategies for participation. The word 'strategies' can mislead, suggesting the preparation of those programmes of activities which too often parade as strategies. What Lowndes and her colleagues appear to be suggesting is a set of principles or guidelines to govern authorities' approach to participation.

Possible principles guiding action include the following:

- *There is no one right approach.* A variety of approaches are required if a habit of citizenship is to be nurtured and participation developed.
- *The best should not be the enemy of the better.* Against any particular approach, it is possible to argue its weaknesses. The issue is not whether an approach is perfect, but whether it can make a contribution to the work of the authority and to building local democracy.

- *Be aware whom one is hearing from and whom one is not hearing from.* When citizens are invited to participate, certain voices may be heard more readily than others. It is important to identify whom the authority is not hearing from.
- *Seek out the voices that have gone unheard.* Once one identifies those unheard, methods can be devised to reach out to them.
- *Make clear the basis of involvement.* Limits on what the council can or will do should be made clear at the outset. The limits can be challenged by citizens but in awareness of them, rather than finding out after views have been put forward.
- *Response is a necessary condition of effective participation.* Participation is ineffective if views are not taken into account and responded to. Even when views are rejected, explanation and openness to discussion are a necessary response for a deliberative democracy.
- *Deliberation is a key test.* Deliberation involves citizens in discussion and reflection and thereby gives meaning to representative democracy. (Based on Stewart, 1997, pp. 36–7)

Conclusion

The government has highlighted the problem of low turnout in local elections. Turnout should not be regarded as the fundamental problem, but a symptom of deeper problems in the relationship between authorities and the public (matching similar problems in the relationship between central government and the public). Passive concepts of representative democracy have reinforced the enclosed authority. Councillors, who believe they can speak for people merely because they are elected, enclose the organisation against the diversity of the public and of their views. The danger of the local authority being an enclosed organisation is challenged by a concept of representative democracy based on active citizenship built through deliberation.

The government has recognised the need to develop citizen participation, at least for local government if not for themselves. The government has wisely not legislated in detail on this issue. Citizen participation is developing in local authorities and it is at local level that there is experience and lessons to be learnt. If there is a need for democratic renewal at local level, there is an equal, if not greater, need for democratic renewal at national level, but citizen participation almost inevitably takes place at local level. Central government, if concerned with its own democratic renewal, has to draw upon the potential strength of participation at local level – a theme returned to later in the book.

Much work has still to be done to develop effective participation at local level. The work has begun, but is very far from building the deliberative democracy advocated in this chapter. The aim should be to ensure that all citizens have the opportunity, at some point in their life, to take part in a citizens' jury or other form of citizen deliberation. Involvement breeds involvement. The best way to build a deliberative democracy is to extend that experience from the few to the many.

Strong local democracy is critical for effective local government and democratic renewal as a main theme is a clear strength of the modernisation programme. The main weakness of the government's programme and a limitation on its effectiveness is that through its legislation, it has focused the attention of local authorities on new political structures rather than on the need for the involvement of citizens in the work of local government.

4 The Main Options for Political Structures

As stressed in the last chapter, the government, while rightly giving importance to democratic renewal, has placed its emphasis on new political structures rather than directly on the relationship between local authorities and their citizens. The government argued that new political structures were required because the traditional culture was expressed in and reinforced by political structures based on the committee system enclosing the authority rather than opening it up for the public.

The background

The committee system had been part of local government since the introduction of elected municipal government in the early nineteenth century and was based on the statutory precept that the council was a corporate body, responsible for all that happened in the authority. The council exercised that responsibility through a series of committees, between whom the work of the council was divided, normally according to the main functions or services of the authority.

The government argued that the committee system had basic weaknesses: 'The current system is confusing and inefficient, with significant decisions usually taken elsewhere. Many councillors have little influence over council decisions, yet spend a great deal of their time at council meetings. The result is that people do not know who is running the council' (DETR, 1998a, p. 7). The government stressed that these weaknesses had been highlighted in past reports of committees of inquiry. Yet, in the more distant past, the committee system had been celebrated as one of the strengths of local government. One distinguished writer concluded, 'its achievements become the more remarkable the more closely they are scrutinised' (Laski, 1935, p. 97).

The Maud Committee's report on the management of local government highlighted the time-consuming nature of the committee system and the volume of paper involved, but their main criticisms were directed at the lack of coordination. 'The general conception is that of an assemblage of committees, each carrying out its own special duties and championing its own causes, with reliance on horizontal committees, personal contacts, party machinery and the efforts of officers to achieve co-ordination' (Maud Report, 1967a, para. 60). The Maud committee's main recommendations on committee structures were designed to overcome these problems of coordination. They proposed the elimination of the executive responsibilities of committees and the establishment of a management board of between five and nine councillors as the executive of the council, or in today's terms the cabinet.

The Maud Committee saw strengths as well as weaknesses in the committee system. Committees kept 'members informed' and gave 'them an understanding of the working of the various services. These values are not to be lightly cast aside' (1967a, para. 163). They proposed that committees should continue as deliberative rather than executive bodies, making recommendations to the management board and reviewing progress. To overcome the problems of time and paper, the committee recommended there should be no more than six such committees.

The proposal for the management board was too far beyond existing practice and was rejected by every local authority in the country. Nevertheless the report had an influence. Many authorities accepted the need to reduce the number of committees and to improve coordination. Instead of a management board and deliberative committees, a policy committee was established along with a streamlined committee structure, an approach which was to be advocated in the Bains Report for the political structures in the new authorities created in 1974 (Bains Report, 1972). These proposals were almost universally adopted, although the role of what were now called policy and resources committees varied and there was a tendency, over time, for the streamlined committee structures to spawn new committees and sub-committees.

The Widdicombe Committee considered alternative political structures including the Maud proposals and ministerial models. The committee decided there was no need to change the basis of the existing structures, recommending that:

the system of decision taking in local government should continue to be one in which:

(i)   the council is a corporate body;
(ii)   decisions are taken openly by, or on behalf of, the whole council without any separate source of executive authority;
(iii) officers serve the council as a whole. (Widdicombe Report, 1986, p. 77)

The main change recommended was that membership of decision-making committees reflect the party balance on the council, although deliberative committees could be composed of one party, recognising thereby the reality of political control and the existence in many authorities of a leadership group based on the majority party. The Conservative government rejected this latter recommendation and introduced legislation requiring the membership of all committees to be proportionate to party strength on the council, unless there was unanimous agreement to the contrary (Local Government and Housing Act 1989, s. 15).

The Audit Commission renewed criticism of the committee system, highlighting the time taken by committee work and a tendency to focus more on detail than on issues of policy and strategy. *We Can't Go On Meeting Like This* was the title and message of its first report (Audit Commission, 1990), reinforced by a second report (Audit Commission, 1997).

Criticism of the committee system was contained in a 1991 consultation paper prepared by the Department of the Environment, at the initiative of Michael Heseltine, the then Secretary of State, although it recognised the strengths of the system in involving all councillors in the business of the council (DOE, 1991b). The paper put forward various executive models as alternatives to the committee system. It proposed legislation allowing councils to introduce these models, but not requiring them to do so. These models were later elaborated in the report of a working party on the internal management of local authorities. The report proposed enabling legislation to permit experiments by local authorities (Working Party on the Internal Management of Local Authorities in England, 1993). Such legislation was not introduced until 1997 after the election of the Labour government. Lord Hunt of Tanworth introduced a private member's bill in the House of Lords with government support. It failed to make progress in the House of Commons because of Conservative opposition on procedural grounds.

Strengths and weaknesses of the committee system

The starting point for the government's proposals on political structures was its analysis of the weaknesses identified at the start of this chapter. The inefficiency derived from the time taken, from duplication of work by different committees and from the proliferation of paper. In the words of the Audit Commission, 'committees can be unnecessarily slow and cumbersome' and 'the system is also expensive in terms of the opportunity cost of senior management time' (Audit Commission, 1997, quoted in DETR, 1999e, p. 8). The committee system was seen as opaque because 'despite the time and resources councils devote to running it, their major decisions are in reality taken outside it' (DETR, 1999e, p. 8). The dominance of party politics and group discipline meant that in many authorities decisions were taken in private group meetings and enforced by the whips at committees.

The government argued that the result was 'a lack of clarity about where decisions are taken and by whom. The role of the council's officers to provide professional advice to the decision takers is clouded. People do not know who to praise, who to blame, or who to contact with their problems' (DETR, 1999e, p. 8). Public confusion meant the system weakened local accountability. It is uncertain whether people were as confused as this quotation suggests. People were probably aware of the reality of political control from their experience of local elections and many were aware of the possibility of contacting councillors with their problems. The government was merely reiterating what had come to be the conventional wisdom about the committee system.

The government summed up its analysis of the committee system:

the traditional committee system, designed to provide an open and public framework for decision taking, has grown into an opaque system with the real action off stage. People lose confidence in their council's decisions, individual councillors become disillusioned with their ability to influence local decisions and people are discouraged from standing for election.

Opaque and unclear decision taking weakens the link between local people and their democratically elected representatives.(DETR, 1999e, p. 8)

The government appeared to see the committee system as a major cause of the weakness of local democracy and change in political structures as the critical step forward in democratic renewal and in changing the traditional culture.

While the government was correct in identifying weaknesses in the way the committee system operated, that did not necessarily require fundamental change. Streamlining the committee system was possible and had been undertaken in a number of authorities. In so far as problems arose from excessive group discipline, change could have been considered, and the government's own proposals sought such a change in the overview and scrutiny role. Analysis should have gone beyond the weaknesses of the committee system. While it was important to overcome weaknesses, it should have been equally important to identify strengths to be maintained in any new structure.

The committee system meant that formal decisions were made in public. Even when the actual decision had been made beforehand in the party group, the decision could be challenged by opposition councillors in public and had to be justified by the chair or other members of the party. Practice varied and in some authorities decisions were modified or 'taken back' in the light of the discussion. Even where that was unknown, the fact that formal decisions had to be made in public and could be challenged in public was a clear strength.

The committee system enabled councillors to gain experience, making contact with officers and learning about the workings of the authority and its services. It also provided a mechanism for testing councillors, from whom the future leadership could emerge. The development of councillors was a strength, and any new structures would need to provide alternative mechanisms if that strength was to be maintained.

The committee system enabled specialisation by councillors, building up their experience and knowledge of particular services. That experience and knowledge provided an important resource for the authority, although not always fully used. While specialisation was a strength, it was a weakness if carried too far. Councillors could come to regard themselves as more responsible for the service than responsible to the communities who elected them. Any new structures should enable the strengths of specialisation while overcoming the weaknesses.

The committee system provided roles for all councillors, establishing their position in the authority and giving them access to information and to the working of the authority. Whether those roles were fully utilised can be disputed, but a new structure should provide effective roles for all councillors if they are to make a contribution to the work of the authority.

The government's proposals enacted

The government ignored the strengths and focused on the weaknesses of the committee system. Because of those perceived weaknesses, the government proposed that all local authorities be required to adopt new structures

characterised by

- *efficiency*, where decision can be taken quickly, responsively and accurately to meet the needs and aspirations of the community;
- *transparency*, where it is clear to people who is responsible for decisions;
- *accountability*, where people can measure the actions taken against the policies and plans on which those responsible were elected to office; and
- *high standards of conduct*, by all involved to ensure public confidence and trust. (DETR, 1999e, pp. 10–11)

The requirement for high standards was met by the new ethical framework described in Chapter 6. To meet the requirements of efficiency, transparency and accountability, the government proposed that all authorities introduce new political structures based on what was described in the early days as a separation between the executive and scrutiny functions. Three possible structures were put forward for the executive:

- a directly elected mayor and cabinet;
- a leader appointed by the council with a cabinet; or
- a directly elected mayor with a council manager.

The Local Government Act 2000 required all authorities in England of over 85,000 in population to introduce one of the three models. The introduction of a political structure with a directly elected mayor has to be endorsed in a binding local referendum. Such referendums can be called by the council, by a petition signed by 5 per cent of the electorate or by a direction of the Secretary of State. A fall-back position has to be specified and adopted in the event of a rejection of the mayoral proposal and this has normally been the leader and cabinet model. Authorities under 85,000 in population can opt for the 'alternative arrangements' of an enhanced committee system. The Act also applied to Wales, but regulations have been used by the Welsh Assembly to allow alternative arrangements to be chosen in all authorities in the form described below.

No requirements for new political structures have been introduced in Scotland, although the Executive set up a Leadership Advisory Council to encourage authorities to review their political structures within the parameters set by existing legislation. That legislation does not permit the option of a directly elected provost – the title used for the nearest equivalent to mayor in Scotland.

The Local Government Act 2000 was followed by a series of detailed regulations and directions and many pages of guidance, to which section 38 requires authorities 'to have regard'. The extent of prescription indicates the government's distrust of authorities and fear that without prescription the dominance of the traditional culture meant authorities would find ways of avoiding the main thrust of the legislation.

Under the Act and regulations, the council is responsible for agreeing the policy framework and the budget of the authority (DETR, 2000-2, para. 2.7), normally but not necessarily on the proposal of the executive, although in the mayoral options a two-thirds majority is required to overturn the executive's proposals. Within that policy framework, the executive in all its forms has taken over responsibility for exercising most of the functions of the authority, although certain functions can be delegated to area committees. An exception was made for certain regulatory functions, such as development control and licensing, which remain the responsibility of the council, normally delegated to committees.

Cabinets need not be constituted proportionate to party strength and can be composed solely of members of one party. The cabinet has to have between three and ten members (including the mayor or leader). Individual members of the cabinet can be given responsibility for specific services or cross-cutting themes, with delegated authority to make decisions. The council is required to set up at least one overview and scrutiny committee composed of councillors outside the executive. Such committees and the regulatory committees have to be constituted proportionate to party strengths. Overview and scrutiny committees have a wide responsibility to review the work of the executive and of the council generally and to explore issues facing the authority and its communities.

The government argued that the abolition of the committee system, as well as securing efficiency, transparency and accountability, would free up the time of councillors to develop their representative role, as well as undertaking important roles in overview and scrutiny. 'Councillors will be able to concentrate on bringing the views of local people to bear on the council's decision-making process, rather than, as is so often the case today, spending their time on justifying the council's decisions, on which they often have no real say, to their people' (DETR, 1999e, p. 26). No evidence was produced that this was how councillors behaved in dealing with their constituents and it is hard to believe that they all behaved in this way, including members of the opposition. The government argued that 'the majority of councillors will have greater freedom and a greater impact on the direction of the council and the services it provides to local people than is currently often the case' (ibid.). Many councillors were unconvinced that this would be achieved by the work of overview and scrutiny committees, which could be ignored by the executive.

Local authorities were required to consult widely before deciding which option to adopt. The government indicated its preference for the mayoral options, at least in major towns and cities, and clearly believed that consultation would support those options, drawing support from surveys of public opinion. It is doubtful that questions asked in surveys without any prior discussion of the issues involved can give a reliable guide to considered opinions. Even the question itself can be misunderstood, as the word 'mayor' suggests the traditional and well-understood social and ceremonial role. Experience to date in referendums, in the majority of which mayoral options have been rejected, suggest that views formed after time are more hostile to the mayoral options than suggested by surveys.

Under the alternative arrangements, authorities in England of fewer than 85,000 in population could opt for an enhanced committee system based on up to five policy committees, which in addition to the quasi-judicial and regulatory committees are enough to cover the limited functions of shire districts and more than some of them had previously. Such councils are required to appoint at least one overview and scrutiny committee and to provide for the council to determine the policy framework. These arrangements were a concession to Liberal Democrats in the House of Lords to avoid their supporting a Conservative amendment that would have removed prescription from the legislation. While it is easy to understand the political necessity for this provision, it is hard to justify the dividing line, particularly to authorities a few thousand or so above 85,000 in population. The only exceptions to that dividing line in England are Brighton and Hove and Harrow, as a result of a provision, no longer available now councils have adopted their constitutions, allowing authorities to specify an enhanced committee system as the fallback position in a mayoral referendum.

In Wales, the alternative arrangements differ from those in England. They provide for modified executive arrangements, with a Board constituted proportionate to party strength exercising executive functions. The authority of the council over executive functions is maintained, unlike the main executive models. 'Nothing in these regulations shall prevent a local authority from exercising those functions delegated to a Board' (Statutory Instrument 2001, No. 2284, W 173, s. 7.2).

The three options

The choice is between the three executive options, except for those authorities eligible for the alternative arrangements, 59 of which have adopted them. All but eleven of the others have adopted the leader and cabinet option. Those that have chosen mayoral options have held referendums and referendums have been held following successful petitions and once on the direction of the Secretary of State. All these referendums, apart from that in Stoke-on-Trent, have been on the mayor and cabinet option. By December 2002 there had been 30 referendums with the mayoral option being rejected in nineteen of them.

Directly elected mayor and cabinet

The mayor is elected by the whole electorate using the supplementary vote. Voters can exercise a second preference. If no candidate obtains 50 per cent of the votes cast, all candidates except the top two are eliminated, and their second preferences distributed among those two. Mayoral elections for seven authorities were held in May and for four in October 2002. The mayors elected included Independents in Bedford, Hartlepool, Mansfield, Middlesbrough and Stoke-on-Trent or nearly half the elections, a Conservative in North Tyneside, a Liberal Democrat in Watford and Labour in Hackney, Lewisham, Newham and Doncaster. The Greater London Authority also has a directly elected mayor under separate legislation, currently Ken Livingstone who was elected as an Independent.

Directly elected mayors become members of the council, although not the chair, the council choosing a separate chair. After the initial term, which can be less to fit electoral cycles, the mayors are elected for four years. They have substantial powers. The mayor appoints a cabinet from among the councillors, and does not require council approval for their appointment. The mayor can at any time remove members of the cabinet and make new appointments. The mayor can determine the powers to be exercised by the cabinet, by individual cabinet members, by officers or by themselves. A leader of the council can have similar powers, but only if so decided by the council, whereas the mayor's powers are prescribed by the Act. The mayor's proposed budget and policy framework can only be altered if two-thirds of the council vote against it (Statutory Instrument 2001, No. 3384, Schedule 1, Part 1, s. 7 and s. 13). The government has argued that because the mayors have a mandate from the electorate as a whole, it is right that they have substantial powers to carry their policies. But the council also has a mandate which may be more recent than the mayor's mandate. If the council rejects or amends these proposals by a majority of less than the two-thirds, there is gridlock that presumably can only be overcome by negotiation between the mayor and all or some of the councillors.

Under the legislation, the mayor cannot be removed from office within the four-year period, other than by disqualification through imprisonment, bankruptcy or similar provisions. The mayor is in a fundamentally different position from other political executives in the United Kingdom. Prime ministers can be removed from office or be forced to call an election by a vote of no confidence carried by a simple majority in the House of Commons. Even if a council unanimously passed a vote of no confidence in the mayor, they would not have to resign. Mayoral elections could return a popular local figure with no experience of politics or of management who could be a great success or a great failure. In the latter event, there would be nothing that could be done about it until the four years were up, either by the council or the electorate.

In countries where there are directly elected mayors, there are often procedures by which they can be removed or forced to stand for reelection. Such a procedure is not easily initiated, since the removal of a mayor should only be possible if major problems are encountered. One method is by a vote of no confidence carried by a two-thirds or other special majority of the council. The other method is by the right of recall, which allows a specified percentage of the electorate to petition for a new election (Clarke *et al.*, 1996; Cronin, 1989). These procedures are rarely used, but are a significant safeguard against mayoral abuse of power or sheer incompetence. The government resisted all attempts to include any such provisions in the legislation, arguing that any mayor who was ineffective would resign – a rather over-optimistic view! The strong position of the mayor reflects the government's belief in individual leadership. Whether the dominance of a single individual is appropriate to the governance of complex urban communities is open to question. The government's thinking harks back to simplistic models of urban change or of industrial entrepreneurship that may be outdated in present society.

There are strong arguments for directly elected mayors and strong arguments against. The key argument for and against is the same – it creates one clear point of responsibility and accountability. The concentration of power can be seen as a strength, creating a focus for power and influence both within the authority and within the community. The concentration of power can be seen as a danger, raising issues of corruption at the extreme, but more generally of an authoritarian approach and the possible neglect of issues that do not command mayoral attention.

There are counter arguments for each of the arguments put forward for directly elected mayors. It is argued that turnout will be increased because of the interest aroused by mayoral elections. There is no clear evidence that mayoral elections increase turnout (Clarke *et al.*, 1996, pp. 15–16). In the United States turnout can be below that in the United Kingdom, when low registration is taken into account. Despite the media publicity given to the first mayoral election in London, turnout was slightly lower than in the preceding London borough elections. Mayoral elections have not so far led to a significantly increased turnout, although one would have expected the first elections to have aroused particular interest. In the four October 2002 mayoral elections, turnouts were below the most recent council elections even when the mayoral elections were held by post.

It is argued that the election of mayors will lead to national prominence for local politicians, giving them attention in the national media and establishing their position in national affairs. The attention given in the media to Ken Livingstone is quoted, but the media paid similar attention when he was the leader of the Greater London Council before its abolition by the Conservative government. This attention reflects the media's focus on London. It is doubtful if even directly elected mayors in Birmingham or Manchester would receive anything like the same degree of attention, never mind Lewisham, Watford or North Tyneside, particularly if there were many rather than few such mayors. There has been little national media attention paid either to the mayoral elections or to the mayors elected. If the government really wished to give national prominence to local government figures, there are simpler ways of doing so: by involving them in national affairs on commissions or in task forces or by membership of the House of Lords.

It is argued that directly elected mayors will provide dynamic leadership in urban regeneration, giving new vitality to towns and cities. They might, although it could be physical development centred on prestige projects at a cost to the complex of social and environmental and even economic issues that are equally critical to the vitality of urban areas. Bullman and Page concluded in their account of German experience:

> There is however a danger that if current moves to 'personalise' local politics through direct elections for key officials are pushed forward, the advantages of the parliamentary system will be lost. And such moves may reflect a desire to stifle the lively political debates about basic issues of economic, social and environmental policy taking place at local level rather than any real commitment to improve the quality of local self-government. (Bullman and Page, 1994, p. 52)

In any event, leadership in urban regeneration does not depend on directly elected mayors, as the example of leaders in many towns and cities shows.

After greater experience it may be easier to make a judgement, but there does not appear to be an overwhelming case for the degree of concentration of power and security of tenure espoused by the government. Ironically, while advocated for the big cities, the directly elected mayor may prove to be more suited to the smaller town than for the big city with its complex issues and mixture of communities.

The use of the title of mayor has been a source of confusion, as people naturally associate the title with the traditional social and ceremonial role of first citizen and chair of the council, and not that of political leader. The government has decided that the title of mayor should be reserved for the directly elected mayor, where that option is adopted. The government has made an exception where the title of mayor as chair of the council derives from ancient custom or royal charter. Confusion could be created because some authorities are entitled to retain the title of mayor for the traditional role, while others would have to abandon it.

The loss of the title for the traditional role will create expectations that the elected mayor will play that role. That is unlikely to be possible in practice. In many towns and cities the roles of the mayor and of the political leader are full-time or almost full-time. It would not be possible for the elected mayor, carrying out all the functions of the leader and probably more, to take over the mass of engagements carried out by past mayors, nor would it be desirable for that to be the case. An elected mayor could undertake major public duties which normally involve leaders. It is uncertain whether it would be appropriate for an elected mayor to wear the robes and chain which are associated with the traditional role. The chair of the council could carry out the remaining duties but there might not be the same interest as in a mayoral visit and even less if the chair could not wear the mayoral chain.

It seems likely that there will be a loss of or at least a marked reduction in the traditional role. That loss may not seem important. The mayoral role has been virtually ignored by most recent academic writers. In the main texts on local government the role receives almost no mention. Yet to many organisations and community groups the role is important. Schools, residential homes and local firms welcome mayoral visits. The position and its role are widely appreciated by the public and the mayor is always greeted with warmth – not always the case with the leader! It is difficult to understand why the government resisted attempts to retain the title for the traditional role and insisted on the mayoral title for a very different role – a source of confusion in sounding public opinion about new political structures.

Leader and cabinet

The leader and cabinet option is seen as the nearest to the previous structure. In many authorities, there had been an unofficial executive based on the leadership of the majority party. Yet even so, the leader and cabinet option represents a fundamental change with the abolition of most decision-making committees.

A major difference between the leader and the mayoral options is that the leader necessarily has the support of the council. If the leader does not have that support, the council can and probably will remove him or her in a way that is not possible with elected mayors. The government suggested possible leadership models that approach the mayoral model in powers and in relative security of tenure. The guidance outlines two alternatives for the appointment of the cabinet:

- where the cabinet is appointed by the executive leader and the executive leader determines the scheme of delegation; or
- where the cabinet is appointed by the full council and the council determines the scheme of delegation. (DETR, 2000–2, para. 4.62)

The former approaches the mayor and cabinet option, while the latter follows past practice. The guidance suggests a number of hybrid arrangements. For example, the council could determine the membership of the cabinet, but the leader would determine the responsibilities of cabinet members. Research has shown that in the councils covered by a survey the council appoints the cabinet members in 62 per cent of authorities, but determines their portfolios in only 45 per cent (Stoker *et al.*, 2002, pp. 34 and 37).

The guidance also suggests that the leader and cabinet could be given a term of office extending beyond a year. The government was seeking a leadership model that approached the elected mayor model, limiting the dependence of the leader on continuing council support, although it is difficult to see how, in practice, a leader could continue without such support even if given a longer term. The leader and cabinet model is distinguished by the dependence of the leader on the support of the council. A close link between the council and leader is a defining feature of this model. To make the leader into an elected mayor by the back door would challenge what many have seen as the merit of the leader and cabinet option.

Mayor and council manager

Stoke-on-Trent is the only authority to have introduced this option, following a referendum initiated by a petition from the electorate. Nearly every other authority has dismissed the mayor and council manager model as beyond serious consideration. The combination of an elected mayor, itself unpopular with councillors, and a council manager has been automatically ruled out by councils. To councillors this option seemed the greatest threat to their role, but this view underestimated the extent to which a council manager is directly responsible to the council.

The mayor and council manager option differs significantly from the mayor and cabinet option. Whereas in the mayor and cabinet model, the executive powers are given to the mayor who determines how those powers are delegated, that is not the case in the mayor and council manager model, where the executive powers are given to the council manager (including the responsibility for the appointment of all staff) who determines how they are delegated. While the mayor is elected directly and cannot be removed by the council, the council manager is appointed by the council and can be dismissed by the council. The council manager is, therefore, as set out in the guidance, 'responsible to the council as a whole' (DETR, 2000–2, para. 4.82) in a way elected mayors are not.

There is no cabinet in this model and the Act describes the mayor and council manager together as the executive. The mayor can appoint one or more committees to advise the executive whose membership need not be proportionate to party strength on the council. The legislation does not, however, give the executive any direct powers, since these are given to the council manager alone. The council manager can delegate those powers to the executive, but not to the mayor alone or to the advisory committees. In determining the delegations, the council manager 'must have regard to any advice given by the elected mayor' (Local Government Act 2000, s. 16.3). One would expect the council manager to follow that advice except where it is contrary to the guidance issued by the Secretary of State that 'the authority must have regard to' (s. 38.1). That guidance states: 'The council manager should generally not delegate to the executive, except that she or he should delegate decisions on the broad shape and content of draft plans and strategies before their submission to the council for consideration.' Even on these issues the mayor cannot impose his or her views and if the mayor and council manager disagree 'they should each put their views separately to the council" (DETR, 2000–2, para 4.90). One presumes the council then decides between the proposals by a simple majority, rather than the two-thirds majority, required to make changes in proposals on which mayor and council manager agree.

The mayor in this model is in a very different position from the mayor in the mayor and cabinet model. The mayor has the standing that comes from direct election, but lacks executive powers. Those lie with the council manager who is responsible to the council. The elected mayor's role is to give broad political guidance to the council manager in line with manifesto commitments and the policy framework. However, all of the executive decisions for delivering and implementing the framework will be the responsibility of the council manager. The council manager is expected 'to have regard to any political steer from the mayor' (DETR, 2000–2, para. 4.17) and will naturally respect the mayor's views, but will also wish to have regard to the views of the council, to which the manager is responsible. Problems will not arise where the mayor and council are in agreement, but if the mayor does not command a majority on the council he or she may lack an effective role, since in these circumstances, the council manager will probably have to pay attention to the views of the council and its leadership.

In giving the council manager the executive functions, along with responsibility to the council, the legislation makes the role similar to that of the city manager in the United States. The legislation appears to confuse the position by making the elected mayor part of the executive along with the council manager, although all the executive functions are given to the council manager – a confusion not found in the United States. The council manager form in the United States did not originally allow for an elected mayor and still does not involve one in 30 per cent of authorities adopting the council manager form. Even where there is an elected mayor they are not a member of the executive. The mayor is important by virtue of leading the council, but has no formal authority separate from the council.

The council manager form in the United States is based on the authority of the council. Unlike the executive mayor form, there is no separation of powers. The Model City Charter set out by the National Civic League for the council manager form emphasises that 'The council is to be the pivot of the municipal system. It is to be the final source of local authority, but delegating some of them' and 'all of the powers that can be exercised by the city rest in the popularly elected city council' (National Civic League, 1992, p. 6). The manager should recognise that 'responsibility for policy execution rests with members' (ibid., p. 28). William Hamsell, the executive director of the International City Management Association, stresses that 'the council manager form provides a system in which there is no separation of powers' and 'all power is concentrated in the council'. 'An appointed manager must be aware that the powers of local government belong to the council. Any authority or responsibility assigned to the manager by the council or by the citizens can be removed at any time, or for any reason' (Hamsell, 1993). The council manager is, in the words of the Charter, 'continuously responsible to the city council' (National Civic League, 1992, p. 28). The position of the mayor and council manager option in the United Kingdom approaches the American model, although it is not identical with it and is confused by the description of the mayor and council manager as the executive even though giving the executive functions to the council manager.

It has not been sufficiently recognised in the United Kingdom that there is a fundamental difference between the role and powers of the mayor in the mayor and council manager model and in the mayor and cabinet model.

Conclusion

This chapter has set out the main provisions of the legislation on political structures. The next chapter discusses the issues raised in implementing the legislation with a conclusion covering both chapters. At this stage it is only necessary to highlight the extent of prescription, limiting as it does the scope for local choice that is a condition of effective local government and a means of learning how political structures can be made more effective.

5 Making New Political Structures Work

The emphasis given by the government to the role of political structures in democratic renewal has been stressed in the preceding chapters. This chapter focuses on the problems of implementation – due in part to the inadequate preparation of the government's proposals.

The process of legislation

The legislation on political structures was not based on any substantial study of the workings of executive models in local government in Europe or America. The government did not undertake any significant research into how such models operated. Nor had any major research been undertaken by academics in Britain. It was well-known that many countries had executive mayors, although it was not always appreciated that in countries such as France or Spain, the mayors were appointed by the council. There was, however little information on how such systems worked and, above all, on the role of the council.

The government began the preparation of legislation with little firm basis beyond the statement that the new structures would be based on separation of the executive and scrutiny roles and that the three broad options would give expression to that principle. As the process of legislation proceeded through consultation and pre-legislative consideration of a draft bill, ideas had to be worked out as issues arose. During the passage of the bill through Parliament, further issues arose and had to be dealt with. There were nearly one thousand amendments moved by the government during the legislative process – the implications of which had not always been thoroughly thought through.

In the course of the preparation and enactment of the legislation, major changes were made in the government's approach. The simplistic idea of the separation of the executive and scrutiny roles lost its dominance, as understanding grew about the nature of executive models in local government and of the problems involved in their operation. Many authorities did not appreciate the fundamental nature of these changes. As a result there were a series of misunderstandings about the new political structures, as developed in the legislative process.

The misunderstandings

The basis of the new structures

The speeches and the writings of the advocates of the new structures had inculcated the belief that the basis of the new structures was the separation of the executive and scrutiny roles. It misled many in local government who failed to appreciate that that was no longer the main principle underlying the new structures that had emerged from the legislative process. Nor is it the principle underlying executive structures in other countries. There, structures are based on a distinction between the role of the council in determining policy and the role of the executive in implementing that policy, as well as being the main source of recommendations on policy. The structures now prescribed by the legislation are largely based on that distinction and therefore on the supremacy of the council in the determination of policy – at least, in the leader and cabinet model.

The Local Authorities (Functions and Responsibilities) (England) Regulations 2000 prescribe that the policy framework, the budget and capital programme have to be adopted by the full council. The policy framework, within which the executive has to act, consists of the community plan, the best value performance plan and a series of other statutory plans such as the education development plan, the land-use development plan and the community care plan. The local authority can place certain other plans in the policy framework, including the council's corporate plan and the local agenda 21 plan covering sustainable development. The regulations prescribe that, with the exception of special provisions for urgent matters, only the full council can make a decision contrary to the policy framework. The monitoring officer is responsible for identifying such decisions, which are *ultra vires*, that is, beyond the powers of the executive.

These provisions make clear that the authority for the policy framework rests upon the council, even though the executive will normally propose the various elements of the framework. The council has to decide whether to accept, amend or reject the plans and the budget and capital programme. There have to be provisions for conflict resolution where the council and the executive are not in agreement. These have to provide an opportunity for the executive to object to any changes made by the council, but the final decision rests with the council. The guidance states that in the leader and cabinet model the council's decision can be made by a simple majority, although a council's constitution could require a greater majority. Councils generally have laid down that the council makes its decisions on the policy framework by a simple majority, expressing the principle that the council has the responsibility for determining the policy framework in the leader and cabinet model. In the mayoral models a two-thirds majority of the council is required to amend the executive's proposals, which weakens the council's role.

The meaning of scrutiny

Misunderstanding arose because the word 'scrutiny' suggested a focus on specific decisions or on critical appraisals of performance. Councillors saw those roles as limited and negative. The government recognised that the word was misleading and the legislation prescribes not the expected 'scrutiny committees', but 'overview and scrutiny committees', a rewording designed to suggest a wider role. *Local Leadership: Local Choice*, the government paper presenting the draft legislation, suggested four roles:

- consider and investigate broad policy issues and make reports and recommendations to the executive or council as appropriate;
- consider the budget plans, proposed policy framework and other plans of the executive, and make reports and recommendations, including recommendations proposing amendments to the executive or council as appropriate;

- provide advice to the executive on major issues before final decisions are made; and
- review decisions taken by the executive and how it is implementing council policy, and make reports and recommendations, including proposals for changes to policies or practices, to the executive or council as appropriate. (DETR, 1999e, p. 28)

Section 21.2 of the Local Government Act 2000 adds to the overview and scrutiny role:

- make reports or recommendations to the authority or the executive on matters which affect the local authority's area or the inhabitants of that area.

The Health and Social Care Act 2001 gives local authorities with social services functions a responsibility for overview and scrutiny on matters relating to health services with powers to require attendance of representatives of the health authorities. In addition overview and scrutiny can undertake best value reviews under the Local Government Act 1999.

Some councils did not appreciate the positive role that could be played by overview and scrutiny in policy development and in supporting community leadership, as well as reviewing specific decisions and performance.

Separation of the executive and overview and scrutiny

The emphasis given to separation between the executive role and what was originally called the scrutiny role led to misunderstandings about how the new structures could operate. It would, indeed, be strange if an overview and scrutiny committee included a cabinet member in a review of its decisions or an individual cabinet member in a review of his or her performance. The early emphasis on separation suggested to many, however, a total division of the council into the executive with the main body of councillors limited to a narrow scrutiny role in the council and a representative role in their electoral areas. An over-emphasis on separation can mean the executive is deprived of the support and help of other councillors.

Total separation has been avoided in many authorities, but in some it is still believed to be required by the new structures, although it is not what the legislation prescribes or the guidance suggests. An emphasis on separation neglects the importance given to the council in the new structures. The guidance describes the council meeting, even in the elected mayor options, as 'All councillors and an elected mayor, acting *together* as the full council' (DETR, 2000–2, para. 2.7; my italics). The government has stressed that the executive can and should seek views from overview and scrutiny committees prior to making decisions (ibid., figure 7.2). *Local Leadership: Local Choice* said, 'Frequent and effective dialogue between the executive and other councillors would be essential' (DETR, 1999e, p. 31).

Even in transitional models introduced prior to the legislation, many authorities recognised the executive's need for support and help. In North Tyneside most members of the cabinet were associated with a reference group of councillors on whom they could draw for support. In Bedfordshire, councillors were asked to designate areas of expertise which could be used by the cabinet or by the council. Different approaches have developed as executives have recognised the need to use the experience and abilities of other councillors. Some councils have appointed advisory committees for cabinet members. The Transport, Local Government and the Regions Select Committee's report on *How the Local Government Act 2000 is Working* stated they had 'received evidence that the new arrangements are working best where the split between executive and scrutiny is blurred and that non-executive councillors are more satisfied when scrutiny is used to inform the decision-making process' (Select Committee on Transport, Local Government and the Regions, 2002a, p. 15). Councillors giving support to the executive cannot themselves make decisions – that is reserved for the executive and its members. They can investigate problems, monitor developments, build up knowledge and give advice. A cabinet member responsible for education might ask a councillor to take a special interest in nursery education and give advice on issues arising, since there may not be time to keep in touch personally with all the matters within his or her remit.

Executive members often want to work with other councillors on policy development and on community issues. While it might be possible to find ways of working through overview and scrutiny, this need is often met by other mechanisms. Policy panels or working groups have been set up on which a cabinet member sits with other councillors. To allow greater flexibility, authorities can set up only the one overview and scrutiny committee required by legislation, using a variety of other means for many of the roles suggested for overview and scrutiny.

Difficulties and dangers

Effective ways of working are not easily established in new structures. Old habits have to be overcome. The adoption of a new structure embedded in a council constitution is only the start. A process of learning and adaptation has to take place, as local authorities face up to problems in making the structures work effectively and in seeking the efficiency, transparency and accountability aimed at in the modernisation programme. In describing these problems and how they might be overcome, the focus of this chapter will be on the cabinet and leader model adopted by nearly every authority with a population over 85,000 and some with less, although many of the issues raised are relevant to the mayoral models and some to the alternative arrangements open to authorities with a population under 85,000.

Executive overload

The executive is the most easily established part of the new structure. Many authorities already had unofficial executives, although they could not be given formal recognition if composed of members of one party, as was normal in majority-controlled councils. Executives are now part of the formal structure and make and have to make most of the council's decisions. Many members of the executive are used to the decision-making role from their previous experience as committee chairs. The significant change is in the number of decisions executives are required to make. The executive has taken over responsibilities previously exercised by committees and inherited all the decisions those committees made.

Cabinets face overload in many authorities as they wrestle with long agendas composed of the detailed issues the previous committees dealt with. The meeting of the executive can become a setting for 'getting through the agenda', as members nod through items, just as in the worst form of committee. In such meetings the executive has little time to develop policy, work on strategies or face the challenge of community leadership. There is no space for these roles on the agenda or even if they were on the agenda there is no time for the in-depth discussion required.

There are ways of dealing with these problems, provided they are faced. Executives need different forms of meeting for different roles. Some executives have combined formal meetings for on-going business with other meetings focused on a specific policy or on issues raised by community leadership. That change although desirable is not sufficient. The burden of agendas remains, often overloaded with a mixture of the important and the unimportant. Delegation is the solution. The legislation allows three possibilities: to individual cabinet members, to officers and/or to area committees. There has been reluctance to increase delegation to officers and reluctance in some authorities to delegate to individual members of the executive, in part because of a fear of reinforcing departmentalism, but the inevitability of delegation is being recognised as executives face the reality of overload.

The government did not see any need for area committees when it first put forward its proposals. It came to recognise the contradiction between an emphasis on democratic renewal on the one hand and centralisation of decision-making on the other. The legislation now allows, but does not require, the appointment of area committees to which the executive can delegate functions. About half of the authorities – more than had previously done so – have delegated certain responsibilities to area committees, both to overcome overload and to avoid undue centralisation.

Overload is also being overcome by the use of councillors in support of executive members as described above. While these developments cannot reduce the number of decisions to be made by an executive and its members, support and background work can help in the preparation for decisions.

Too much scrutiny?

Local authorities can have too much scrutiny, as well as too little. In some authorities best value reviews are undertaken separately from overview and scrutiny. The result is that the same activity can be reviewed for best value, again for overview and scrutiny and yet again in inspection by one of the inspectorates discussed in Chapter 11, with the best value review itself being subject to a review by the best value inspectorate.

Overview and scrutiny committees can themselves undertake too much work, particularly if focused on the narrower forms of scrutiny. They have the power to call in decisions of the executive after they are made and to ask for them to be reconsidered before they are implemented (Local Government Act 2000, s. 21.3). Committees that concentrate on this task will have little time to develop work on policy or to give advice to the executive on decisions they are considering. Yet, work carried out before decisions are made is more likely to influence decisions than challenging them after the executive has made its decision.

Making overview and scrutiny effective

Overview and scrutiny has presented difficulties in authorities, being seen as new to local government, for that was how it was sold, although this ignored the long experience in many authorities of performance review and in policy panels and working groups. Authorities have had to find appropriate ways of working.

One danger is that overview and scrutiny committees adopt the pattern of traditional committee working, with its regular cycle of meetings, its routinised agenda and a style of chairing focusing more on getting the business through than on facilitating discussion. Such an approach is clearly inappropriate for overview and scrutiny. Yet in some authorities the habits of committee working and the adoption of a committee cycle have moulded the work of overview and scrutiny. The agendas look very much the same and reinforce past ways of working, rather than drawing on experience of more flexible ways of working on policy panels.

Where the need for new ways of working has been recognised some authorities have taken oral evidence sessions of select committees of the House of Commons as the model of overview and scrutiny. Select committees take oral evidence through formal question and answer sessions rather than through discussion with those giving evidence. Overview and scrutiny committees have the opportunity to find better ways of working.

One mistake is to assume that the committees have to adopt a standard way of working applicable to all their tasks. The style required for a review of performance is different from that required for reviewing policy, or exploring community issues. Question and answer sessions are only one possible form of meeting. They may be more appropriate for reviewing perform-ance than for developing policy. The seminar involving free-flowing discussion may be more appropriate in the development of policy, although effective working will use a variety of approaches. New ways of involving the public can be explored. In Hartlepool the public were encouraged to take part in discus-sion by the format adopted.

Overview and scrutiny requires officer support and that can be difficult in a small authority with limited staff. Two different types of support are required. The first is committee servicing which has to be much more flexible than the necessarily rou-tinised procedures of traditional committees. The second is research and analysis to help the committees investigate issues. There can also be support by external advisers not merely in giv-ing evidence or taking part in discussions, but as members of an overview and scrutiny committee considering a particular topic.

The guidance recommends that overview and scrutiny should be free from whipping, although recognising that it is a matter for the political parties to decide both locally and nationally. What actually happens will depend on the national parties and on local circumstances. The Labour Party model standing orders have been revised to recommend that overview and scrutiny (and meetings of the cabinet) should be free from whipping. Research into the operation of overview and scrutiny committees concluded, 'It is rarely the case that formal whipping or discipline is applied to overview and scrutiny councillors' (Snape *et al.*, 2002, p. 42). Although that is the formal position, the reality can be different, as the research recognised. Where a committee is considering an issue on which there is clear party policy, it is unlikely that members of the committees will feel free to dissent from that policy. Even if there is no formal discipline, self-discipline can apply. Members of the majority party will be reluctant to criticise their leadership in public with the opposition present and with the press ready to highlight party divisions. Informal pressure can be brought to bear to ensure party positions are supported. Such problems are not necessarily common. On many issues no deep party divides exist. Overview and scrutiny committees find that they are free from party conflict for much of their work. In a number of authorities the chairs of overview and scrutiny committees are shared between parties, although in others the majority party has taken all the chairs.

Authorities have to consider how the overview and scrutiny work programme is determined. Each committee should have the right to decide on work to be undertaken, but by itself that could lead to gaps and overlaps. Some authorities have set up coordinating committees to overcome these problems. In addition, the council itself may decide that overview and scrutiny should consider an issue, or the executive ask for advice on an issue.

Reports of overview and scrutiny can go to the executive or to the council. One would expect reports on policy and on investigations asked for by the council to be considered by the council, with the executive having the opportunity to comment. Reports on matters within the responsibility of the executive will go to the executive, and need only go to the council if the overview and scrutiny committee is not satisfied with the response. Overview and scrutiny committees cannot enforce their views on the executive even if they have council support, unless it is on an issue about the policy framework or a decision contrary to that framework. However, an executive that paid no attention to reports from overview and scrutiny could soon face difficulties, particularly if it had to be reappointed by the council each year. Conflicts between executives and overview and scrutiny committees are mainly likely to arise where overview and scrutiny is being used for faction fighting within or between parties.

Over time most authorities are working out their approaches to all these issues. Problems arise where an authority has not been ready to learn by experience and adapt and change their approach.

Open government

The guidance sets out high hopes that 'there should be greater dialogue between all councillors, the public and other stakeholders than has often been the case in the past' (DETR, 2000–2, para. 7.10). Yet the legislation as originally drafted allowed executives to meet in private and was challenged, as defeating the stated aim of increasing transparency in decision-making. The government met these objections by amendments and subsequent regulations requiring cabinets to make key decisions in public, unless the decision involves matters that are exempt or confidential under the legislation applying to all council business. Reports for meetings involving key decisions, but not earlier draft reports, must be made available publicly at the same time as they are made available to cabinet members. The provision for key decisions to be made in public is 'not intended to extend to early collective discussion where the executive may decide to narrow the options under consideration' and it also allows the executive to have a political discussion without officers present provided that a key decision is not decided at that meeting (DETR, 2000–2, para. 7.37). In Wales a simpler solution was adopted, requiring all cabinet meetings to be held in public except for normally exempt business (Statutory Instrument 2001, No. 2290, W 178).

The regulations require the preparation of a forward plan covering the key decisions expected over the next four months. It should set out:

- a short description of matters under consideration and when key decisions are expected to be taken;
- who is responsible for taking the decisions and how they can be contacted;
- what relevant reports and background papers are available; and
- how and when the decision-maker intends to involve local stakeholders in the decision-making process. (DETR, 2000–2, para. 7.13)

These provisions create problems for authorities and are widely seen as imposing unnecessary bureaucracy. It is not easy to anticipate the key decisions to be made over the coming four months, so the plans have to be updated monthly.

The provisions only cover key decisions, which are defined as involving 'significant expenditure' or are 'significant' in their effect on communities. Significant expenditure will be expenditure above thresholds specified by each authority. A significant effect on communities is defined as an effect on communities living and working in two or more wards, but is not restricted to decisions having such an effect. It is recognised that some decisions affecting a single ward could be regarded as key decisions having a significant effect on communities (DETR, 2000–2, para. 7.20). Key decisions can be taken by the cabinet, by its committees, by individual members of the executive or even by officers although that would be unusual. The concept of key decisions is deeply ambiguous and can be subject to different interpretations, as the government found in seeking to give greater precision to the word 'significant' – an attempt now largely abandoned at national level, being left to local authorities to decide.

Yet after all these efforts, the provisions do not fully meet concerns about open government. It is far from certain that any definition of key decisions can be satisfactory. Whether or not a decision is a key one can always be argued about. An individual may regard a decision as important even if the authority does not. One person's minor decision is another person's key decision. There are too many loopholes for an authority that wishes to evade the need for open government. Decisions made by individual members of the executive are not subject to the requirement that key decisions have to be made in public. In the mayor and cabinet model some of the most important decisions are likely to be made by the mayor. Meetings for political discussion can be held in private without officers present. In such meetings the decision may well become clear even though the formal decision cannot be made there.

The problem with the whole complex of provisions about key decisions is that they do not meet the real issue, because attention was focused on the weaknesses of the committee system and its strengths were neglected. It is true that decisions at committee meetings have often been predetermined by group decisions made in private as can still be the case with the new political structures. Those decisions were subject to challenge by and discussion with the opposition in a way that may not be possible with meetings of the cabinet. Cabinets, in most although not all authorities, have been constituted from the majority party or the parties forming an administration in hung authorities.

Public meetings of the executive can be relatively formal occasions. Many decisions are nodded through. The reality is that most decisions are not made at a fixed point, but grow in informal discussion. If debate takes place at the meeting, it is likely to be for form's sake. Members of the executive are not likely to disagree strongly with their colleagues when the press and public and even the opposition are present. It is argued that the opposition can challenge decisions at overview and scrutiny committees through the exercise of call-in powers. Such a provision, if much used for this purpose, would consign overview and scrutiny to a negative role and create the party conflicts it is hoped overview and scrutiny can avoid. The simplest way for authorities to resolve these issues would be to hold all decision-making meetings in public, whether concerned with key decisions or not, and for the opposition to be invited to attend with the right to speak if not to vote.

All decisions taken by members of the executive whether individually or collectively, as well as key decisions taken by officers, have to be published as soon as possible, along with the reasons for the decision. The reasons could be difficult to establish, since members of the executive might have different reasons for making the decision. Any reports on which the decision was based have to be made available at the same time as the decision.

Can something be done about the council meeting?

There is a danger that the council meeting has gone unconsidered by authorities, along with other issues. It has been assumed too readily in some authorities that they had modernised if they had established an executive and overview and scrutiny committees, without realising that changes in political structures should have an impact on the whole working of the authority.

The nature of the council meeting is one of the most important issues raised by the new structures. The role of the council as the authority for the policy framework is the basis of the structure, giving a new importance to its meetings. It is the only setting where all councillors are involved in decision-making and the decisions are the most important made by the authority.

Misled by a focus on the executive and overview and scrutiny roles, some councils reduced the frequency of council meetings, whereas councils are now finding more frequent meetings are required if the policy framework is to be given proper consideration. It is significant that authorities abroad operating executive models often have council meetings much more frequently than in the United Kingdom. In the United States, 56 per cent of councils in authorities with a population of between 250,000 and

500,000 meet once a week, with 69 per cent of all councils meeting at least twice a month (Renner and De Santis, 1998, p. 30).

There has long been a case for redesigning council meetings. The council meeting could be the forum where the elected representatives of the citizens discuss key issues facing local communities. In most authorities, however, the council meeting considered reports from committees, or even the minutes of committees, discussing again matters already much discussed. In addition, motions could be put down for debate on party lines. The council meeting, far from arousing public interest, stifled it and received little attention even in the local press.

New structures provide the opportunity and create the need for redesign of council meetings. Three roles for council meetings merit consideration:

- the determination of the policy framework;
- the opportunity to provide community leadership; and
- holding the executive to account.

The legislation places the responsibility for determining the policy framework on the council meeting. If that is to be done seriously it should involve reconsideration of council procedures. I have put forward one approach (Stewart, 2000b): plans in the policy framework could be subject to consideration at more than one meeting. There could be a preliminary discussion or first reading, at the conclusion of which the plan could be referred to an overview and scrutiny committee and/or for public hearings before being taken with any proposed amendments for a second reading in a subsequent meeting. A similar approach is found in the United States for local legislation or ordnances (National Civic League, 1992).

The local authority's role in community leadership merits recognition in council meetings. The council can hold a state-of-the-area debate focusing on key problems and opportunities and on directions for the future. Special council meetings can be held to discuss key community issues, such as crime and community safety. The meeting can become a forum for the community.

Accountability involves both giving an account and being held to account. The executive is accountable to the council, at least in giving an account of its stewardship. Procedures are required for reports by the executive and its members, which can then be discussed. The council procedures should also make provision for the discussion of overview and scrutiny reports. The extent to which the executive can be held to account depends on the form of political structure. The council can hold the leader and cabinet to account in authorities adopting that model. While councils can require accounts from elected mayors, they have no means of holding them to account, since mayors are assumed to be accountable to the electorate.

The importance of the council meeting, along with the creation of an executive, makes the role of its chair of great importance. The chair has a vital responsibility for maintaining the position of the council against encroachment by the executive and protecting the rights of the opposition and of backbenchers. It should no longer be sufficient that the holder of the position is determined by seniority as has been the case in some authorities.

Some authorities have considered these issues, but in others the council meeting has remained virtually unchanged. Such authorities have not appreciated the full implications of the new political structures.

The role of officers

In some authorities it was assumed that the position of the officers and even of the chief executive and chief officers would remain unchanged in the new structures. This assumption was encouraged by the government's guidelines, which describe the role of officers in traditional terms: 'Officers should be responsible for day-to-day managerial and operational decisions within the local authority and should provide support to both the executive and all councillors in their several roles' (DETR, 2000–2, para. 2.8). The role of the chief executive is 'under-pinned by the fundamental principles of political neutrality and service to the whole council' (para. 8.15).

There has always been an ambiguity in the relationship of officers to a majority administration and to the general body of councillors. The doctrine that officers serve the whole council did not sit easily with the reality of control by a majority party, which was recognised as forming an administration long before the adoption of executive structures. The opposition has often suspected that chief executives and other chief officers were closet supporters of the majority party because they worked closely with its leadership. This suspicion has occasionally resulted in the forced retirement of the chief executive when control changed, although the chief executive and chief officers had merely been loyally serving the council majority. The wise chief executive maintained contact with the opposition parties, for the opposition of today may be the majority of tomorrow. Chief executives as servants of the whole council have had to insist on the right of the council to information, but will have done so with finesse, so as not to lose the confidence of the administration. A delicate balance had to be maintained.

The new structures can make the situation more difficult. While the previous structures often had 'administrations', they were not part of the official structure. Now there is an official executive with wide-ranging powers. It will be hard for chief executives and chief officers to see their responsibilities to the whole council having even as much importance as before. Consider the position of a chief officer appearing before an overview and scrutiny committee, being asked 'what did you advise', when they had advised against the executive's decision or a decision by an individual member of the executive. The executive will not welcome the officer describing his or her reasons for advising against the decision. It can be argued that advice on a key decision made by the executive will have been given in public, but this need not be true about decisions made by individual members of the executive nor about advice given privately before papers are prepared.

Over time, if individual members of the executive are given authority to make decisions, they may come to see themselves as the equivalent of ministers responsible for their departments, challenging the role of chief officer. The position of leader, or even more of a directly elected mayor in the mayor and cabinet model, could weaken the position of chief executive. The same word 'executive' being used to describe both roles is a pointer to future difficulties. The role that chief executives, chief officers and other officers will play is one of the uncertainties about the new structures. In the short term there has been relatively little change as old ways of working retain their influence. In the longer run, service for the whole council is likely to become less meaningful in many authorities. If structures are adopted drawing on parliamentary models, it is no surprise if officers come to regard themselves as no more responsible to the whole council than civil servants are to Parliament.

Authorities need to consider whether and how the relationship between councillors and officers has changed, is changing with the new structures and should change. Following such consideration protocols can be developed covering the relationship, giving expression to the results of such consideration which should involve both the executive and other councillors. Such protocols can be a point of reference, as some of the difficulties suggested above have to be faced.

The representative role

The government argued that the abolition of the committee structure would allow councillors time to develop their representative role. This argument showed a failure to appreciate the amount of time taken by overview and scrutiny, if developed seriously, as has now been found in those authorities with an effective way of working. In these authorities, overview and scrutiny is proving more time-consuming than traditional committee work. As the Select Committee's report into the operation of the Act recognizes, 'non-executive councillors report that they are attending more meetings' (Select Committee on Transport, Local Government and the Regions, 2002a, p. 19).

The emphasis on the representative role raises issues about how that role could be made effective in influencing the decision-making process. If councillors were, indeed, to have more time to consult their constituents and contact local organisations, it would only lead to frustration both for councillors and the public if nothing happens about issues raised. One solution lies in the development of area committees, consisting of the councillors for the area and attended by the public. These committees can be given executive powers for local matters within the policies of the authority. They can also be forums where local issues can be considered. An alternative approach is through area or neighbourhood forums, which can provide a setting for representatives of local organisations and other local people to consider issues along with local councillors.

Setting up area committees or forums is not enough. Procedures are required to link their views to the decision-making process and hence to the executive. Members of the executive could meet with each area committee on a rota basis. The preparation of the policy framework could draw upon work of area committees or forums, provided there are clear procedures for doing so. There is no point in developing the representative role unless that role has an influence on decisions, and that requires settings and procedures through which it can be secured.

The role of councillors

Authorities that have not considered how the role of all councillors could be developed risk widespread dissatisfaction. Neglect of the role of those councillors not in the executive deprives the authority of the resource their experience and abilities can provide. The council is operating far short of its potential if all but a few councillors are under-utilised. In the past, in order to give councillors a role, authorities had to find a committee or sub-committee for them to chair or be members of. The new structures provide opportunities to stimulate new thinking about councillors' roles. There is no need for these roles to be limited to those prescribed in the legislation, although they can be developed in a wide range of ways as the discussion on overview and scrutiny has shown.

Councillors can play a variety of roles. There are the six roles for overview and scrutiny set out earlier in this chapter, not all of which need be carried out by overview and scrutiny committees, if the authority considers other settings more effective. Apart from those roles, the new structures provide for:

- membership of the council meeting, which gains importance in the new structure;
- membership of regulatory committees and of the standards committee; and
- the representative role.

and can involve:

- membership of an area committee exercising executive powers; and/ or
- membership of an area or neighbourhood forum, considering community issues.

In addition the guidelines make clear that councillors can be:

- council representatives on outside bodies and partnerships.

There are new possibilities including:

- advisers to executive members;
- councillors appointed as policy experts on particular topics;
- councillors appointed to make contact with outside groups and to advise the authority, for example a councillor for the disabled; and
- rapporteurs appointed by the council to prepare a report on an executive proposal or an issue of concern to the council.

There are likely to be other possibilities for individual roles to develop. Some, but not all, councils have come to appreciate that while legislation requires authorities to have an executive, regulatory committees, and an overview and scrutiny committee, and prevents executive functions being given to other councillors apart from area committees, they are still able to develop other structures and procedures provided they do not breach the requirements of the legislation. Some councils have created new committees to keep the workings of the new structures under review, to ensure the coordination of overview and scrutiny or to oversee council business. Councils can pursue innovation if they consider not merely what is required and what is prohibited, but also what is possible under the legislation.

Group working

In some authorities there has been virtually no consideration given by political groups to how their organisation and way of working should change. It has been assumed, implicitly if not explicitly, that groups will as far as possible function as before although the issue of group discipline in overview and scrutiny has been recognised. Failure to recognise the need to reconsider ways of working by political groups can lead to tensions in the structures and create barriers to effective working.

Copus has argued:

It is inconceivable that councillors do not rethink the role and activities of the party group, at the same time they are reconfiguring a whole new set of political relationships and interactions within the council that executive arrangements entail . . .

The current dynamics of the group system can not be left unchanged; the inward focus it encourages of councillors conflicts with the requirements of community leadership. Group loyalty and discipline closes down, rather than stimulates public debate and involvement and can damage councillors' willingness and ability to hold an executive to account – preferring, if in the majority, to do that in group meetings. The legitimacy councillors grant to the group as a place in which to debate issues and make decisions damages openness and transparency. (Copus, 2001, pp. 13–14)

Not all will agree with these conclusions, but the need to review group working is clear. The role of the group in relation to the council's consideration of the various plans in the policy framework is of particular importance. A proposal for first and second readings was set out above. Group discipline could be relaxed on a first reading, since the only motion would be that the plan be referred to a committee for detailed consideration. The group decision on the plan would then be made after discussion on the first reading and after the committee's consideration of the plan. This suggestion is only one possibility, but illustrates the possibility of new thinking about the group and its relationship to the council and the executive.

Political groups have issues to decide about the operation of the new structures. The majority group or groups in a hung authority can offer places on the cabinet to the opposition, who have to decide whether to accept. Opposition representatives can be given the right to attend and speak at cabinet meetings. Opposition councillors have been offered and have accepted chairs of overview and scrutiny committees in some authorities.

Conclusion

The early advocacy of new political structures was based on the separation of the executive and scrutiny roles. In working out what this meant in practice, the government was inevitably influenced by the parliamentary model, which appeared to be based on the same principle. The cabinet was the executive and select committees provided the scrutiny function.

The weaknesses of the parliamentary model were ignored by advocates of the new structure, but were immediately recognised by many councillors who saw the relative powerlessness of MPs and of the House of Commons in relation to the government of the day. Councillors feared that unless they were in the executive they would be reduced to the position of the backbencher in the House of Commons. Their fears were reinforced by the emphasis given by ministers to the representative role without any indication of how that role would influence decision-making. This emphasis conjured up images of those MPs who devote themselves to constituency work with little or no influence on government policy. The model of select committees was unfortunate since select committees often have limited influence. The influence of national models on the government's proposals was also seen in the original proposals that would have allowed all cabinet meetings to be held in private.

The problems encountered in developing the new structures were due in part to lack of research into how executive models operated in countries where there was long experience of such models. What little information was available focused on mayoral systems and on the role of the mayor. Some mayors were invited to speak in the United Kingdom, but they were rarely asked about the role of the council or the division of powers between the mayor and the council. Few in the United Kingdom appreciated the frequency of council meetings in the United States, reflecting the amount of business for which they are responsible.

There was a failure in analysis. There was a failure to identify the strengths as well as the weaknesses of the committee system, paralleling the failure to identify the weaknesses as well as the strengths of the parliamentary model. The committee system brought councillors into the working of the authority. Councillors had regular contact with officers in a way that does not happen with MPs. The routinised agendas, which were seen as a weakness, built up understanding and knowledge about the authority. Too little was done to retain the strengths of the traditional system in the involvement of all councillors in the work of the authority, avoiding the frustrations of the backbencher in the House of Commons. Group meetings gave an opportunity for councillors in the majority group to make decisions even if those opportunities were not always taken. Admittedly group meetings were held in private, but committee meetings were held in public and the opposition challenge was immediate in a way that certainly does not happen in central government with Cabinet decisions made in secret.

The original positions taken by the government were modified in the process of preparing and carrying through legislation. From consultation paper to the Act, provisions changed significantly. It was difficult to defend replacing public decision-making in committees by private decision-making in cabinets when the new structures were being promoted as increasing transparency. Parliamentary pressure and opposition by the press in support of open government led to the provision that the cabinet had to meet in public when making key decisions. Even so the opportunity for decision-making by individual cabinet members raises questions as to whether transparency is decreased rather than increased by the new structures.

The government recognised that the original presentation of the new structures based on separation of the executive and scrutiny roles was inadequate. The word 'scrutiny' was changed to the phrase 'overview and scrutiny' and its meaning widened. Emphasis on the separation of the executive lessened with the recognition that the executive could draw on the advice and support of other councillors. Most important of all the role of the council in determining the policy framework was asserted, reflecting experience in other countries and perhaps the recognition that in the parliamentary model Parliament set the statutory framework. There was a continuing process of change as amendment succeeded amendment, regulation succeeded regulation and pages of guidance mushroomed.

Some local authorities have learnt that there are choices to be made and developments possible that can overcome some of the problems encountered and can maintain some of the strengths of past structures, while overcoming their weaknesses. Among the most important developments have been the establishment of advisers or advisory groups for the executive, the formation of area committees and area or neighbourhood forums and the development of other new roles for councillors. Some but not all councils have recognised that the new importance of the council meeting requires new procedures, giving the general body of councillors a meaningful role in determining policy. A process of adaptation and innovation is improving the working of the structures, although some councils have not appreciated the choices that exist both within and beyond the prescriptions of the new structure.

The government's production of many pages of detailed guidance has been a factor in the failure of councils to appreciate the scope for innovation, since they appeared to provide a comprehensive prescription. This guidance is based on limited experience of the workings of local authorities, being largely drawn up by civil servants. It reflects a fear that local authorities will evade the requirements of the legislation, if not tied down by detailed prescription. That is to emphasise the negative of evasion rather than the possibility of innovation, reflecting a command and control model of the management of change.

Many problems have been and will be encountered in the new political structures. These problems are the result of over-hasty legislation and the rejection of the alternative of learning through enabling legislation allowing, but not prescribing, new political structures. The gradual evolution of new political structures that enabling legislation would have permitted could have led to change that overcame the weaknesses of traditional structures without undermining their strengths. However, where authorities break out of perceived limitations to new possibilities, they can realise those strengths by developing roles for all councillors that build on their potential by involving them effectively in the work of the council.

The challenge to local authorities to review their political structures and legislation to open up new possibilities are strengths of the modernisation programme. The main weaknesses derive from the extent of prescription and the failure to carry out adequate preparation, making such prescription an even greater problem for the modernisation programme. The extent of prescription reflects the government's suspicions of local authorities and their view that new political structures were necessary to challenge the traditional culture, but would be evaded by authorities without such detailed prescription. Yet even within that prescription, authorities can find ways of overcoming many of the problems faced in making the new structures work, if they are not bemused by its extent or misled by the early stress on separation of executive and scrutiny. Not all have appreciated these possibilities because of the way the government advocated and implemented its proposals.

6 Councillors and the Modernisation Programme

The role of the councillor is critical in the search for democratic renewal since local democracy rests upon the effectiveness of councillors as elected representatives, – a role that distinguishes the local authority from other public bodies at local level. Yet the modernisation programme devoted relatively little attention to councillors as opposed to the political structures in which they work.

Modern Local Government did recognise the need for councillors to be more representative of the population generally: 'Fewer councillors are employed, fewer are drawn from the ethnic minorities, many more are over 45 and many fewer are women, than is the case generally' which 'cannot be healthy for local democracy'. It went on to state, 'The Government wishes to see more councillors drawn from each of these groups in future. In particular, there is a need for more talented, vigorous young people in local government able and willing to make a difference to the world around them' (DETR, 1998a, p. 36). The use of the phrase 'more talented' is significant as a code for 'calibre' generally, although used in the context of young people. The government's wish for councillors to be more representative of the population is welcome, although the groups concerned are under-represented to an even greater extent in the House of Commons.

Modern Local Government also proposed a new ethical framework for councillors, but beyond that little was said. While this chapter considers the government's proposals and the resulting changes, it starts with a wider consideration of the background of councillors and of issues about their recruitment and retention, necessary for an understanding of local government as the modernisation programme develops.

The make-up of councils

The government focused attention on the under-representation of women, ethnic minorities and young people. In England and Wales in 2001, only 27.9 per cent of councillors were women, 2.5 per cent came from ethnic minorities compared with 3 per cent of the population and there were very few young people, as Table 6.1 shows.

Since the 1960s there has been an increase in the number of women on councils – although only to a limited extent. In 1964 the percentage of women councillors was 12 per cent. There were very few ethnic councillors. The trends for women and the ethnic minorities have been in the right direction, although at a relatively slow rate. On the other hand, the number of councillors under 35 in age has remained virtually unchanged and the average age of councillors has increased from 55 in 1964 to 57 in 2001 (Maud Report, 1967b; IDeA, 2002).

In 2001, the councillors in England and Wales had the occupational status shown in Table 6.2. Of those working, 61 per cent were in the private sector, 33 per cent in the public sector and 6 per cent in the voluntary sector. The largest group of those in employment came from managerial or executive positions (36 per cent) or from professional or technical positions (28 per cent). Fifteen per cent came from administrative, clerical, secretarial or sales. Only 11 per cent came from manual or craft employment (IDeA, 2002). The managerial and executive and the professional and technical groups are over-

Table 6.1 *Age range of councillors in England and Wales*

Age range	%
Under 25	0.1
25–34	3.2
35–44	10.9
45–54	24.3
55–64	34.5
65–74	22.9
Over 75	4.1

Source: Data from IDeA, 2002.

Table 6.2 *Occupational status of councillors in England and Wales*

Status	%
Full-time employment	27
Part-time employment	9
Self-employed	16
Retired	38
Unemployed	2
Other not working	8

Source: Data from IDeA, 2002.

represented with other groups under-represented. Yet that is far from the general impression and has not been remarked on in *Modern Local Government* or in later government statements.

The political background

The dominant fact about councillors is that they are almost all elected for a political party, making political groups and party discipline key factors in the role of councilors – factors that remain important in the new political structures.

There are 22,319 councillors in Great Britain. In 2000–1 their party affiliations were as shown in Table 6.3. Party membership dominates most councils. There has been a continuous decline in the number of Independents. In county councils the number of Independents elected reduced from 12 per cent in 1973 to 3 per cent in 2001 and in the shire districts from 25 per cent in 1973 to 11 per cent in 1999. There were always few Independent councillors in the metropolitan districts and the London boroughs. There were, however, still significant numbers of Independent councillors elected in 1999 for the unitary authorities in Wales (23 per cent) and in Scotland (16 per cent).

The dominance of Independent councillors in an area was often associated with unopposed returns since there was a reluctance to challenge sitting councillors. In some cases, particularly in the past, although probably not to the same extent in Scotland and Wales, Independent councillors were party members,

Table 6.3 *Party affiliations of councillors in Great Britain*

	Number	%
Conservative	6,941	31
Labour	8,487	38
Liberal Democrat	4,382	20
Nationalists	418	1
Independents and others	2,091	9

Source: Wilson and Game, 2002, p. 278.

normally Conservative, who chose to stand as Independents in local elections. Part of their decline in numbers was due to national party pressure to stand under the party label.

The period since 1973, when the new local authorities were elected, has seen a growth in the number of councillors from parties other than Conservative and Labour. In England there was a general increase in the number of Liberal (later Liberal Democrat) councillors:

- in London Boroughs from 1 per cent in 1974 to 16 per cent in1998;
- in metropolitan districts from 7 per cent in 1973 to 23 per cent in 2000;
- in shire districts from 7 per cent in 1973 to 22 per cent in1999; and
- in counties from 6 per cent in 1973 to 18 per cent in 2001.

Because of reorganisation the figures for counties and shire districts are not directly comparable, but if the figures for shire districts and unitary authorities are added together Liberal Democrats account for over 20 per cent of councillors, confirming the extent of the increase. The period since 1973 has also seen a marked increase in the number of Scottish National and Plaid Cymru councillors as well as an increase in the number of Liberal Democrat councillors. In 1999, the Scottish National Party gained 17 per cent of council seats in Scotland and Plaid Cymru 16 per cent in Wales, compared with 6 per cent of Scottish districts in 1974 and 3 per cent of Welsh districts in 1973 (Rallings and Thrasher, 1997, 1999–2001).

There are exceptions to the dominance of the main parties, of which the most remarkable is Epsom and Ewell where the great majority of councillors have, since the 1930s, come from local resident associations with the majority of households in membership. In 2002, Resident Association candidates gained control of the adjoining authority of Elmbridge. A relatively little noticed change has seen new parties or organised groups making headway in local elections. In 2002, the Green Party had five councillors in Lancaster, four councillors in Stroud, three in Brighton and Hove, Kirklees, Oxford and Leeds, and councillors in seventeen other authorities. In addition three members of the London Assembly were elected for the Green Party from the added list. In Wyre Forest, Health Concern, a party formed to oppose the closure of a local hospital, controls the district council as well as winning six seats on the county council and the parliamentary seat in 2001. In Birmingham, the Justice Party (formerly the Justice for Kashmir Party) has three seats. In Stoke-on-Trent, the Labour Party, having won every seat in the first election for the unitary authority, is no longer in the majority, mainly because of seats won by the Independent Group, which has the same number of seats as Labour in what is now a hung authority. The Liberal Party, based on Liberals who opposed the formation of the Liberal Democrats, the Socialist Alliance and other groups have seats on a few councils. These admittedly limited developments show it is possible to challenge the dominance of the main parties in local elections and may reflect an emerging trend reflecting disillusion with that dominance.

Is calibre an issue?

It is common, sometimes even amongst senior councillors and officers, to speak of the low calibre of councillors. Officers speak highly – with some exceptions – about those councillors holding positions in the cabinet who they work with and have come to know well. It is as if there are a few councillors of calibre holding the leading positions, while the others are seen as of low calibre or 'purely parochial' in attitude. Yet the latter councillors may be playing an effective representative role and the former may not have had the opportunity to show their potential in the work of the council.

Views about the low calibre of councillors are widespread in central government and Parliament. The cabinet minister, Charles Clarke, then Chairman of the Labour Party and a cabinet member, spoke shortly after the 2001 general election about too many councillors being 'inarticulate'. MPs generally, and particularly those who once were councillors, look down on local councils with which in the United Kingdom, unlike in France and other countries in Europe, they are anxious to sever their relationship in order to establish an identity on the national stage. Civil servants' attitude to councillors can show the same elite contempt that often characterises their attitude to local government generally. In the corridors of Whitehall and Westminster attitudes reinforce each other. The press often speaks disparagingly about councillors. The low calibre of councillors becomes an accepted problem, reinforced by a belief that calibre has declined, looking back to a golden age when great men, and it was men, walked the stage of local councils.

There are many problems with the assumptions underlying this commonly held view. The first is the assumption is that calibre and only calibre matters in the elected representative, whereas the council should be representative of the community, able to make judgements on behalf of local people. Pity the council composed only of people of high calibre. Issues would arise as to whether such a council was truly representative.

The second assumption is that one knows what the word 'calibre' means, but that is far from clear. Does calibre reflect a considered judgement on the abilities of councillors or does it reflect a judgement on their social or economic status or on their educational qualifications? Looking back to the past councillors of calibre believed to have inhabited council chambers, one suspects it is the industrialists and landowners that are assumed to have been people of calibre. It is an assumed lack of councillors from business and management that is regretted as the nearest equivalent to the mythical great men of the past.

Calibre is too loose a concept. A council needs a mixture of abilities, skills and experience and needs them more because of the variety of roles that new structures have created. Different qualities are required for the executive, the regulatory committees, overview in policy exploration, local decision-making on area committees, the representative role generally, scrutiny in all its forms and the determination of policy in council meetings.

The average council contains councillors with a mixture of abilities, skills and experience, but has not always been able to realise their full potential, because of the dominance of one role – membership of a service committee – and because of inadequate provision for training and development. The variety of roles possible in the new structures makes commitment to training and development even more important.

The decline in calibre is normally asserted without evidence in support. One possible response to such assertions is that it has always declined or rather been said to have declined. Looking back to the press even of the late nineteenth century, one finds editors lamenting the loss of the 'great men' assumed to constitute the councils of the past. Local political figures of the past – or at least all that can be remembered, for even in the Birmingham of the 1870s not all councillors were Joseph Chamberlains – will always seem more impressive than councillors engaged in the controversies and problems of today.

What can be said about calibre today when compared with the recent past, if not the nineteenth century? Reporting impressions formed in working for over thirty years with councillors, I respond that the general body of councillors are today more assertive, more ready to challenge both the leadership and council officers, and more ready to take part in discussion to express their views. Whether this means an increase in calibre I hesitate to say, because of the uncertain meaning of the word, but it is unlikely it means calibre has declined.

Statistics show there has been significant change in councillors' educational background. In 1964, 44 per cent of councillors had no school or educational qualifications. By 1993, only 18 per cent lacked such qualifications. These figures are not exactly comparable since the 1964 figures do not include Scotland, but they indicate a trend and a trend likely to have continued. The numbers with degrees and professional qualifications increased over the same period from 21 per cent to 50 per cent (Maud Report, 1967b; Young and Rao, 1994). Whether this indicates an increase in calibre is again uncertain because of the lack of clarity about what the word means. It probably means, however, a more articulate and assertive group of councillors, in the same way as the spread of education generally in society means an electorate less ready to give political parties and politicians an unquestioning loyalty.

The Government's proposals

The government made relatively few proposals as to how a better balance of representation was to be achieved. It proposed changes in the methods of financial support for councillors. It urged councils to consider scheduling meetings to suit people with jobs, implying evening meetings. The main contention was that the new structures created 'new rewarding roles for councillors'. It argued that the combination of these measures 'will encourage a wider crosssection of the community – more employed people, more women, more people from ethnic minorities, more young people and people with young families – to serve their communities in future' (DETR, 1998a, p. 36). These proposals were not based on any analysis of factors determining councillor recruitment and retention. The lack of such analysis could mean that the hopes placed in the limited measures proposed will prove misplaced. A wider examination is required both of recruitment and retention and the factors influencing them.

Recruitment and retention

Game and Leach have argued there are growing problems in securing candidates and in retaining councillors, over and above problems of the under-representation of certain groups. They concluded:

> there is *a perceptibly looming crisis of councillor recruitment and retention* . . . or an approaching precipice. The pool of potential candidates – to change the metaphor slightly – is drying up, as otherwise qualified and predisposed individuals are no longer drifting as in the past through the precipitant filters of time availability, compatible employment and personal circumstances and, above all, a sufficiently positive regard for the councillor role. At the same time, sitting councillors are making similar calculations and filtering out of the pool. (Game and Leach, 1993, p. 58: original emphasis)

Processes of recruitment and retention determine the trends in membership. Policies designed to increase the number of councillors from under-represented groups and to increase the number of would-be candidates generally require an understanding of those processes. Only then can adequate policies be developed, not merely to enhance the representativeness of councillors, but to increase the number of people seeking to become councillors and to avoid the early loss of councillors.

In 1999, Alice Brown and her colleagues analysed the factors that had to be taken into account in explaining the under-representation of certain groups. They argued that there was no simple explanation but that the factors involved were 'varied, multi-dimensional and interlinked' and reflected '*systemic factors* such as the political, electoral and legal context and structure of opportunities in which selection takes place . . . *recruitment factors* such as selection procedures for candidates . . . and '*individual supply and demand factors*' (Brown *et al.*, 1999, p. v: original emphasis).

The selection process

Recruitment is normally from a limited base in party membership and a base that has become even more limited in recent decades. As party control over local authorities has grown, membership and the number of party activists have declined. This means that the number of potential candidates has fallen. Although party membership has declined, membership or involvement in campaigning groups has not declined but that wider pool of political activists is not drawn upon as a source of candidates unless they become members of a political party.

Barron and her colleagues suggest that many people become candidates through a cumulative process of drift:

> Some individuals who eventually become councillors engage initially in sporadic community activity, may become party members, hold party office and stand for an unwinnable seat before successfully contesting a local election. For these people, the final decision to stand for election may be seen as the culmination of an extended process, which begins long before the formal selection stage. There is, however, no inevitability about this progression. People may drift between activity and inactivity. Some individuals may move to candidature, others may strongly resist, whereas others again may be catapulted on

to the council with little or no prior involvement in party politics. (Barron *et al.*, 1991, p. 43)

If drifters rather than intenders are the dominant group, one issue is how the process can be encouraged and resistance lessened, particularly among the under-represented groups.

Game and Leach (1993) found in their research that all parties had difficulties in recruiting candidates, with the Conservative Party facing the greatest problems. They pointed out that legislation preventing senior officers of one authority standing for election in another authority had robbed the Labour Party in particular of some able councillors. Trade unions no longer encouraged officials to stand for election as councillors. The Liberal Democrats probably had least difficulty in finding candidates and their candidates tend to be better balanced in terms of gender, age and occupational background, although there are sometimes problems in retaining successful candidates, especially those who did not expect to be elected.

The reason for the under-representation of certain groups is due more to under-representation in those putting themselves forward than to bias in the selection process, although there is evidence of a slight tendency for women to be selected in less winnable seats (Rallings and Thrasher, 1997). Those from ethnic minorities probably have greater difficulty in selection outside the areas with large numbers in the population.

To understand the under-representation of women more information is required on the factors that lead to candidates putting themselves or not putting themselves forward for selection. The reason may have 'as much if not more to do with the political culture within parties and society as with the formal rules and procedures of party business' (Brown *et al.*, 1999, p. 18). Family commitments and attitudes have probably deterred some women from standing. The dominant political style may not attract many women and some men. The under-representation of ethnic minorities in certain areas may reflect racist attitudes amongst some of the electorate and even the selectorate. For young people the problem begins with a failure to recruit many into membership of the political parties.

No single action will be sufficient to counter the under-representation of significant groups in society and to overcome the general problems of recruitment. While local authority and party procedures and structures are relevant, there are problems of culture and attitudes to be faced in local authorities, in political parties and in society generally.

Does the electoral process discriminate?

Rallings and Thrasher have examined whether people discriminate against women in elections. They conclude there is no evidence that the electorate discriminate against or in favour of women candidates. They also report unpublished research by Michael le Lohe that where over 10 per cent of the population come from ethnic minorities there is usually a proportionate representation of the Asian population (often predominantly male), although not always so in the case of the black population (Rallings and Thrasher, 1997). The overall under-representation of the ethnic population is probably mainly due to authorities where there is a smaller ethnic population without the concentration of population that provides a strong basis for representation in the authorities with larger ethnic numbers. Data were not available to Rallings and Thrasher to test whether there was discrimination by the electorate against or in favour of candidates from ethnic groups.

Retention and turnover

Councillors once recruited do not necessarily stay long on the council. Electoral defeat is a possibility faced by all councillors, although more likely for some than for others. Deselection is a possibility, more commonly discussed in relation to the Labour Party, but not unknown in the Conservative Party (Game and Leach, 1993). Turnover is, however, more due to councillors deciding to leave the council than to electoral defeats or deselection. Electoral turnover was:

- 6.8 per cent in English counties in 1989;
- 4.6 per cent in London boroughs in 1990;
- 13.6 per cent in metropolitan districts in 1992
- 8.9 per cent in English shire districts in 1991;
- 9.9 per cent in Welsh counties in 1989; and
- 8.6 per cent in Welsh shire districts in 1991.

Non-electoral turnover in the same years was:

- 33.7 per cent in English counties;
- 48.9 per cent in London boroughs;
- 27.4 per cent in metropolitan districts;
- 31.7 per cent in English shire districts;
- 23.0 per cent in Welsh counties; and
- 18.0 per cent in Welsh shire districts. (Game and Leach, 1993, p. 19)

Deselection is included in these latter percentages, but is not a major factor. The levels of turnover had been relatively constant since the 1974 reorganisation with the highest levels in London. More recent data are not available, but there is no reason to believe there has been significant change.

The figures are difficult to interpret. A degree of turnover is not only inevitable as councillors retire, but is desirable so councils have a continuing intake of new councillors. If the under-represented are to be recruited, other councillors must leave, but one of the problems is that turnover is high amongst younger and more recent councillors.

Figure 6.1 *Main reasons for leaving the council*

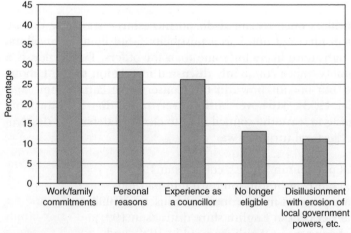

Source: Adapted from Bloch, 1992.

The main reasons for leaving the council found by Bloch are indicated in Figure 6.1. These results were broadly in line with other research (Game and Leach, 1993; Young and Rao, 1994), although the way reasons are classified varies, with Young and Rao giving excessive time commitments, frustration at lack of local autonomy, family commitments and lack of influence on council decisions as the dominant reasons (1994, p. 16).

Leaving for the personal reasons identified by Bloch reflects a normal process of retirement and does not require special comment. The largest group left the council because of conflicting demands. For these, the solution may be more support and more consideration of how workload can be adjusted to suit personal circumstances. The other main group found their experience unsatisfactory. Both these groups raise the issue of whether the workings of councils are a major factor in increasing turnover and whether that is likely to be lessened or intensified by the new political structures.

The government's proposals appraised

The impact of new political structures

The government believed that the new political structures would prove attractive to existing and to would-be councillors. This belief was not confirmed by the general reaction of councillors. Many councillors outside the executive felt the new structures deprived them of an effective role. The committee system was valued, not because of the time spent, but because it involved them in the work of the authority. The way the structures were presented, and hence the way in which they were implemented in some authorities, appeared to separate off councillors from the main work of the authority. There is hearsay evidence that some councillors have retired because of the new structures, although that could be welcomed by the government as removing councillors immersed in the previous culture. More serious from the government's perspective are executive members who have found it impossible to combine the greater demands on their time with their jobs and their family commitments – a problem likely to be greater with younger councillors. The Select Committee report on the working of the

Local Government Act 2000 recorded evidence from a number of witnesses 'that councillors are citing the new executive and scrutiny arrangements as their reason for not standing for office again' (Select Committee as Transport, Local Government and the Regions, 2002a, p. 19).

The government argued that the new structures would give councillors time to develop a more satisfying representative role: 'Backbench councillors will spend less time in council meetings and more time in the local community at residents' meetings or surgeries' (DETR, 1998a, p. 34). The committee system 'results in councillors spending too many hours on often fruitless meetings – a recent survey showed on average 97 hours per month. It distorts councillors' priorities: 70% of councillors in a recent study felt that representational work directly with the community was their most important role, yet they spent an average of only 30% of their time on it' (ibid., p. 15). The argument was that the new structures would enable councillors to spend more time on what they regarded as their most important role and would therefore prove attractive to existing as well as to new and aspiring councillors.

The figures are misleading. The 97 hours reported was from a survey by Nirmala Rao (Rao, 1992) and was not the time spent on meetings, but the total time, including time spent on the representative role. Table 6.4 shows the results of this survey and a later larger-scale survey by Young and Rao (1994).

It is not clear which survey was used by DETR to show that only 30 per cent of time was spent on representational work with the community, since this depends on how the figures are inter-

Table 6.4 *Time spent by councillors on the representative role (per month)*

	Rao	Young and Rao
Attending council meetings	30 hours	22 hours
Preparation for such meetings	23 hours	16 hours
Travelling	12 hours	8 hours
Attending party meetings	6 hours	5 hours
Dealing with electors' problems	14 hours	13 hours
Meeting external organizations	9 hours	7 hours
Public consultation	3 hours	3 hours
Total	97 hours	74 hours

preted. Within each category some or all of the time may be spent on the representative role – including time spent on council meetings. It is difficult to see how the representative role can be made effective in influence on the council without some form of meeting. After all, the representative role must involve making representations!

The surveys probably underestimate the time spent by councillors. Research based on diaries, recording time as it was spent, gives higher figures than surveys asking councillors to recall time spent (Barron *et al.*, 1991). Underestimates are likely to be greatest in the informal work of conversation, phone calls and dealing with letters that make up much of the representative role.

Even taking the figures as correct, the statement that in the survey 70 per cent of councillors saw representational work as their most important role does not necessarily mean that 70 per cent of their time should be spent on it. More significance should be given to the finding in the same survey that only 28 per cent of councillors thought that too little time was spent on dealing with electors' problems (Young and Rao, 1994, p. 23). In any event these views were not necessarily those of the 'talented young people' the government seeks to attract. Dealing with electors' problems would probably not attract the aspiring management-focused people, whom one suspects the government hopes will become councillors.

The government's view that the new structures would enable councillors to devote more time to the representative role was never convincing to councillors who believed they were already deeply involved with their constituents and with community organisations. There are problems too in the view that the new structures would give councillors more time for the representative role. As argued in Chapter 5, the overview and scrutiny role is at least as time-consuming as traditional committee work, and probably more so when carried out effectively. To investigate policy issues and community problems in depth requires more time and effort than nodding through agendas, as is alleged happened in committees.

Whether the new structures are likely to make councillors' roles more attractive remains at best uncertain. The long-term impact will depend on the extent to which the issues raised in Chapter 5 are resolved. The new structures are more likely to be attractive both to existing and to would-be councillors if the variety of roles suggested there are developed; if the widest possible meaning is given to overview and scrutiny; if individual roles for councillors are developed in support of the executive; and if structures and processes give real influence to the representative role. A variety of roles opens up choices for councillors. The roles can be combined in different ways to suit both the interests and the time available of both present and future councillors. A councillor who had only limited time need only serve on the council – a vital role in the new structure – and carry out the representative role, although that suggestion will surprise those used to the committee role. Councillors with more time available could have a wider range of roles.

Financial support

Modern Local Government suggested new possibilities of financial support for council work. The government originally proposed to make possible 'pensionable salaries' for certain roles (DETR, 1998a, p. 35). In practice, the allowance system has been maintained, but with the removal of the attendance allowance, felt to encourage unnecessary meetings, so that the arrangements now consist of a basic allowance and a special responsibility allowance for defined roles. The legislation allows for the provision of pensions, and the government has now decided pensions could be extended to all councillors if councils so decide (ODPM, 2002f), having previously wished to restrict its application to members of the executive and chairs of overview and scrutiny committees (DETR, 2001c). The legislation provides for payments covering childcare and other forms of care, about which there had been doubts over authorities' right to pay.

The legislation requires authorities to appoint independent panels to draw up recommendations for allowances which do not necessarily have to be accepted by the council. Councils would, however, be very reluctant to exceed the proposed levels, for fear of a public outcry. Some councils have paid less than the panel recommendations, perhaps because of concern about the public reaction, although in places the public have been surprised as to how little councillors have actually been paid. Authorities can join together to appoint panels. The Welsh authorities joined together to appoint a panel whose recommendations can be quoted as typical of the level in some, but by no means all, of the unitary, metropolitan district, London borough and county authorities. The basic allowance was set at £9,907 of which £900 was for specified expenses. The special responsibility allowances (SRAs) for the population range 100,000–200,000 are shown in Table 6.5.

While there were variations in the SRA with the size of authority, the basic allowance proposed was the same for all authorities in Wales. The basic allowance was calculated on the assumption of a workload of 90 hours per month at the Welsh average non-manual salary of £12.51 per hour with the result then reduced by one-third to allow for the voluntary factor in public service. The panel also recommended a dependant and childcare allowance and an individual learning account to be drawn on for training and development (INLOGOV, 2001). The combination of a basic allowance with special responsibility allowances recognises the role of all councillors, while taking account of the special responsibilities of certain roles. The rates are not overgenerous. The leader of a unitary authority has greater responsibilities than a member of parliament and yet is paid significantly less.

The system of allowances is a necessary, but not a sufficient condition for resolving problems of councillor retention and recruitment. There is a special problem in filling executive positions. The role of executive member in a major authority is likely to be demanding in time and therefore incompatible with a full-time employment outside the council, yet the position is vulnerable to the electoral process and to decisions by the council or

Table 6.5 *Special responsibility allowances for the population range 100,000–200,000*

	SRA	Total including basic allowance
Elected mayors	£31,913	£41,820
Leaders	£25,530	£35,437
Deputy leaders and cabinet members	£12,765	£22,672
Overview and scrutiny chairs and principal opposition group leaders	£7,659	£17,566
Chairs of other committees and vice-chairs of overview and scrutiny	£5,106	£15,013
Vice-chairs of other committees and leaders of minor opposition groups	£2,553	£12,460

the political group. A cabinet member might lose the position within a year or two of being appointed. That is an uncertain basis for a councillor to abandon a job with career prospects. This problem was highlighted in Birmingham when, after a new structure of allowances was agreed, the leader indicated he would expect cabinet members to become full-time. Because of the reaction of some cabinet members who were unwilling to give up their outside employment for what might be a short period in the cabinet, he did not press the point. A cabinet member being appointed for longer than a year would not remove the problem, since the electoral process could mean individual defeat or a change in political control.

The Local Government Association's and other views

The LGA shares the government's concern over the representativeness of councillors. In *Representing the People*, the LGA set out policies on the recruitment and retention of councillors with a stress on women, the ethnic minorities and young people. (LGA, 2001a).

The LGA argued that local authorities could do more to promote council membership by open house sessions for the public and by inviting people to shadow councillors. Effective citizenship work in schools was stressed. The government should promote the little-known Employment Rights Act which requires that councillors be given reasonable time off work. The LGA proposed legislation for a wider public involvement entitlement covering public services. Consideration should be given to compensation for employers who encourage and support staff with roles in public service. Councils were urged to develop further training and support for councillors to reduce turnover, particularly among the under-represented groups.

The recommendations go much further than the government's own proposals. Brown and her colleagues went still further. Their suggestions include:

- the political system (proportional representation; legal changes to allow positive action; limited terms of office)
- recruitment process (taster events; training of candidates and selectors; equal opportunities; selection procedures; self-nomination in political parties)

- supply of candidates (changing working conditions; secondment opportunities)
- demands of gatekeepers (getting away from images of the typical councillor; political will). (Brown *et al.*, 1999, pp. 30–5)

Their analysis shows the need for a wide-ranging approach if council work is to prove attractive to greater numbers, particularly from the under-represented groups.

The reputation of local government can be a factor influencing the readiness of candidates to come forward and for those elected to seek to remain on the council for at least more than one term. This raises issues about the powers and responsibilities of councils and the place of local authorities in the system of government, discussed in Chapter 11. Equally relevant are the ethical standards of local government, critical to its public reputation, with the danger that perceptions of the few can hide the high standards of the many.

The ethical framework

Modern Local Government proposed a new ethical framework as an important element in the desired culture of local government. 'In a council which puts people first, the culture will be one where personal service is valued, and where the highest standards of personal conduct are the norm.' (DETR, 1998a, p. 49). The Local Government Act 2000 established that new ethical framework and a similar framework was established in Scotland by the Ethical Standards in Public Life Act 2000, although with a wider application covering other public bodies. The framework was stated to reflect the third report of the Committee on Standards in Public Life. The committee's starting point was:

As with all the other sectors we have examined we found an enormous number of dedicated and hard-working people. We are of course well aware of the relatively few, but highly publicised, cases where things have gone wrong or people have behaved improperly. But it is important to set such cases in the context of more than 20,000 councillors and 2,000,000 employees in local government. (Nolan Report, 1997, p. 3)

The committee pointed out that in their two previous reports they had commented 'that attempting to enforce good conduct through detailed rules, especially where these are based on presumptions that people will naturally misbehave, can itself contribute to wrong-doing. Nowhere is this more true than in local government. Local government is far more constrained by rules than any other part of the public sector we have examined'. (Nolan Report, 1997, p. 3). The proliferation of rules had created confusion.

The committee's key conclusion was that 'responsibility for the maintenance of standards had moved away from local government'. They therefore recommended placing the 'leading responsibility with local government itself' (Nolan Report, 1997, p. 3). The Committee recommended that the government draw up a statement of general principles of conduct to be approved by Parliament and that each local authority should adopt a code of conduct, based on a model reflecting these principles to be developed by the Local Government Association, and approved by Parliament. Each authority should appoint a standards committee with powers to recommend disciplinary action by the council for breaches of the code, including suspension from the council for up to three months. There would be a right of appeal to an independent tribunal. The committee also recommended the abolition of the powers of surcharge, which had made councillors and officers in local government personally liable for expenditure contrary to law, unlike others in the public service. Instead the committee recommended the introduction of a new statutory offence of misuse of public office, applicable to all holders of public office and not just to local government.

The government accepted the recommendations on the code of conduct and in 2001 Parliament approved the statement of principles and a model code of conduct, developed with the Local Government Association. Local authorities are required by section 51 of the Local Government Act 2000 to adopt local codes, which include the mandatory provisions of the model code, and councillors are required by section 52 to give a written undertaking they will observe the authority's code. New provisions were introduced clarifying declarations of interest. The abolition of surcharge was included in the Act and came into operation in 2002.

The main difference between the Nolan recommendations and the government's legislation is in the role of local authorities. The government rejected the main recommendation, giving responsibility not to local authorities as the committee proposed, but to national bodies. Local authorities have to appoint standards committees with at least one independent member from outside the council, and the general function of 'promoting and maintaining high standards of conduct by the members and co-opted members of the authority' and 'assisting them to observe the authority's code of conduct' (Local Government Act 2000, s. 54.1). But the Act places the main responsibility for enforcing standards on new national bodies. The Standards Board receives complaints that the code of conduct has been broken. If it considers there is evidence to support that view, it refers the complaint to an ethical standards officer for investigation. The ethical standards officers can also investigate cases at their own initiative. They cannot impose penalties, but can decide whether further action is required. If the ethical standards officer after investigation decides the case is serious, it will be referred to the President of the Adjudication Panel, who will appoint a case tribunal to determine the action to be taken, with powers to suspend or partially suspend councillors for periods of up to six months or to disqualify them from being a councillor for up to five years.

The ethical standards officer can refer less serious cases to the authority's monitoring officer, either before or after an investigation. The monitoring officer can conduct an investigation and can make a report to the authority's standards committee. The government is considering the powers to be given to local standards committees by regulations. The government's consultation paper suggests these committees should have power to suspend councillors for up to six months as well as lesser penalties. There would be a right of appeal against the decision of the committee. The appeal would be to a tribunal appointed by the President of the Adjudication Panel (DTLR, 2002d).

These complex arrangements raise issues about the relationship between the different bodies and officers and about the role of the Standards Board whose members must wonder if they have a meaningful role. The main issue raised, however, is that responsibilities are not placed on the local authorities as recommended by the Nolan Committee. Instead the main responsibilities for enforcing standards are given to new external bodies, adding to the number of external bodies scrutinising local authorities.

Should the number of councillors be reduced or increased?

Some commentators have seen a reduction in the number of councillors as a necessary element in the process of modernisation. Leading members of the New Local Government Network, an unofficial organisation generally committed to support of the modernisation programme, have argued for such a reduction, phased over a ten-year period (Filkin *et al.*, 2001b), although with the introduction of elected neighbourhood councils. Peter Hetherington of the *Guardian* has suggested a reduction of two-thirds in the number of councillors (Hetherington, 2000).

Advocates of a radical reduction in the number of councillors have not thought through the implications of the new political structures. It would be difficult to reconcile the government's emphasis on the representative role with such a reduction. Problems would also be created for the workings of the new structures. A reduction of two-thirds could mean many councils of only twenty members or less. The executive can consist of ten councillors, who will normally come from the majority party. If that party held only twelve seats it is difficult to see how the overview and scrutiny committees could be constituted on the proportionate basis required by legislation. It is equally difficult to see how the range of roles discussed in Chapter 5 could be carried out. The only possible solution would be a much smaller cabinet with an extreme concentration of power and even greater burdens on cabinet members.

The advocates of reduction have given no weight to the relatively small numbers of councillors in the United Kingdom, as shown in Chapter 3. If anything there is a stronger case for increasing the numbers of councillors rather than reducing them. If one is concerned to attract people to stand as councillors, lessening the burden of work on individual councillors is likely to increase the pool of those willing to stand. Certainly an increase in the number of councillors is more likely to do so than reducing the number of councillors and sharply increasing the workload involved in the representative and other roles, even though fewer councillors would be required. Yet in Scotland, where the number of councillors was proportionately less than in England and Wales, the Kerley Report on *Renewing Local Democracy* (Kerley Report, 2000) recommended a reduction in the number of councillors, which is taking place in certain authorities.

Conclusion

The government highlighted the need to improve the representativeness of councils, raising issues about councillor recruitment and retention and the need for a new ethical framework, while neglecting a wider discussion of councilors' role and background – apart, that is, from new political structures. It argued that changes in the allowance system and greater support for councillors, coupled with the new political structures, would help to resolve these issues. The changes in the allowance system are less important than the acceptance by the government that past levels of allowance were inadequate, particularly for what is becoming a full-time role for members of executives in some authorities. There is more dispute about the impact of the new political structures. The new structures could aggravate the problems and will only help to resolve them if the issues identified in Chapter 5 are overcome and a wide range of councillors' roles are developed. The opportunity to develop differing roles and work patterns with differing time commitments could enable councillors to fit their roles to their personal circumstances, avoiding some of the loss of councillors after only a short period on the council. Roles and work patterns could change for individuals as their personal circumstances changed. The political parties could emphasise the varying roles and work patterns in encouraging potential candidates.

The government's analysis did not and probably could not cover the role of political parties even though they are the main source of recruitment. Increasing party membership is critical to councillor recruitment, but raises much wider issues. The contrast between declining party membership and developing political activity outside party politics raises issues about how those so active could be drawn into the pool of potential candidates. Could political parties draw candidates from a wider group allowing supporters to stand? Political parties have to consider their relationship to a wider group than members if they are to be effective generally and not merely in councillor recruitment.

Stimuli, suggestions and persuasion are powerful means for recruiting candidates. Normally these happen informally and are effective for that reason. Yet political parties could do more in bringing forward candidates. Councils too have a role to play. Councils and political groups could develop 'Find out about being a councillor' sessions and opportunities for those interested to shadow a councillor. Potential recruits can be identified among those who have already begun to play a public role as school governors or in other roles.

The more that can be done to build up public appreciation of the importance of the role of the council, the more potential candidates are likely to come forward. The government has a responsibility to build up that role both in its legislation and in its public statements. Over-emphasis on 'failing councils' or 'poor performance' is hardly a message to encourage recruits. Councils can put over a positive message. Open days and learning weekends can give messages about the councillor's role, since their work and responsibilities are rarely fully appreciated.

Change in political structures can provide the opportunity to consider the style of meetings. The confrontational style found in council meetings and sometimes even more in political group meetings can be a factor in some councillors deciding not to stand again. Excessive group discipline with its constraint upon discussion has been a deterrent for some. One test of overview and scrutiny will be whether it permits a style of meeting that encourages freer discussion.

Most of the changes discussed above are intended to make the position of councillor attractive to a greater number of potential candidates. That does not necessarily resolve the problems of under-representation. It could mean merely that there was more of the same. It is important that the measures outlined are particularly directed at the under-represented groups and the style of the council and its meetings could be important for this issue.

The modernisation programme was generally limited by the relatively little attention paid to the council and councillors that distinguish the local authority as a political institution. It was a strength of the modernisation programme to raise the issue of the need for more councillors from the under-represented groups, but it was a weakness that its analysis of how this could be achieved was so limited. A critical test of the modernisation programme should be its success in increasing the pool of potential councillors both generally and from the under-represented groups. For the more representative the council becomes, the hope is the better it can comprehend the need and aspirations of its communities and the wider the source of initiatives and innovations, building thereby effective local government.

7 Best Value and Improving Performance

Improving performance is the third main aim of the modernisation programme, and high standards of performance in meeting community needs and providing services are an important contribution to effective local government. *Modern Local Government* emphasised that successful councils 'strive for continuous improvement in the delivery of local services' (DETR, 1998a, p. 12) and proposed the introduction of the best value regime as the main means of securing that improvement.

The background

The best value regime replaced compulsory competitive tendering (CCT) – the requirement to put out to competitive tender specified services or functions – introduced by the previous Conservative government. The consultation paper on best value had seen benefits in CCT: 'It required authorities to consider the standard and cost of the services for which they were responsible, and widened the choices available as to how the services were provided', as well as focusing attention on how the services were managed. But the government's conclusion was that 'compulsion has . . . bred antagonism, so that neither local authorities nor private sector suppliers have been able to realise the benefits that flow from a healthy partnership. All too often the process of competition has become an end in itself, distracting attention from the services that are actually provided to local people' (DETR, 1998c, pp. 5–6). *Modern Local Government* argued that the 'current framework for service delivery [compulsory competitive tendering] has proved inflexible in practice, often leading to the demoralisation of those expected to provide quality services and to high staff turnover. Concentration on CCT has neglected service quality and led to uneven and uncertain efficiency gains. In short this framework has provided a poor deal for local people, for employees and for employers' (DETR, 1998a, p. 16).

The government replaced CCT with the best value regime through the Local Government Act 1999. That Act placed a duty upon local authorities to 'make arrangements to secure continuous improvement in the ways in which its functions are exercised, having regard to a combination of economy, efficiency and effectiveness' (Local Government Act 1999, s. 3). The duty was enforced by procedures to be followed by local authorities and by external inspection. In Scotland legislation was not enacted until 2003 when the Local Government in Scotland Act placed a similar requirement on Scottish authorities. A best value regime had previously been developed on a non-statutory basis through a partnership based on a best value task force including representatives of the Scottish Executive, local authorities and the Accounts Committee, responsible for the audit function in Scotland.

The government's commitment to improving performance has led on to further action. Beacon councils were identified as models to be followed by other authorities. Public service agreements were introduced committing local authorities to targets for service improvement. *Strong Local Leadership* set out a comprehensive performance framework for service improvement involving national priorities and targets, along with performance assessments of individual authorities and related incentives and penalties. The government has given an emphasis to the involvement of the private sector thorough partnerships and other means. This chapter focuses on best value with these developments being covered in the next chapter.

The policy

The commitment to improving services has driven best value:

> A modern council – or authority – which puts people first will seek to provide services which bear comparison with the best. Not just with the best that other authorities provide but with the best that is on offer from both the public and private sectors. Continuous improvements in both the quality and cost

of services will therefore be the hallmark of the modern council, and the test of best value. (DETR, 1998a, p. 64)

Local authorities shared these aspirations for quality services and continuous improvement. The concept of best value derived from ideas put forward by the local government associations and adopted by the Labour Party in their election manifesto (Labour Party, 1997).

There are, however, problems with the concept of best value as expressed by the government. Pedants can point out a tension between best value and continuous improvement. The phrase 'best value' implies it can be achieved, and if the best is achieved then there can be no further improvement. It would have been more consistent to use better value as the aim in the same way as the government in its modernisation programme for central government set its aim as better rather than best government (Cabinet Office, 1999).

Pedantry apart, best value, good service, excellent performance and even service improvement are not precise or easily defined concepts. There can be disagreement between stakeholders or between political parties about the definition of good service or excellent performance, dependent on which aspect of the service is most highly valued. In many services a balance has to be struck between different values and interests. In transportation the need for rapid transport has to be balanced with environmental and safety considerations. In the care of the child, social control and support for the family can both be involved. In some services equity can be in conflict with consumer satisfaction.

In its original guidance on best value, the government set a target for continuous improvement. 'As far as possible comparisons should be made on the basis of outcomes, although detailed comparisons of inputs and outputs will be required to assess the scope for greater efficiency consistent with the Government's overall target of 2% p.a. efficiency improvements for local government as a whole' (DETR, 1999a, para. 30). While recognition is given to the importance of outcomes and hence of effectiveness, this quantitative target puts an emphasis on efficiency. Yet it is possible to be efficient in providing an ineffective service, which can hardly be regarded as providing best value.

The 2 per cent target for increases in efficiency derives from discussions between the Treasury and DETR and other departments. It is not clear on what it is based other than folklore that all organisation are capable of such increases each year. Such beliefs have little relevance to local authorities, which involve many services delivered in interaction between staff and those for whom the service is provided. A reduction in the number of staff or an increase in the number of clients served is likely to decrease effectiveness, even if it can be regarded as an increase in efficiency. If class size increases, it can be regarded as an increase in efficiency as measured by the number of children taught per teacher, but it can hardly be regarded as desirable and certainly not an increase in effectiveness.

The guidance recognised that the scope for achieving the 2 per cent increase in efficiency varies from service to service but fails to recognise how many of the services depend on the intensity of staff involvement, making the overall target difficult, if not impossible, to achieve without harming the service. If such services are exempt from the requirement and the overall 2 per cent target remains unchanged, the target for the remaining services becomes impossibly high. Few in local government have challenged the target, because to challenge it opens up an attack on the complacency of local government, giving ammunition to its critics. Yet the 2 per cent target can and should be challenged.

The emphasis on efficiency reflects the difficulty of measuring outcomes and even when they can be measured of assessing the outcome in the light of differing values and interests. Some will consider that good service can be recognised when one sees it, but what one person sees is not necessarily what others see.

The procedures of best value

The guidance set out a framework for best value:

- establish authority-wide objectives and performance measures;
- agree programme of best value reviews and set out in local performance plan;
- undertake best value reviews of selected areas of expenditure;
- set and publish performance and efficiency targets in the best value performance plan;
- independent audit inspection and certification;
- areas requiring intervention referred to the Secretary of State. (DETR, 1999a, para. 9)

The first four stages involve the local authority's own actions; the last two involve external action and possible action. For the local authority there are two key products – the best value reviews and the local best value performance plan.

Best value reviews

Local authorities were required to review all their functions over a five-year period, with priority being given to poorly performing services. The reviews covered cross-cutting themes as well as specific services. The guidance laid down requirements for the approach to the reviews:

- *challenge* why, how and by whom a service is provided;
- secure *comparison* with the performance of others across a range of relevant indicators, taking into account the views of both service users and potential suppliers;
- *consult* local taxpayers, service users, partners and the wider business community in the setting of new performance targets; and
- use fair and open *competition* wherever practicable as a means of securing efficient and effective services. (DETR, 1999a, para. 10; original emphasis)

The evaluation of the pilot projects for best value commented that collaboration was not one of the four Cs (Martin *et al*., 2001, p. 116). This omission is surprising given the commitment to partnership in the modernisation programme and to the inclusion of collaboration in the government's 5Cs for modernising central government (Cabinet Office, 1999). Equally strangely those to be consulted did not include citizens, although citizens are emphasised in the government's approach to democratic renewal.

The government elaborated its guidance, stressing that authorities should:

- take a sufficiently long-term perspective;
- involve elected members;
- seek advice from outside the authority;
- involve those currently delivering services;
- question existing commitments;

- engage with users and potential users of services;
- address equity considerations; and
- give effect to the principles of sustainable development. (DETR, 1999a, para. 17)

The reviews had to 'set demanding targets for service improvement, and action plans to deliver these to a realistic time-table, including decisions on *the best value option for future service delivery*'. The main options listed were:

- the cessation of the service, in whole or in part;
- the creation of a public–private partnership, through a strategic contract or a joint venture company, for example;
- the transfer or externalisation of the service to another provider (with no in-house bid);
- the market-testing of all or part of the service (where the in-house provider bids in open competition against the private or voluntary sector);
- the restructuring or repositioning of the in-house service;
- the renegotiation of existing arrangements with current providers where this is permissible; and
- the joint commissioning or delivery of the service. (DETR, 1999a, para. 44)

These options suggest that best value reviews should focus on who delivers the service, rather than on how the service should be delivered or on what sort of service is required. This emphasis was reinforced by the attention given in the guidance to developing markets and encouraging a diversity of suppliers (paras 37–43). The issue of service redesign has not received anything like the same emphasis from the government as choice on who delivers.

The guidance devoted relatively little attention to how the choice on who delivers should be made beyond a statement that it 'will depend on an objective analysis of what has emerged from the Review' (para. 45). Little was said about what that analysis should involve. It is, of course, expected that the 4Cs of challenge, compare, consult, and competition will be applied, but in making the choice criteria are required to guide judgement on the options being considered. The guidance said authorities will be expected to demonstrate that they 'have selected the options most likely to deliver best value to the public' (ibid.), leaving open the criteria to be used with the danger that criteria of efficiency are given greater weight than criteria of effectiveness.

Best value performance plans

Section 6 of the Local Government Act 1999 requires authorities to prepare a best value performance plan each year. The guidance set out what the plan 'must' include:

- a summary of the authority's objectives in respect of its functions;
- a summary of current performance;
- a comparison with performance in previous financial years;
- a summary of the authority's approach to efficiency improvement;
- a statement describing the review programme;
- the key results of completed reviews;
- the performance targets set for future years (using both local and national indicators);
- a plan for action (how those targets are to be met);
- a response to audit and inspection reports;
- a consultation statement; and
- financial information. (DETR, 1999a, para. 54)

The complexity of the performance plan had dangers. Preparation of the plan could become a bureaucratic routine that has to be carried out, rather than a challenge to improved performance. The plan is supposed to be based on consultation with the public, but it was always unlikely that members of the public would be sufficiently interested or that the completed plan would receive much public attention, and so it has proved. The information in the plan has different audiences, which was obscured by the comprehensive requirements laid down in the guidance.

The government specifies national indicators authorities are required to use in their performance plans along with local indicators chosen by the authority. There are two types of national indicators – corporate health indicators and service delivery indicators. The latter are designed to cover five dimensions of performance: strategic objectives; cost efficiency; service delivery outcomes; quality; fair access (DETR, 2000c, para. 2.1.2). Local authorities are free to set their own targets for most of the indicators, subject to the requirement to improve performance. The government has specified that for a limited number of indicators – eleven in 2001 – the target set over a five-year period should at least equal the level of performance currently achieved by the top 25 per cent of authorities. Section 4.10 of the Local Government Act 1999 also allows the government to set standards that <u>must</u> be met. The government has said it will only use these powers 'sparingly and where there is a legitimate national interest' (DTLR, 2002a, para. 4.2). It has set such standards for recycling and composting, and for the time taken to determine planning applications.

Enforcement procedures

Local authorities are under a statutory duty to pursue best value and to carry out the procedures laid down in the legislation and regulations. The government has powers to enforce those requirements by audit, inspection and direct intervention.

The performance plan is subject to audit of whether the plan meets statutory requirements, the information is accurate and 'the targets set are realistic and achievable' (DETR, 1999a, para. 63). Checking the accuracy of the data on current and past performance can properly be regarded as an audit function. The audit of targets raises issues as to whether the auditor is substituting his or her judgement for that of the elected council and as to the basis on which the judgement is made.

These issues are raised even more sharply by inspection of best value reviews. Each review has been subject to inspection by the newly created best value inspectorate under the Audit Commission or by one of the specialist inspectorates. The inspectors assess the quality of the service reviewed and whether it is likely to improve. Marks are awarded on a scale of 0 to 3.

Quality of service		*Future improvement*	
0	Poor	0	Will not improve
1	Fair	1	Unlikely to improve
2	Good	2	Likely to improve
3	Excellent	3	Will improve

The first 500 inspections judged that the quality of service found was 'good' or 'excellent' in only 40 per cent of reviews and that only half would probably or definitely lead to better services (Audit Commission, 2001a, p. 7). These inspections are, in effect, reviews of reviews. The Audit Commission has developed a checklist for challenging best value reviews, asking such questions as 'Is "compare" encouraging new relationships that support change and transfer of "good practice", skills and techniques?' or 'Are benchmarking exercise going deeper than [PIs] [performance indicators] and cost data and asking "how" and "why"?' (Audit Commission, 2001a, p. 49). While such questions are designed to test the depth of the review, it is not clear that the answers given by the inspectors form a reliable basis for a judgement on either the quality of service or the likelihood of improvement. To form that judgement, inspectors also undertake a quasi-review, contacting members of the public in what can be regarded as an attempt to second-guess the results of the real review. The issue is whether these judgements can be regarded as reliable and, where they differ from those of the authority, whether they should be given greater or even as much weight as those of the authority.

The inspection process is important in its own right, but is of special importance as the main trigger for intervention by central government. The Local Government Act 1999 gives the Secretary of State powers to intervene where authorities are judged to be failing to deliver best value. These powers include general powers to give directions and powers to remove a function or functions from the control of the authority for a period of time. The government has said the use of these powers will be limited. But even if little used, the existence of the powers gives greater weight to the inspection and audit processes as possible triggers for intervention. Behind each inspection, the threat of intervention lies and although most authorities need have no fears, it can turn inspections from a helpful and supportive exercise into a potentially coercive mechanism. The government and the Local Government Association have agreed a Protocol on Intervention, which seeks to lessen the dangers in the process by specifying the procedures to be followed.

The Protocol states that the removal of a function or use of the powers of direction will normally be enforced only after authorities have had a full opportunity to make representations and if necessary take action to improve performance. The Protocol confirms the Secretary of State would only use the intervention powers 'when there is clear evidence that an authority is failing either to discharge its functions adequately or failing to meet its statutory obligations' (DETR, 2001c, para. 6). The auditors and inspectors are the main sources of evidence described in the Protocol, confirming the reliance placed on their judgement. These issues have become more important because of the changes brought about by the comprehensive performance framework described in the next chapter. The implications of the growth of inspection and of central government's powers of intervention are further considered in Chapter 11. In Scotland, the Local Government in Scotland Act 2003 gives Scottish ministers powers of intervention through enforcement directions, but these powers do not appear to be as wide-ranging as those applying in England and in Wales, making no specific reference to the removal of functions from the authorities.

The government's contribution to best value

The government has recognised that existing legislation, regulations and its own procedures can be obstacles to improving performance in local authorities, as can the lack of relevant powers. It has taken powers to remove by order 'an enactment that prevents or obstructs the achievement of best value' (Local Government Act 1999, s. 16.1), to confer any powers 'necessary or expedient' for that purpose (s. 16.2) and to extend the powers of authorities to contract out functions (s. 18). These powers complement the powers of community well-being described in Chapter 2.

The government did not lay down any procedures for authorities to apply for the use of these powers. The development of public service agreements described in the next chapter provides an opportunity for authorities to highlight obstacles to improving performance in relation to the targets set in those agreements. In the consultation paper on *Working with Others to Achieve Best Value* (DTLR, 2001b), the government indicated its readiness to use these powers to facilitate partnership working in new forms as well as considering other uses of these powers, a readiness confirmed in *Strong Local Leadership*.

Problems in implementation

Problems have arisen both with the best value regime itself and with the procedures for inspection and audit. These can be summed up as a tendency for best value to become a burdensome process occupying the time of management without equivalent returns. Put another way, the best value regime has not provided best value. The performance plans were regarded as overdetailed and the danger of their preparation becoming a bureaucratic routine has already been highlighted. Best value reviews have been time-consuming and there has been general recognition that too many reviews were being carried out, some of them on issues that did not merit the time and cost involved. There have been relatively few reviews of cross-cutting issues, in part because of the guidance's emphasis on services.

The government accepted, in *Strong Local Leadership*,

> the case for streamlining the best value regime, to enable authorities to use it as an opportunity for radical challenge rather than a bureaucratic process, and to engage citizens and staff in improving services.
>
> Best value reviews are becoming more strategic and fewer in number. We will introduce further measures to reinforce a more challenging and strategic approach. (DTLR, 2001a, p. 34)

> These [performance] plans need to be better focused on service delivery priorities, councils' capacity to deliver and financial performance. To achieve this we and councils need to be clearer about the intended audiences for the plan. It is unrealistic to meet the needs of Government, local people and stakeholders, inspectors and auditors in one document. (Ibid., p. 36)

The government has introduced new regulations (Statutory Instrument 305/2002) and proposed additional guidance (ODPM, 2002a) to overcome these problems. The new regulations have removed the requirement to review all of an authority's functions over a five-year period. The new additional guidance argues that the change enables authorities to focus reviews on priorities and to take a proportionate approach taking account of identified weaknesses and opportunities for improvement. 'Authorities should balance the effort and work put into a review, against the potential gains arising from it' (ODPM, 2002a, p. 10).

The government said in *Strong Local Leadership* that it had decided the public should be sent a summary of the performance plan with the council tax bill, although many members of the public, the author included, already find themselves overwhelmed by the sheets of paper sent with that bill. Fortunately the additional guidance has now laid down that instead the method of communicating performance information should be decided by local authorities in the light of local circumstances. The performance plan itself should be directed at 'staff and elected members of the authority, groups and organisations with an interest in the authority, and central government' (ODPM, 2002a, p. 18). It should focus on information of corporate importance. The need for an efficiency summary and consultation statement has been removed, reducing the amount of material required. The number of performance indicators has been reduced. The government has indicated the content of the plan will be kept under review.

The ambiguities of best value

While few would dispute the desirability of seeking best value or at least better value, it has already been pointed out that it is not immediately obvious what best value is. The Local Government Act 1999 defines best value as economy, efficiency and effectiveness, but does not indicate their relative importance. There is a danger that the more easily measurable efficiency is emphasised at the expense of effectiveness, while there is doubt about the meaning of economy and whether it should be regarded as an end in itself.

There is a deeper uncertainty about the concept of best value raised by the question of 'who judges?' People can differ about the value placed on a service. If one considers different aspects of a service, people can differ in the weight or even the desirability of particular aspects. Value in local government cannot necessarily be taken as given. It can be the subject of disagreement or political dispute, which is one reason why such services are the responsibility of a political institution.

Local authorities see some benefits in inspections as a stimulus to change, giving a focus to the need for improvement, and it is accepted that inspections have correctly identified poor performance in certain authorities. But authorities also see problems with the inspection process. It is widely felt that the inspection process adds to the burden on authorities. Inspection of reviews has been a costly process both in its direct costs and in time taken from other tasks. Inspection can be demotivating for staff, influencing attitudes to best value. The problems were aggravated by the requirement to inspect each review. Many authorities felt there was inadequate linkage between the inspection and audit regimes. There has been concern among some chief executives about the quality and experience of certain inspectors.

The government and the Audit Commission recognised some of the problems with the audit and inspection regimes. *Strong Local Leadership* states the government's intention to 'establish a new model of inspection', based on coordination of inspections and ensuring 'the amount and nature of inspections' is based on 'performance assessment and risk analysis, taking account of local priorities', but the government remained committed to the view that inspection must be 'an effective component of intervention measures where services are failing' (DTLR, 2001a, pp. 29–30).

The Audit Commission is integrating audit and inspection and has piloted single client managers for authorities. A joint statement by the Best Value Inspectorate Forum and the Local Government Association states:

Arrangements for best value inspection should ensure effective inspection on behalf of service users while minimising the burden on inspected bodies by:
- complementing and reinforcing the development of robust best value processes in authorities;
- ensuring a consistent evaluation of best value arrangements by different inspectorates and auditors;
- targeting inspection on the areas where the risks involved are the greatest. (DTLR, 2001c, para. 5)

The best value regime assessed

While some of the immediate problems have been recognised, there remain fundamental issues to be faced in any assessment of the best value regime. The duty to pursue best value has been widely accepted by authorities. Both the process of setting targets and the best value reviews have led to significant improvements in performance and the way services are provided in some authorities. The Audit Commission believes those improvements are far from universal due to the lack of challenge in too many authorities. There are, however, problems about the best value regime itself. Some of the problems relate to the implementation of the regime, and as shown above are being faced, but there are also fundamental problems reflecting tensions in the government's approach to best value and to the modernisation programme generally.

Local or national requirements

The guidance on best value stresses the need for authorities to consult widely both on the performance plan and on the reviews. This stress reflects the emphasis in the modernisation programme on providing responsive services and on democratic renewal. Yet the best value regime involves a high degree of external control, both in the procedures laid down and in the process of inspection, which can encourage conformity to inspectoral or government views rather than to the views of local people.

The evaluation of the pilot projects concluded that 'one of the most important tensions underlying the pilot programme has been, and remains, the apparent contradiction between central control and the encouragement of local autonomy, responsiveness and diversity' (Martin *et al.*, 2001, p. 36). The report on the evaluation suggests that there has been more emphasis on exemplars to be followed than on experimenters. Even the widely accepted need to spread good practice can be a means of encouraging uniformity rather than stimulating innovation.

The tension between building local democracy and central requirements underlies the whole modernisation programme and is critical to the best value regime, because it raises the issue of whose best value and who judges whether it has been achieved – the government, the inspectors or local councillors and/or local people.

The possibility of disagreement on the meaning of value can easily be forgotten in the apparent certainty of procedures or the assumed rigour of inspections. The search for best value should encompass the exploration of meaning through debate, discussion and even political dispute, recognising that in the end there may not be agreement on best value, although there may be more on better value.

The dominance of measures

The best value regime stresses performance management, the comparison of performance and the use of targets. The issues raised by performance management will be dealt with in Chapter 9. There are special issues raised by the stress on comparison and the use of benchmarking. The guidance stated that authorities should 'compare their current and prospective performance against other public sector bodies, and those in the private and voluntary sectors' (DETR, 1999a, para. 29). As a result benchmarking has developed within the best value regime.

There is a danger of a simplistic approach to benchmarking, if the measures used become overdominant and it is assumed they can be read off automatically to compare performance, The ambiguities of best value mean that value cannot be assumed to follow from the measure alone. Consultation and local views can run counter to benchmarking. The hard data of benchmarking can drive out the softer data of opinion.

These dangers were recognised in the guidance in so far as it suggested 'there will rarely be a process of exact comparison, rather the intelligent exploration of how analogous services or elements of such services perform' (DETR, 1999a, para. 29). Best value reviews should not be dominated by measures; rather measures should be set within a reflective process or an 'intelligent exploration'. The danger is that these cautionary remarks have little impact against the general tenor of the guidance; the quantitative drives out the qualitative and measures dominate reflection.

Procedures as the priority

The best value regime was developed as a means of improving performance. The danger is that the focus is on procedures, which although designed as a means of improving performance can become ends in themselves. The government has recognised some of the problems with performance plans in its proposals for simplification, although they do not go very far in that direction. There is an equal danger in best value reviews, reinforced by an inspection process designed to ensure procedures are properly carried out.

The Audit Commission's checklist for scrutinising best value reviews has the danger of becoming, as the word suggests, a series of boxes to be ticked. The aim for the authority can become getting the right ticks in the boxes. Questions such as 'Is "challenge" just a stage of the process or do all elements of the BVR [best value review] challenge existing views and means of delivering the service and provide an honest and accurate assessment of what improvements are required?' (Audit Commission, 2001a, p. 49) are presumably designed to avoid the danger of the process being an end in itself. Yet the checklist approach suggesting a 'yes' or 'no' answer almost makes a tick box approach inevitable. The evaluation report on the pilots commented that the audit of performance plans was seen by many councillors and officers as 'a largely "tick box" approach to auditing', and reinforced 'fears that the Best Value regime was becoming increasingly process-driven with a standard set of approaches being applied to all authorities regardless of their current performance or the approaches that they took to implementing Best Value' (Martin *et al.*, 2001, p. 2).

There is a dilemma. Procedures are needed to challenge existing practices, but the procedures can become the new practice, which in turn needs to be challenged. Auditors, inspectors and central government, as well as officers and councillors, should guard against these dangers. The recognition of the need to simplify the performance plan and to reduce the number of reviews is a welcome step in avoiding both being merely routines to be carried out, but it is necessary to go further.

The Welsh Assembly has departed from the approach laid down in England and placed the emphasis in best value on authorities carrying out a corporate diagnosis of the overall need for improvement leading to an authority improvement plan. Cirell and Bennett point out that the Welsh approach has 'exposed a fundamental flaw in the way the [best value] regime has been embraced – that the focus has been on performance in disparate service areas rather than on what the local authority as a corporate whole is seeking to achieve, and how Best Value can support and advance that vision'. They argue that there are lessons to be learnt from 'the need to focus on the corporate diagnosis as opposed to treating Best Value as a heavily bureaucratic exercise of research on how services are provided' (Cirell and Bennett, 2002, p. 30). A similar benefit may be obtained in England from the self-assessment that is part of the corporate performance assessment described in the next chapter.

Is improvement the focus?

The goal is improved performance, yet it often seems that the emphasis is being given not on how the service can be improved but on who delivers the service. The guidance stresses the importance of decisions on the options for service delivery, and those options are mainly about which organisation should deliver the service. The focus on who delivers the service can distract attention away from the issue of how the service can be improved by better service design.

Performance improvement would be even more likely to be achieved if the guidance had focused on better ways of meeting need, rather than on better ways of providing services. The guidance does suggest as an option 'the cessation of the service, in whole or in part' (DETR, 1999a, para. 44), but does not focus on alternative forms of service or on alternative ways of meeting needs.

Limited range of options

When considering options on who delivers the service, the original guidance emphasised the involvement of the private sector, although it also included partnerships and the involvement of the voluntary sector. The latest guidance extends the range of options:

> The 'make or buy' decision is often seen as a choice between in-house delivery and out-sourcing, but there are a wide variety of service delivery options and partners available, all of which need to be considered. Inviting external tenderers to compete with the in-house team is one such option. Others include internal re-organisation, service out-sourcing, private finance initiatives, public sector consortia, pooled budgets, joint commissioning, joint ventures, non-profit distributing organisations, as well as partnering contracts and legal partnerships. (ODPM, 2002a, p. 14).

The government has now recognised, as discussed in the next chapter, that partnerships can take many different forms, but the options are dominated by forms of private sector involvement. The new guidance still fails to give an equal attention to, or in some cases even to mention, approaches such as self-help or mutual aid. The omission of self-help and to a less extent mutual aid is probably due to the focus on who delivers rather than on ways of meeting need.

Discussion of options for service provision and for meeting needs has been wider in the United States. An International City Management Association (ICMA) report lists seven alternatives to direct provision:

- contracting;
- franchising;
- subsidising;
- vouchers;
- volunteers;
- self-help; and
- regulation and tax incentives. (ICMA, 1989)

Criteria of choice

Choice on the means of service delivery or of meeting need has to be guided by appropriate criteria. This key issue is barely touched on in the guidance. Choice, one is told, should be based on 'objective analysis'. There should be a 'written policy on evaluation and appraisal'. 'Authorities will be expected to demonstrate that they have explored the full range of alternatives and selected the options most likely to deliver the best value to the public' (DETR, 1999a, p. 15). The stated criteria in the legislation are economy, efficiency and effectiveness, with effectiveness, in particular, having many facets, although that is not recognised by the guidance. But these should not be the only criteria. The ICMA lists criteria to be used when considering service contracting:

- cost;
- effectiveness, quality of service, service level;
- impact on other local services' potential for service disruption;
- responsiveness to citizens' needs and expectations;
- legal constraints;

- personnel issues;
- political support;
- availability of providers;
- administrative control;
- transitional factors;
- potential for waste, fraud and abuse;
- capital investment requirements;
- service equity; and
- size of government. (ICMA, 1989, p. 5)

Nor is this list comprehensive. Other criteria could include:

- allocation of risk;
- the flexibility required over time;
- the diversity of service required;
- specialist skills and knowledge required by the authority for the client role;
- learning about future needs and service requirements;
- responsiveness to political control;
- public accountability; and
- market conditions.

There are also authority-wide criteria to be considered. Service-by-service review can mean little consideration is given to the cumulative impact of decisions made on separate services, with each decision being made on its merits for that service. The guidance sees a value in 'real variety in the way services are delivered and genuine plurality among service providers' (DETR, 1999a, para. 37). Yet if the forms of provision vary and each is subject to separate contracts or agreements, joined-up government can become more difficult, since each arrangement has its own limited focus. The danger of fragmentation has led some authorities and the government to favour strategic service partnerships embracing many functions in a single partnership, but they can bring their own problems, as discussed in the next chapter.

Problems of accountability grow as the forms of provision extend. Accountability depends on comprehensibility and transparency. As the variety of forms of provision and of providers grows it becomes more difficult for the public to find out where responsibility lies. Transparency is limited unless private sector

organisations accept the obligations of open government and
public accountability, or, put another way, unless these organisations accept they have, in part, been 'publicised'.

These considerations mean that choice on the form of service
provision or on the way to meet needs involves many criteria,
some related to the function and some to the overall impact on
the authority. No one criterion should dominate. Different
criteria have to be weighed against each other. There should be
no reading off of the choice as if from a calculation. What is
required is judgement formed after reflection and discussion.

Conclusion

It is a strength of the modernisation programme that improving
performance and the search for best value were recognised as a
condition of effective local government. Best value should be a
means both of ensuring high standards of performance and of
relating the work of the authority to the needs and aspirations of
the community and its citizens. As with so much of the modernisation programme, problems have arisen not so much with the
concept but in applying it in practice. The government has now
recognised some of the dangers of bureaucratisation of the best
value processes enforced by over-elaborate inspection. Some of
the weaknesses in the approach to best value have still to be
faced, including the ambiguities of best value, the criteria for
evaluation, the relative neglect of service design and the importance of judgement based on discussion and reflection. What has
happened, however, is that the government no longer sees best
value as the only route to improved performance in local authorities. The next chapter discusses the other approaches developed
by the government in what can be described as the restlessness of
the modernisation programme.

8 Beyond Best Value

The government has gone beyond the best value regime as the means of improving performance in the modernisation programme. Rather than relying upon experience for both local authorities and central government to learn how to make effective use of the best value regime to improve performance, it has taken a series of further initiatives, which make the best value regime almost redundant.

Beacon councils

The government set out a scheme for beacon councils in a prospectus issued at about the same time the best value regime was established. The beacon council scheme was designed to identify examples of excellence in service provision and thereby provide models for other authorities to follow. The prospectus said the scheme aims to 'recognise the best performing councils and spread best practice' (DETR, 1999b, p. 8). Beacon authorities would shine light on what was too readily assumed to be the outer darkness of the rest of local government.

The scheme was to have two phases. The first phase concentrates on excellence in particular services or in dealing with particular cross-cutting issues with the proviso that beacon councils should also 'be good across the board' (DETR, 1999b, p. 11). Beacon councils spread good practice through a national programme of dissemination for which they receive a small grant. The incentive for authorities to apply for beacon status in this phase is not the hope of financial reward, but publicity of their work and the national prestige it is assumed to bring. An advisory panel assesses applications after preparatory work by officials and service experts, who reduce them to a number that can be effectively handled by the panel. Ministers make the final decision and have normally, but not invariably, accepted the panel's recommendations. A variety of means are used for

141

dissemination. Roadshows give broad presentations. Open days in the beacon authorities give an opportunity for a wider exchange of information and ideas. Beacon councils also provide other dissemination activities, including site visits, secondments and consultancy.

The first phase of beacon councils began in 2000, but the second phase has yet to begin and may now never begin, being overtaken by developments described later in this chapter. The second phase was to have covered overall beacons or 'councils which are excellent across the board'. (DETR, 1999b, p. 22). This phase would have brought councils more than prestige since the beacon councils were to have been awarded new freedoms from and flexibilities in statutory and other central government requirements. These freedoms and flexibilities were to have included powers to raise additional business rates, a relaxation of controls on capital investment as well as freedom for councils to take their own decisions in areas where there is a consent regime, and powers to take initiatives where councils have no power to do so (DETR, 1999b, p. 25).

There are problems with the beacon council scheme. The scheme rests on judgement and judgement can be disputed. Judgement is not easy, as the panel recognised in recommending 37 applications covering 46 councils for 2000/1. It may be that the most important stage in making the judgement was the process of reducing 269 applications to 65 for the panel to consider (DETR, 2000d). The panel was to a large extent dependent on the officials and service experts to carry out this reduction, although the panel could and did subject their conclusions to critical appraisal. Judgement can be challenged and the reaction of some councillors and officers to the presentations made by the beacon authorities has been that there was nothing exceptional about the processes and practices presented, although others welcomed the opportunity for learning.

The main problem is the assumption that excellence is a rare quality and only a very few authorities merit beacon status. As stressed in the opening chapter, this assumption has underlain the government's approach to local government and to the implementation of the modernisation programme. The world of local government is very different from the world implied by this assumption. There is probably very little to distinguish services in the beacons from those in several or even many other authorities. If this is probably true of the first phase, it would certainly have been true of the second phase. The alternative assumption is that most authorities and their services contain a mixture of excellent, good, fair, weak and even poor activities, as they are later to be described. It is misleading to single out particular authorities or their services as a special category of beacons to shine out on the unenlightened in the darkness beyond. Rather than the many learning from the few, all can learn from each other, and there is a strong tradition in local government of learning from other authorities.

The Improvement and Development Agency (IDeA) set up by local government has initiated an approach based on peer review, involving shared learning. Local authorities can invite the IDeA to arrange for a peer review in which a team is sent into an authority to review its workings and to prepare a report with recommendations to be considered by the authority. The teams are composed of a councillor, officers including a chief executive and others from the private and voluntary sectors. The team is supplied with documentation. The key part of the review is the week-long visit by the team for interviews and discussions. The team operates within a framework setting out issues to be explored and criteria to guide the work of the team.

These peer reviews have generally been seen as helpful by the authorities where they have taken place. Authorities have learnt from them, but so have members of the teams, who often say they have learnt as much as those being reviewed. For there are few, if any, authorities from which nothing can be learnt and few, if any, authorities that have nothing to learn from others. Peer reviews can have much more to contribute to improving performance than the carefully selected beacons.

Local public service agreements

Local public service agreements (PSAs) are agreements between individual authorities and central government. Authorities undertake to deliver specific targets and the government undertakes to reward the authority for achieving those targets and to consider giving the authorities new freedoms and flexibilities to assist that achievement. No similar developments have taken place in Scotland, but in Wales policy agreements are playing a related role.

The Local Government Association proposed local public service agreements under the title Local Challenge as an approach balancing national objectives with local autonomy (LGA, 1999, 2000c). The government welcomed this initiative. After pilots in twenty authorities, the government has rolled out the approach for all shire counties, metropolitan districts and London boroughs, with arrangements, where agreed locally, for shire districts to be included in the county PSA.

PSAs brought together two lines of thinking for the LGA. PSAs drew upon the experience of pathfinder authorities under the LGA's New Commitment to Regeneration, which developed the role of councils in formulating strategies for regeneration with local partners and with central government and its agencies. Contrats de Ville in France influenced the LGA in the development of the New Commitment. Contrats de Ville are agreed between a local authority and central government based on a local strategy tackling urban problems. They commit both parties to implementing the strategy and cover the implications for mainline programmes (Le Galès and Mawson, 1995). The New Commitment did not go so far as the legally binding Contrats de Ville; it did, however, give expression to the principle of partnership between an authority and central government. Writing about PSAs, the LGA said, 'Like the LGA's *New Commitment to Regeneration*, they offer a further means to engage the government as an active partner locally; and to work with the government to remove rules and regulations which stand in the way of tailoring policies to meet local needs' (LGA, 2001c).

The LGA also drew on the experience of public service agreements made between the Treasury and other central government departments and setting targets covering a three-year period. The ideas put forward by the LGA brought together that experience with experience of joint working in the New Commitment. The LGA argued that local PSAs would resolve the tension between government's national targets for policy priorities and local councils' awareness of local circumstances, recognising that local solutions are often the best way to achieve national targets. 'Nationally prescribed programmes all too often become straight [*sic*] jackets, hindering delivery on the ground' (LGA, 2000c).

Among the advantages seen by the LGA were the involvement of local authorities in discussions with central government departments and the possibility of new freedoms and flexibilities, which it hoped would be wide-ranging in scope. For central government, PSAs are a means of meeting targets for national priorities. The government makes significant financial resources available as rewards for achievement and as support in preparation for achieving the targets, although these resources are presumably taken from funds that could have been part of the general revenue support grant.

The pilot projects were regarded as confirming the value of PSAs both for local authorities and for central government, leading to the decision to extend the approach. The discussions leading to PSAs in the pilots had been time-consuming and for this reason the rollout of PSAs was phased over two years. The pilot projects had not fulfilled all the hopes of new freedoms placed on them by the authorities concerned. A process evaluation carried out for DTLR concluded, 'In general, authorities were disappointed with the freedoms and flexibilities they achieved, although the commitment to further discussions on matters of mutual importance has been welcomed' (OPM, 2002 Executive Summary).

There were, nevertheless, examples of significant freedoms for authorities. Camden successfully negotiated with the government freedom to allow joint working with the police on traffic enforcement and to pilot a lane rental scheme for utilities to pay a daily charge when they dig up roads. In Sunderland flexibility was allowed in the use of Youth Justice Board project funds. In many PSAs, however, all the authority obtained was a commitment to explore an issue further. The government agreed to explore with five authorities, judged to have good planning processes, whether an overarching education plan can be produced meeting the purposes of the many separate plans. The government agreed to explore with Kent whether there were ways of limiting the divergence in the VAT regimes applying to health and local authorities where it inhibits the potential of pooled budgets. These and other commitments have led to continuing joint work, which has been argued to show the value of the process. It is a commentary on past relations between central government and local authorities that it has required PSAs to bring about such joint discussions. The test will be the outcome of the discussions.

The rollout of PSAs began in 2001. The first stage involves discussions in which the authority presents its strategies within which the PSA will be set. There follow negotiations expected to last about six weeks covering both the targets and the proposed relaxations in the requirements of central government. The PSAs have to include about twelve performance targets, expressed as outcomes, with an emphasis on national priorities. The targets for national priorities include at least one relating to each of education, social services and transport and a measure of overall cost-effectiveness. In addition there should be at least one more relating to either education or social services. The local targets should cover 'the main issues of substance that consultation indicates are important local concerns but which might not be sufficiently reflected in the national priorities' (DTLR, 2001e, p. 9). Authorities have to produce supporting evidence from the best value performance plan or from other plans to show that the targets are 'stretching' and beyond what would otherwise be achieved. Achievement of the targets is monitored through the audit of performance plans.

A pump-priming grant of up to a maximum of £750,000 plus £1 per head of population is available after consideration of an authority's proposals. Additional borrowing of up to £3 million for an average-size authority can be made available to a council 'which makes a persuasive case', showing the extent to which the borrowing will enable the authority to meet the government's aims of an additional notable improvement in outcomes or a 'particularly convincing instance' of cross-cutting working (DTLR, 2001e, p. 12). These financial arrangements are to help authorities meet the targets. In addition, a performance reward grant is made for achieving the targets – half as capital grant and half as revenue grant. If an authority achieves all its targets, the grant is equivalent to 2.5 per cent of its budget at the start of the PSA. The grant is scaled down pro rata if an authority does not achieve particular targets, and no grant is paid if the authority achieves less than 60 per cent of the targeted improvement in performance. PSAs involve, therefore, grant paid in relation to performance, a principle discussed in Chapter 12.

The LGA attached particular importance to the scope for relaxations in the requirements placed on local authorities and while as shown above these have been limited in scope, it is still felt there is significant potential for local authorities to obtain new freedoms and flexibilities. This potential is recognised by the government. It accepts that submissions by local authorities can be important in building understanding at national level of the impact of government-imposed constraints on performance at local level:

> Some of these [statutory and administrative] requirements may have seemed necessary for the management of administrative processes. But they may limit the scope for improving the delivery of services to a greater extent than departments realise. The Government wants authorities to use the Local PSA to draw attention to adverse consequences of such requirements, and it wants departments to relax or remove requirements where the benefit in the delivery of better services outweighs any possible risks or drawbacks. (DTLR, 2001e, p. 12)

The PSA process reflects more the government's emphasis on targets than the LGA's hope for a wide-ranging discussion about the needs and opportunities of the area. True, the government stresses that the 'greatest value in improved outcomes is likely to come when the Local PSA is part of a concerted plan to achieve the community's priorities, building on Best Value plans to achieve continuous improvement across the board' (DTLR, 2001e, p. 5). What is lacking is an emphasis in the PSA guidance on community strategies, although these are emphasised in the Welsh approach to policy agreements (Welsh Assembly, 2002). There are dangers in the focus on a limited number of targets without the wider perspective of community planning. PSAs can become merely an exercise in target-setting with many of the targets being nationally generated.

Performance management and targets are discussed in Chapter 9. Here it is sufficient to signal the problem that a limited number of separate targets can distort the work of the authority because it can involve relative neglect of other aspects of the authority's work and encourage separatism rather than joined-up working between services. Whether PSAs result in improved overall performance will depend not only on whether targets are achieved but also on that achievement not being at the expense of services or of aspects of service not covered by the targets. It can be easy to achieve a limited range of targets if they receive a concentrated focus, but such a focus can mean a relative neglect of other activities.

The greatest gains from the process are likely to derive from the discussions between central government departments and local authorities. As the process is rolled out, it will be important to avoid the danger of it becoming a routine, not for the authorities for whom it will be an exceptional experience, but for central government departments involved in discussions with many authorities.

The greatest danger is that PSAs become not a partnership between central government and local authorities but an instrument of central control. The emphasis on national priorities and targets to be found in *Strong Local Leadership* highlights that danger, through its proposals to set local PSAs within the national 'comprehensive and integrated performance framework' discussed below (DTLR, 2001a, p. 23), and for the government 'to take a more proactive approach', identifying before negotiations begin 'a small number of areas in which we will expect their local PSAs to include 'stretch' targets' (ibid., p. 32).

Reform of the public services

The government committed itself to reform of the public services in its second term. Some in local government are puzzled by this new stress on reform, since they understood that the modernisation programme in general and best value in particular were regarded as reform of the public services. Reform is now associated with greater involvement of the private sector. The 2001 Labour manifesto stated that 'Where the quality is not improving quickly enough, alternative providers should be brought in. Where private-sector providers can support public endeavour, we should use them. A 'spirit of enterprise' should apply as much to public service as to business' (Labour Party, 2001, p. 17). The stress on private sector involvement has continued as almost the central element in the rhetoric of reform.

These views on reform are presented as non-ideological because the stress is said to be on what works. Yet there does appear to be an underlying ideology, if by that is meant a set of beliefs determining policy and the action that follows. Not that such an approach is necessarily undesirable, for politics is about just that – beliefs influencing action. What is necessary for an effective political process is that the beliefs are made explicit and open to challenge, rather than hidden by an emphasis on 'what works'. Such references can hide an ideological preference for private sector involvement and a belief that such involvement is what works.

There is and has always been considerable private sector involvement in public services. Compulsory competitive tendering (CCT) extended that involvement. Competitive tendering has continued as an option in the best value regime and the guidance stressed that 'such competition is expected to play an essential and enduring role in ensuring best value' (DETR, 1999a, para. 36). The Labour government developed the private finance initiative (PFI), begun by the Conservative government. Private finance has been used to enable the construction or modernisation of buildings and the arrangements can extend to continuing involvement in maintenance work and the provision of support services. Public–private partnerships, of which the private finance initiative is one form, have been emphasised by the government as the main means of involving the private sector.

The government has taken a number of steps since the 2001 election to enable greater private sector involvement. *Strong Local Leadership* welcomed the recommendations of the task force on Local Government Procurement 'and will work with appropriate agencies to strengthen local authority capacity for procurement' (DLTR, 2001a, pp. 48–9). The additional guidance on best value indicates that 'The emphasis needs to shift away from routine market-testing, to robust option appraisal, so that a much wider range of service options are considered' (ODPM, 2002a, p. 14).

The additional options are not exclusively based on private sector involvement, but include use of the voluntary sector and joint action between authorities as well as new ways of working with the private sector. The consultation paper on *Working with Others to Achieve Best Value* (DTLR, 2001b) emphasised that the new powers of well-being enable local authorities to form and participate in companies, trusts or charities, including joint venture companies. These powers are not necessarily available for mainstream functions. The government proposes to use section 16 of the Local Government Act 1999 to give authorities wider powers to form and participate in corporate structures (DTLR, 2001b, p. 20). The government is also examining the scope for social corporate bodies, drawing on ideas about public interest companies: 'an organisational form that is based upon entrepreneurial trading for public service, but that will do so without the need to generate profit for external distribution' (Corrigan, 2001, p. 6).

Government policy is directed at increasing private sector involvement through partnership working, avoiding the adversarial relationships that were the result of some of the short-term contracts developed under CCT. Although the government has stressed that what matters is what works there has been as yet no comprehensive analysis of the experience of public–private partnerships (PPPs) and the private finance initiative although the National Audit Office has reported on *Managing the Relationship to Secure a Successful Partnership in PFI Projects* (NAO, 2001) and on *PFI: Construction Performance* (NAO, 2003) while the Audit Commission has reported on *PFIs in Schools* (Audit Commission, 2003). Data are limited on, for example, the extent to which penalty provisions have been applied by authorities or on the extent to which risk transfer is achieved in practice as opposed to intention. The Commission on Public Private Partnerships set up by the Institute of Public Policy Research undertook an evaluation of the experience of PFIs and PPPs, but was limited by the lack of adequate comprehensive data. The development of public–private partnerships has certainly not been an example of evidence-based policy.

The Commission on Public Private Partnerships concluded that numerous PFI projects had gone ahead because public managers generally were convinced there were no alternative ways of obtaining the necessary resources. The private finance initiative was seen as 'the only game in town' (IPPR, 2001, p. 79), because the rules governing public finance appeared to make it the only way to finance required capital expenditure. The Commission argued that 'privately financed public investment has the same implications for the sustainability of the government's finances as conventionally financed investment' by government borrowing (IPPR, 2001, p. 95). The Commission stressed that the criterion for determining whether to pursue private finance rather than public borrowing should be value for money: 'The pre-requisite for taking the PFI model and other forms of PPP forward is to make value-for-money – defined in efficiency and quality terms – the sole driving force and to remove the incentive for going down this route solely to avoid constraints on public finance' (ibid.).

The Commission supported public–private partnerships as bringing a diversity of provision drawing in new skills and abilities. The Commission argued:

> The Best Value approach to the provision of local services based on the authority acting as strategic planner and purchaser and exploring the merits of a diverse range of public, private and voluntary providers is an attractive one in theory. Its focus on service improvement, user involvement and the encouragement of different models of provision and [*sic*] is laudable. However, it will fall down in practice unless it is underpinned always and everywhere by a level playing field in deciding the type of providers that should be selected and in the system through which capital is allocated. (IPPR, 2001, p. 173).

The Commission saw a number of other problems, such as accountability, but believed that they could be resolved if faced directly.

Allison Pollock and her colleagues have challenged the IPPR report for ignoring or downplaying 'the external realities that affect partnership arrangements, and financial issues and implications of these new forms of public procurement' (Pollock *et al.*, 2001, p. 8). They highlight the difficulties encountered in many of the arrangements made with the private sector. They point out the problem of enforcing penalties for failures or of terminating arrangements, the public authority having become dependent on the private sector supplier: 'The public sector has frequently forgone its legal entitlement to penalty payments for poor performance in the interest of building relationships and due to the lack of a realistic alternative supplier' (p. 7). They argue there is a lack of good evidence of greater value for money through efficiency and effectiveness. Increasingly, therefore, risk transfer is 'the primary way in which local authorities and central government justify PPPs' (p. 11), but value for money through risk transfer can be illusory. Even when risks have been contractually transferred, 'it is not always possible to enforce the contract for a range of practical reasons' (p. 12), in part because of the underlying responsibilities of the public sector for the continuing provision of services. It may well be the public 'as individuals' that bear the risk in the form of poor service (p. 32).

The lack of adequate information and analysis of experience to date hinder assessment of the different contentions about the value of private sector involvement. The argument for private sector involvement that there are greater management skills and abilities in the private sector is to say the least unproven. Private sector organisations seeking work in the public sector often begin by recruiting management staff from the public sector.

The development of public–private partnerships can have a cumulative effect, which is not always appreciated when each arrangement is considered on its individual merits. As new forms develop and an authority enters into a variety of arrangements with the private sector, two issues grow in importance. The first is fragmentation as different activities are conducted under different arrangements with different partners. Almost inevitably, it becomes more difficult to achieve joined-up working. Issues about accountability also grow as the number and variety of relationships grow. The public has increasing difficulty knowing who is responsible for a service. This lack of transparency is increased by the growing practice of subcontracting both under contracts and within partnerships. The issue is how the public as citizens or as users can hold to account those responsible for services, when it is not clear who is responsible for what and how, even if known, they can be made accountable.

The government considers that the development of strategic service partnerships can overcome problems involved in limited short-term contracts. The government sees strategic service partnerships as establishing long-term and wide-ranging relationships between local authorities and a private sector partner. Its consultation paper stated:

> There has been a welcome trend in adopting non-statutory Partnership Boards to oversee strategic partnership arrangements between local authorities and the private sector. The aim is to bring elected members, senior officers and company directors to discuss strategic issues relevant to the partnership such as
>
> - business strategy and policies;
> - future budgets and overall financial arrangements;
> - dispute resolution; and
> - the wider impact and role of the partnership in the local community. (DTLR, 2001b, pp. 24–5)

Strategic partnerships can take many forms: private finance initiative transactions, strategic partnership agreements, joint venture companies, community trusts and franchise agreements (ibid., p. 10).

The government sees strategic service partnerships differing from past contracts because they

- are quality-driven, value-added, arrangements;
- derive from a corporate-wide assessment of service need;
- take a long-term perspective to those needs:
- work back from user views in defining those needs;
- seek to embrace innovation through the full and effective utilisation of new technologies, high-quality design and working practices; and
- adopt a corporate social responsibility to their staff, and to the wider community which they serve. (DTLR, 2001d, p. 9)

This is a good example of assuming that if one specifies perfection then perfection there will be.

There has so far been only limited experience of strategic partnerships in authorities. Filkin and his colleagues have described a number of examples including Lambeth's contract with Service Team covering education and building maintenance, housing repairs, ground maintenance and refuse collection among other services, and Middlesbrough's contract with Hyder Business Services covering reception services, facilities management, property management, payroll services, financial services and public relations and many other services (Filkin *et al.*, 2001a). Strategic partnerships aim to create a relationship that is not confined by the terms of a limited short-term contract. They are designed to build a shared interest in developing and improving services, given expression in the partnership board. Whether that shared interest can be maintained over the longer term remains to be tested.

There are dangers in what the IPPR has described as '"a one-company authority" which sits uneasily with the principle of diversity which is supposed to inform Best Value' (IPPR, 2001, p. 155). The authority can become overdependent on the company and the partnership. Problems can arise if there is failure to deliver and because of the extent of that dependence it is particularly difficult for the authority to enforce penalties or dissolve the partnership. Strategic partnerships appear to be contrary to two of the stated reasons for private sector involvement: the value of competition and the value of diversity in service provision. What is being created could become a private monopoly. The government, while seeing potential in strategic partnerships, recognises there can be 'potential risks associated with entering into long-term, far reaching partnerships' (DETR, 2001d, p. 11). The government clearly believes the benefits outweigh the risks and has set up a Research and Development Programme which it hopes will facilitate the growth of such partnerships.

The comprehensive performance framework

Strong Local Leadership, while reiterating the importance of existing instruments for improving performance, argued that further steps were necessary. The government recognised, implicitly rather than explicitly, that it had created obstacles to improved performance in local authorities by imposing administrative burdens and by restricting their financial freedom unduly. The government accepted the need to remove these obstacles, some from all authorities and others from selected authorities: 'To realise our common aim of improving people's quality of life councils need greater freedom and wider powers to deliver' (DTLR, 2001a, p. 40). The government proposed to reduce the number of plans, area-based initiatives and ring-fenced grants as well as a general reduction in red tape and bureaucracy. Greater control over their own borrowing was proposed for local authorities, subject to prudential rules. These changes, which will be discussed in Chapters 11 and 12, remove some of the obstacles and burdens on local authorities that have prevented them focusing on improving services, having to meet the many requirements of central government procedures and initiatives, although there have been signs of a reluctance by central departments to implement these proposals in full.

Beyond these changes, *Strong Local Leadership* set out a new approach to service improvement in a comprehensive performance framework. The starting point is a statement on 'shared priorities' agreed between the government and the LGA. On the basis of these priorities the government has laid down targets for local government as part of the national spending review process. These targets, unlike the priorities, have not been agreed by the LGA, although it was consulted on the areas covered (ODPM and LGA, 2002a). The government intends that these national priorities and targets should inform local authorities' approach to best value and guide discussions on public service agreements.

The agreement on shared priorities puts the Local Government Association in a false position since it cannot commit authorities to its national priorities. The LGA can state its views, but each authority has its own electoral base and makes its own decisions on priorities. It can be argued the national priorities are unexceptional and few would disagree with 'raising standards across our schools', 'promoting healthier communities and improving health inequalities' or 'creating safer and stronger communities' (ODPM and LGA, 2002b). While few are likely to dispute these aims there may be different priorities at local level. Centrally determined priorities remain centrally determined priorities, whether they are determined by the government, by the Local Government Association or together.

The comprehensive performance assessment

The main change introduced by the framework is the establishment of comprehensive performance assessments (CPAs) of authorities and their allocation on the basis of that assessment to one of five categories: excellent, good, fair, weak and poor. Under the Local Government Bill, these provisions are not to apply to Wales and no equivalent provisions have been introduced in Scotland.

Originally there were to have been four categories: high-performing, striving, coasting and poor-performing. The words chosen to describe the categories were widely seen as unfortunate and there was pressure for change. It was hardly likely that the label 'coasting' would motivate authorities, but then the same can be said about some of the current labels. There must be doubts about whether authorities can be fitted into such boxes however they are labelled. As already stressed, most authorities have varying standards of performance. Different services in the same authority can be excellent, good, fair, weak and poor. To place a single label on that complexity is to distort reality.

The comprehensive performance assessments are made by the Audit Commission, considering both current performance and capacity to improve. The assessment of current performance is based on the combination of judgements on up to six service blocks dependent on the functions of the authority. The judgement on the capacity to improve is based on the corporate assessment introduced as part of the CPA. The whole CPA process uses a variety of data sources including performance indicators, plan assessments by government departments, the results of past inspections and audits and the corporate assessment. Much depends on the weight given to different sources of data, to different services and to different elements in the assessment process and how the judgments on current performance and capacity to improve are combined into a single assessment.

The Audit Commission's consultation paper showed how different weights and different combinations gave different results (Audit Commission, 2002a). It can depend on the weights and combinations whether an authority is in one category rather than another, yet the weights given and combinations made are inherently arbitrary. The Commission consulted on these and other issues. As a result new weights and combinations were put forward for further consultation (Audit Commission, 2002c), yet the ones eventually adopted remain arbitrary. The consultation process showed there was no objective basis for the weights and combinations eventually chosen.

The corporate assessment

The corporate assessment of capacity to improve is carried out by a team composed of a team leader, an appointed auditor, an Audit Commission inspector, a councillor, an officer and a member of the support team, supplemented by representatives of other inspectorates (Audit Commission, 2002e, section 3). The corporate assessment starts with existing evidence from inspections and audits and performance data and the council's self-assessment on which guidance has been given (Audit Commission, 2002d). On this basis the Audit Commission 'will form an initial impression' or so the consultation paper suggested (Audit Commission, 2002a, p. 65). One suspects that impressions once formed are not easily dislodged, although there is onsite fieldwork studying documents, observation, discussions, interviews, focus groups and input from local communities and service users, normally, however, covering not more than two weeks.

The teams have to answer four top-level questions:

- What is the council trying to achieve?
- How has the council set about delivering its priorities?
- What has the council achieved/not achieved to date?
- In the light of what the council has learned to date, what does it plan to do next? (Audit Commission, 2002e)

Each of these questions has two or three associated themes. Thus the first question has ambition, focus and prioritisation as its three themes.

A series of key questions are associated with each theme. The three questions on ambitions are 'What are the council's priorities?', 'What are not the council's priorities?' and 'How does the council try to offer leadership to the local community and its own services?' Key questions on other themes cover capacity, performance management, achievement, investment, learning and future plans. The result for each key question is scored on a scale of 1 to 4, representing very weak, fairly weak, fairly strong and very strong. The scores for the key questions are then given 'appropriate' weightings to determine scores for the top-level questions, which are then used to determine the overall judgement of the council's proven capacity to improve. The teams do not rely solely on this arithmetic process but the consultation paper suggests they may 'change scores for a top level question' (Audit Commission, 2002a, p. 68) if the weightings and scores appear to come up with the wrong answer! There have been suggestions that the comprehensive performance assessments, were adjusted shortly before publication (*Local Government Chronicle*, 13 December 2002); If true, this is presumably because the whole complex process had also come up with the wrong answer!

The assessment of performance

The assessment of performance combines separate assessments of the constituent service blocks. These assessments, again on scores of 1 to 4, are made largely by the appropriate inspectorate or by auditors for the resources block. The assessments are carried out with similar frameworks to that used for the corporate assessment, although varying with the nature of the inspection processes on which they are based. The separate scores for the service blocks are combined with the education and social services blocks, being given weights of four times the other blocks, and subject to rules preventing authorities being given overall scores of 3 or 4 if their scores on the education and social services blocks are too low (Audit Commission, 2002c).

Making the overall comprehensive performance assessment

The separate scores from 1 to 4 for the performance assessment and the assessment of capacity to improve are combined to place authorities in one of the five categories, according to a table setting out the possible combinations, Thus an authority scored 2 on performance and 3 on capacity to improve would be categorised as fair. There are again limitations placed on the categorisation of good and excellent if authorities have low scores for education and social services.

The first comprehensive performance assessments were published in December 2002. These covered counties, metropolitan districts, unitary authorities and London boroughs with shire districts to follow in 2003. The 2002 results were:

- excellent: 22 authorities
- good: 54 authorities
- fair: 39 authorities
- weak: 22 authorities
- poor: 13 authorities

These results had more authorities in the excellent and good categories than previous work by the Audit Commission on best value had implied (Audit Commission, 2001a), highlighting the variability of inspection and assessment processes.

The overall comprehensive performance assessment rests upon the inevitably challengeable judgements of inspectors and assessors and the process of weightings and combinations. It cannot be assumed that an assessment built on such an uncertain base can justify authorities being placed in a particular category with a single simple label attached. Yet the label given largely determines the relationship between individual local authorities and central government. Authorities assessed as excellent are given a three-year inspection holiday except where there are statutory requirements or 'grounds for concern' (ODPM, 2002e, para. 30) and are given, as described in Chapters 11 and 12, freedoms and flexibilities beyond those given generally to all authorities. Authorities assessed as good are also given some of these additional freedoms and flexibilities. Excellent authorities are, in addition, invited to join an Innovation Forum called by the government as a collective means of considering further freedoms and flexibilities (ibid., para. 13). For those in the poor and some in the weak categories, the government will intervene in improvement planning.

Improvement planning

A process of improvement planning has been introduced for all authorities, although 'the processes are likely to be less complex' for authorities judged to be higher-performing (ODPM, 2002e, para. 13). For each authority there is an external evaluation of the priorities and improvement programme judged to be required following the CPA. This evaluation will take place through a round-table discussion, coordinated by the Audit Commission and attended by representatives of the inspectorate and of the Office of the Deputy Prime Minister acting for the government. These discussions will review the authority's plans for a response to the CPA, agree an appropriate inspection regime and identify possible requirements for capacity building.

The government elaborated its approach towards authorities judged to have poor performance in a consultation paper entitled *Tackling Poor Performance in Local Government* (ODPM, 2002c):

> The basis for organising action in all cases will be the recovery plan. This will be the centrepiece of a poorly performing authority's improvement planning process. It will identify the key actions and solutions that are necessary to deliver essential improvements to service delivery. It will need to tackle all the weaknesses identified in the CPA. It will address any problems of leadership and management, failings of financial and other corporate systems, and the shortcomings of core corporate services as well as specific service areas. (Ibid., p. 11)

The Office of the Deputy Prime Minister appoints relationship managers as the main point of communication with the authority. They assess the capacity and commitment of the authority to prepare the recovery plan and recommend any government action required. Where, in what it expects will be only a few cases, the government considers that would not be successful it can use its statutory powers of intervention: 'Where there is a clear risk to the public . . . the Government may wish to move decisively to put alternative arrangements in place' (ODPM, 2002e, para. 62a). The government has emphasised that 'The powers in Section 15 of the 1999 Act and in other legislation should be sufficient to ensure that the action needed to make key improvements is not frustrated by a reluctant or obstructive council' (ODPM, 2002c, p. 14). These powers enable the Secretary of State 'to appoint a nominee to carry out specified functions including those that are integral to its corporate effectiveness' (ibid., p. 15).

Where the government considers the authority is capable of preparing and implementing the recovery plan it charges the authority with the task. Authorities are then expected to draw up the recovery plan with 'key priorities, targets and milestones' within eight weeks (ODPM, 2002e, para. 62b). These authorities are expected to appoint a partnership or improvement board. It could include experts in areas of identified weakness and those with 'relevant operational experience – for example, chief executives or chief officers, business executive, elected members, or someone with local community knowledge' (ODPM, 2002c, p. 12). Its role is 'likely to be more of advice or external challenge: a board may help oversee the production of the recovery plan or may be part of the plan itself, and will play an important part in advising [an authority] on the range of support and delivery options available to it' (ODPM, 2002e, para. 62b). Guidance from the board can become an imperative for an authority threatened with the possibility of further action by the government. Such an appointed board could become more important than the elected council in the workings of the authority.

A small government team led by the relationship manager will monitor progress. The relationship manager 'will need to make recommendations to Ministers as to whether there is any need to request amendment to the plan or to consider using formal intervention corporately or more selectively or to provide necessary financial assistance' (ODPM, 2002e, para. 62c). While it is recognised that 'recovery plans must be owned and implemented by authorities itself', the government nevertheless provides for a continuing overview by both the relationship managers who, working with the monitoring teams, 'will have discretion in the day-to-day handling of cases' and by separate inspectors who can 'refer cases to Ministers at any time' (ibid., paras 62d and e). External supervision and possible government intervention will inevitably become dominant in the workings of these authorities.

Although relationship managers have been appointed initially for only a limited number of authorities, the government is considering appointing them generally to develop 'a more direct involvement with individual councils . . . to facilitate the improvement planning process' (ODPM, 2000c, para. 21). Such a development has a potential for much wider involvement by central government in the workings of many authorities, with the danger that greater weight can be given by the government to the views of the relationship manager than to those of the local authority.

The new comprehensive performance framework has major implications for authorities, ranging from new freedoms for authorities judged to be excellent to unparalleled intervention in those judged to be poor, and a new degree of involvement in many other authorities, involving major changes in central–local relations. These developments are based on the principle of selectivity, distinguishing the relationship between the government and authorities according to that judgement on performance, The significance of this principle for central–local relations is considered in Chapter 11. Here it is sufficient to stress that underlying these developments is an implicit assumption that external actors know better than those within the authority how services can be improved. The consequences can be a weakening of local accountability and of local initiative.

Conclusion

This chapter has described four developments: beacon councils, public service agreements, 'reform' bringing greater stress on private sector involvement and the comprehensive performance framework, all following on from the best value regime described in the preceding chapter. In addition central government departments have taken continuing and continuous initiatives on particular services.

The continuing flow of initiatives reflects restlessness in the modernisation programme, ever creating uncertainties as authorities take on board the latest initiative and try to work out its relationship to previous initiatives. There is a felt imperative by the government to intervene with new steps, rather than to allow steps already taken to develop. Changes as significant as best value are not easily introduced, and need time and organisational space to develop before authorities have to cope with new and yet more new developments. Recent developments have made the best value regime almost superfluous. It is unlikely it will be abandoned, but if public service agreements and the comprehensive performance framework had been introduced first, it is unlikely that the best value regime would have seemed necessary.

The government assumes that change has to be imposed and has to be continuously imposed, not recognising that too many changes following rapidly upon one another can be counterproductive. There is no recognition that local government could be capable of achieving the goal of performance improvement by itself, given the stimulus of the best value regime and the modernisation programme. The government's apparent distrust of local authorities reflects the underlying suspicion of local government described in Chapter 1.

The changes described in this chapter have the aim of improving performance, which is a main theme and a strength of the modernisation programme. The danger is that the changes weaken the basis for effective local government, making them counterproductive even for their stated aim. The emphasis of PSAs on national targets can limit local choice and weaken local accountability, both conditions of effective local government. The comprehensive performance framework can make national priorities and external judgement by auditors and inspectors and later by relationship managers more important than the views of local citizens and local councillors, weakening the local democracy that is the basis for effective local government.

9 Management for Modernisation

Effective local government requires effective management. While the modernisation programme did not confront management issues directly, it had obvious implications for management. The vision of modernised local government set out in *Modern Local Government* contained themes for the management of local authorities: outward-looking; working with others; continuous improvement. Within that broad vision, further management ideas have developed in the modernisation programme, in the IDeA's Local Government Improvement Programme (IDeA, 2000) and in the comprehensive performance assessment (Audit Commission, 2002a). These include:

- continuous change and innovation;
- effective leadership;
- a customer focus;
- targets and performance management;
- partnership working; and
- the development of e-government.

Each idea has a contribution to make to management, but each brings problems if over-emphasised and if countervailing approaches are neglected.

Continuous change and innovation

The rhetoric of continuous change and innovation has a natural appeal. The environment is changing and local authorities and their services must change in response. The public is changing too: expectations are growing and both the desire for and the scope for choice is greater. These factors strengthen the case for change and innovation in the workings of local authorities.

The original Local Government Improvement Model designed to guide review teams stated that 'A fully effective local authority . . . is forward looking, innovative, challenges current practice and is prepared to "think the unthinkable", drives for continuous improvement and is not complacent' (LGA/LGMB, 1998, p. 7). This quotation builds an image of an authority continuously challenging, changing and innovating throughout its organisation. The quality of an authority's management is increasingly judged on the extent to which change and innovation are taking place.

Challenge, change and innovation have value in the workings of local authorities, but can be carried too far. There are dangers if a value is placed on change in its own right, rather than on the purpose for which change is proposed. Change cannot automatically be assumed to be desirable. Any particular change may prove to be a mistake, making performance less rather than more effective. It is extremely unlikely that everything that happens in an authority requires to be changed. It is as important to identify what does not require to be changed as to identify where change is required. An over-emphasis on change can mean the abandonment of good practice for worse.

Effective organisations need a degree of stability as well as a capacity for change. Indeed, change itself requires a degree of stability within the organisation so that the changes being undertaken receive the necessary attention. If change is taking place throughout the organisation, particular changes may have unintended consequences, because of the difficulty of anticipating interactions between many changes. Change has costs: the costs of preparing for change; the costs of the transition; the costs of training for the change; the costs of the uncertainty caused among staff and often among the public affected by the change. All these costs have to be taken into account when considering the desirability of any change.

Organisations need established ways of working to carry out their functions. A culture is built up around these ways of working, supporting and expressing them. That culture can be a weakness if it is a barrier to needed change. That culture and the established way of working can, however, be a strength enabling staff to carry out work without detailed supervision. Together they enable the organisation to work effectively and even to adjust gradually without the necessity of dramatic change.

The existing culture and ways of working have to be understood before undertaking change that unthinkingly undermines them. Organisations need to balance change and stability. The all-changing, all-innovating organisation will cease to be an effective organisation, being unable to carry out the many routines and apparently mundane tasks that are necessary to its workings and the provision of its services.

None of these arguments should be construed as being against all change. It is an argument not so much against change, but against a rhetoric of change that encourages the assumption that change is inherently desirable. While the environment and public attitudes have changed and are changing, they have not and are not totally changed. The need for change needs careful evaluation along with the need for continuity. Change needs care in preparation and in implementation, and change needs stability if an authority's organisation is not to be overwhelmed.

The consumer and the customer

Local authorities are urged to look outward to the public served. They are encouraged to develop customer care, adopting the language of the private sector. There are dangers in the unthinking use of this language. It is appropriate to regard the public as the customer of the service when the authority is in a market situation, charging for a service in competition with others. But in many of the services for which a local authority is responsible the word 'customer' is misleading. In the past, local authorities have used differing words to describe those on whom services had an impact: client, patient, applicant, defendant, user, passenger, pupil and so on, reflecting the diversity of relationships with the public.

The customer in the private sector is normally the individual or organisation that purchases the service at the price set by or acceptable to the supplier. It is then easy to identify the customer – the purchaser of the service. It is not often so easy to identify the 'customer' of services in the public domain. In some, the service is not provided to a particular individual or organisation, but for the community at large as with action against pollution in its many forms. In other services there are many different 'customers' for the same service, and not merely those who receive the service directly. Children are customers of education in schools, but so are parents as recognised by parental choice and so are future employers who depend upon knowledge and skills built by education. There are many others who will draw upon the benefits of not just their own education, but the education of others. These might all be regarded as 'customers' of education, but it is doubtful if such a use of the word aids understanding. These customers do not necessarily seek the same outcomes from the process of education. The task of the education service is not merely to meet the demands of one particular customer or set of customers, but to balance differing requirements against a concept of the public interest.

Many services in local authorities are provided not according to demand by customers, but according to judgements on the need for the service. The ability to purchase the service does not determine whether it is provided, but a decision by the authority and its staff on the need for the service, although the way need is determined will vary from service to service and can vary from authority to authority. The demand for services will often exceed the resources available. Services have to be rationed and it is hardly appropriate to describe as a customer someone who is refused a service because they are not regarded as needing the service according to the criteria by which need is judged.

In some activities the local authority has to arbitrate between two so-called 'customers'. A planning application by one individual or organisation may be opposed by neighbours or by others in the community. The word 'customer' hardly captures the authority's relationship with those whose views do not prevail. Applicant and objector properly describe the different roles. The local authority inspects many properties, regulates many activities and even prosecutes individuals and organisations. In the exercise of the public powers of coercion the word 'customer' does not describe the relationship, any more than if the police substituted 'welcome you as a customer' for 'take you into custody'!

An over-emphasis on customer focus and customer care can hide the diversity of relationships between a local authority and its publics. Services may be provided on demand, but may be rationed according to need. Services meet individual needs, but can also meet community needs. Services may be compulsory and enforced or may be left to the public to seek for themselves or not, according to their wishes. The emphasis on the customer developed in the 1980s and the early 1990s had a valuable influence in encouraging authorities to look outward. The stage has now been reached when effective management requires a more refined analysis of the relationship between an authority and its publics, discriminating between different services and activities. Authorities should manage rationing, compulsion, market relationships and other relationships in different ways.

The word 'customer', if meant to cover all the relationships with the public, denies the role of citizenship. The role of citizenship underlies the role of local government and its rationale. Management should be developed to support and deepen the relationship between the authority and the public as citizens and indeed to develop citizenship itself, as well as developing the relationship with customers, clients, users and the publics in all their other roles. The real challenge to effective management is denied if the diversity of the tasks is hidden by the undiscriminating use of the word 'customer'.

Effective leadership

The comprehensive performance assessment and the IDeA's improvement model place an emphasis on the need for effective leadership both within the authority and in and with the community. The word 'leadership' can suggest a macho style, which is certainly not the intention of the IDeA, but others, including some of the advocates of elected mayors, suggest that image. '*What a Difference a Mayor Makes*' (Day, n.d.) or the description of the mayor as a 'big hitter' suggests that effective leadership is an individual characteristic, rather than grounded in the situation and dependent on relationships built for that situation.

Situations vary and the nature of effective leadership varies with the situation. In one authority, different chief executives with different styles were appointed at different times to meet changing needs and to carry out different tasks. The authority had seen the chief executive as urban redeveloper, then as change agent and now as consolidator. Each task called for its own style of leadership. The same tendency can be seen in the choices made by political groups in the selection of leaders. Experienced leaders of majority groups do not necessarily take easily to the different demands of the hung situation. If they then retire, the group is likely to seek a leader who will work easily with other parties. Different services present different challenges for chief officers and place different requirements on them as leaders. Leadership in a uniformed force such as the fire service calls for different styles than leadership in social services or in a treasurer's department.

Authorities face the difference between organisational leadership within the authority and community leadership beyond in the complex patterns of local governance. Community leadership does not have the authority of an established organisational role, nor can it be assumed that others will necessarily accept the authority's leadership role. A catalytic, facilitative leadership style is required. Luke has described such leadership in facing community issues as involving four tasks:

1. Focus attention by elevating the issue to the public and policy agendas.
2. Engage people in the effort by convening the diverse set of people, agencies and interests needed to address the issue.
3. Stimulate multiple strategies and options for action.
4. Sustain action and momentum by managing interconnections through appropriate institutionalisation and rapid information sharing and feedback.

'The four tasks are more organic and artistic than mechanical and sequential' (Luke, 1998, pp. 37–8).

Leadership can take different forms and different forms are required in different situations. Effective leadership is grounded in context. Rarely will macho leadership by an individual be effective in the complexities of urban government. The days of the city boss are hopefully over. Even mayors will be most effective if they are team builders.

Performance measures and performance management

Systems of performance management have been developed in many local authorities and the modernisation programme has increased the importance of performance measures and performance management in local authorities. In local performance plans, local authorities are required to set targets for their services, covering both the best value performance measures laid down by central government and local targets. Public service agreements are based on targets agreed between central government and local authorities. There is a danger in too narrow a focus on performance measures as a result of central government's stress on particular targets. Performance measures should not be seen as ends in themselves, but as a means of understanding performance, its strengths and weaknesses and the factors that determine them. Improvement can be based on that understanding. Performance measures rarely give that understanding directly in local government services.

Most performance measures are indicators that can be a stimulus to investigation, but do not lead automatically to action. Such measures may only cover certain aspects of the service and if action is taken on the basis of the measure alone, other aspects of the service may be neglected or even harmed. Measures focus attention on the quantitative, and the qualitative aspects of a service can be neglected, even though they may be of equal or greater importance. Achievement or failure to meet targets may be due to factors beyond the control of those held responsible. There may be changes in the environment that make a target out of date. The achievement of a target cannot always be regarded as desirable where circumstances change; the result and how it was achieved need to be explored and assessed.

How measures should be used in performance management is a vital but too little explored issue. More attention has been given to developing performance measures than to how they are used. Performance measures can be an aid to understanding and thereby a basis for improving performance, but that requires processes that go beyond and behind the measure. A diagnostic process is required to ensure that performance is understood. Questions have to be asked about performance in relation to targets and the answers have to be probed. Was the target right? Would we reset the target if given the opportunity? Was the target achieved at the expense of other aspects of the service? Why was the target not achieved? Were there factors not allowed for when the target was set? What has been learnt from experience and what does it mean for the future? These are not necessarily the correct questions, but they illustrate a reflective approach that goes beyond the targets and performance measures to an understanding of performance as a basis for action or for inaction.

Performance measures can mislead if taken at face value without time and space for reflection. There are dangers in the targets set in PSAs. An authority might achieve its targets and as pointed out in the last chapter do harm to its other services, or even to aspects of the services for which the targets are set. There are powerful incentives to achieve the targets. There are considerable rewards in finance and in the way the authority is regarded by central government. Achievement of the targets will mean the authority is seen as a successful authority and that is likely to lead to further benefits as an 'excellent' authority under the comprehensive performance assessment. An authority is likely to devote extra resources, effort and attention to achieving PSA targets; indeed, that is presumably what they are expected to do, but it will be at the expense of other services or of aspects of the targeted services not receiving that attention, effort and resources. Achieving the PSA targets might bring serious problems in its wake as a consequence of this redirection of attention.

The government sometimes sets targets as an immediate response to perceived problems and public pressure. There are dangers if they are set without adequate consideration of what they mean for the workings of the organisation. By setting targets the government transfers a problem from the present to the future. Faced with a problem a target is set without it being worked out whether there is a clear path leading to target achievement without harmful side effects. A rhetoric of targets emerges and setting targets is seen as a sign of decisive action.

The government required over 170 best value performance indicators to be set as targets in local authority performance plans. The multiplication of targets has the advantage that performance in a complex service is not reduced to a single measure, but the multiplication of targets raises issues of whether the targets are consistent with each other. The Audit Commission has highlighted the inconsistency between cost reduction targets for waste collection and targets for recycling (Audit Commission, 2001b). Targets may have harmful effects that were not properly appreciated when they were set. Philpot has argued that adoption targets can distort decision-making in social services: 'What if social service departments do not think that all of the children needed to meet the desired increase in the number of children adopted should be adopted or even want to be adopted ... Serve the child or serve Richmond House [the

Department of Health's headquarters]' (Philpot, 2001, p. 35). Some targets will be met, while some will not. How will this be interpreted? Will the achievement of some targets be regarded as of more or less importance than others? The government has recognised dangers in the multiplication of targets and has reduced the number of performance indicators by a limited extent (DTLR, 2002a), but the number may increase again as central government responds to new problems and pressures by the too easy solution of setting new targets.

The arguments set out in this chapter are not against the development of targets or the use of performance measures. The argument is for care in setting targets and on the need for diagnostic processes in the use of performance measures. Performance measures and targets should be seen as aids to understanding performance as a necessary step in improving performance. The test of the effective use of performance measures is whether they do lead to that understanding which is required for effective performance management.

Partnerships

A rhetoric of partnership is part of the modernisation programme. Partnerships have been discussed in the context of community leadership in Chapter 2 and of improving performance in Chapter 8. Those chapters have highlighted some of the issues raised by the importance given to partnerships in the modernisation programme: the effort involved in building effective partnership working; the problems of accountability; the tendency to fragmentation as partnerships multiply.

In this chapter it is only necessary to reiterate that partnerships have both strengths and weaknesses and are not an approach suitable for each and any problem faced. DTLR-sponsored research stressed, 'partnerships only really work where they produce benefits for all partners'. They can fail where there is 'a lack of a powerful shared agenda and the absence of penalties for failure' and 'especially where the partnership is focused on marginal activities and where there are powerful penalties in the partners' mainstream activities' (Stewart *et al.*, 1999, p. 29). As pointed out in Chapter 2 there is a danger of 'let us create a partnership' being the unthinking response to community problems. There are times when it can be more effective to pin responsibility on a single organisation, rather than diffuse responsibilities among several partners. At their best, partnerships can be a means of sharing responsibility, but at their worst they are a means of avoiding responsibility.

There is a need for careful consideration of whether creating a partnership is the best approach to a problem and of the role of the partnership and the period of time for which it will be required. A partnership may only be required for a limited time in order to establish new ways of working. The danger is that partnerships are considered to be 'a good thing' and therefore favoured without counting the costs of the time and effort involved or allowing for the problems that partnerships can create. Both central government and local authorities should consider the cumulative effect of creating partnerships. A proposal to create a partnership considered on its merits can have considerable attraction, but that partnership will be set in a preexisting overcrowded network of partnerships. It is not surprising that partnership overload and partnership fatigue have become a common complaint among partners.

As partnerships grow in number the system of community governance becomes more, not less, complex. A new partnership adds another actor to the stage of community governance. Two organisations joining in a partnership can mean that there are now three organisations where previously there were only two. While a partnership joins together partners, it does so by creating a new organisation with its own identity or quasi-identity. For the public, a partnership may be invisible or barely visible, reducing further the limited transparency of community governance and making accountability elusive.

These arguments do not mean there is no role for partnerships in the government of local communities. The argument is that partnerships should not be assumed to be necessarily desirable and that in some situations they can be barriers to effective performance. There is a need to consider carefully any proposal for a new partnership, both in its own right and in its impact on the overall pattern of community governance. There is a need too to review whether all existing partnerships continue to be required. It would, however, be equally misguided to assume that all partnerships were undesirable. Fitness for purpose is the test.

E-government

The government gave a pledge, repeated in the 2001 manifesto, that 100 per cent of public services should be delivered on-line by 2005. The government required all authorities to produce a statement on implementing electronic government by July 2001. These statements showed authorities had achieved an average of 29 per cent by that date (DTLR/LGA, 2002). The pledge has been supported by the Local Government Association and, although it has no statutory base, has been accepted by local authorities generally. This target is not the only influence in the movement to e-government. It reflects a general movement as new information technology spreads and develops.

The phrase 'deliver services on-line' is ambiguous. Many services cannot be delivered on-line because they involve personal contact, physical inspection or the receipt of physical goods. School meals cannot be delivered on-line any more than public transport, although electronic processes can play a part in the delivery of such services. Presumably what is meant is that access to all services should be capable of being obtained on-line by 2005. The joint consultation paper emphasises access to services rather than delivery of services, confirming this interpretation. Not everybody will seek such access. Even by 2005, not everyone will have easy access on-line. Some will not have the necessary technology and some will not be happy using it. While authorities can provide facilities in libraries and other locations, there will still be problems for some in access to and use of these facilities. A recent survey showed that only 1 per cent use e-mail to contact a council and only 2 per cent would prefer to use it. There is a danger that the spread of e-government could create a new group of the technology-excluded. Of course, the pledge does not mean that services should only be accessed on-line, but there is a danger that if services are mainly obtained on-line, other means of access will become second-best and relatively neglected.

Putting existing processes on-line for access or where appropriate for service would by itself fall far short of achieving the potential of e-government. A SOLACE think-tank report argues that an e-government strategy should be about:

- transforming business processes;
- providing better seamless services more efficiently;

- customer focus and integrated service; and
- managing information as a resource;

and that it requires top-level involvement (SOLACE, 2001, p. 29).

It is possible to go further. 'Providing seamless services' may be an inadequate characterisation. It appears to make the service an end in itself. The better formulation would be seamless ways of meeting needs. Members of the public may present problems or have needs rather than specific demands for a service. Where a life crisis such as homelessness is faced, different services can be brought together. E-government should develop need-based approaches as well as or even instead of service-based approaches. In this way e-government can help establish joined-up government in local authorities.

E-government has dangers as well as benefits. The danger of a digital divide in society has already been mentioned. Other dangers are subtler. One danger present within any procedure, whether digital or traditional, is that people and problems are fitted into the procedures, ignoring aspects that are not allowed for in those procedures. Unless guarded against, that danger could be greater under e-government, if the procedures are written into programmes that do not allow them to be easily bypassed. The danger is that e-government could embed over-bureaucracy in the application of rules, without room for review. It can be guarded against if the design of the programme and the processes by which its operation is monitored provide safeguards allowing human intervention. The hardness of technology may have to be balanced by the potential softness of human appraisal.

Each mode of communication has its own characteristics. Conversation on a phone is different from conversation face to face. Replying to e-mail is different from replying to a letter, with e-mail encouraging an immediate response and a less reflective mode. Public attitudes to call centres can differ from attitudes to direct calls. Overdominance of e-government could drive out modes of communication that have their own distinctive contribution.

Yet again, the argument put forward is not against the commitment to e-government, but for the need to recognise problems as well as benefits and to recognise the contribution that other modes of operation and of communication have to offer as countervailing forces to the overdominance of one mode.

The private sector model

There is an implicit and sometimes an explicit pressure in the modernisation programme for management in the public domain to follow the model assumed to be dominant in the private sector. 'Entrepreneurial approaches' are to be encouraged; 'competition' will increase efficiency; the 'customer' is to be king. The language reflects the private sector model or what is believed to be the private sector model.

Private sector language can be used without regard to its meaning in the public domain. Chief executives who call upon their staff to be entrepreneurial and to take risks may believe they are spreading the message of modernisation, but the message can mislead. It is a message that can leave engineers wondering why they are expected to design a risky bridge or social workers why they have to put a child at risk. This example may seem unfair, but it illustrates the unthinking use of private sector language. The challenge is to the adoption of what is often a caricature of private sector management. Sometimes it seems that public sector managers who see themselves as the equivalent of private sector managers take their model more from TV dramas than from the real world where managers have to understand and to respond to the distinctive purposes, tasks and conditions of their organisations.

The services of local government, while each having distinctive purposes, conditions and tasks that the effective manager has to appreciate, share certain purposes and conditions because they are part of local government in particular and of the public domain in general. The dominance of the private sector model has meant that management approaches in local government have paid too little attention to those distinctive purposes, conditions and even tasks, with the result that management approaches have tended to ignore or even distort them.

Thus it is widely recognised that training and development of staff is necessary in, for example, staff selection and performance appraisal, where processes in local government and the private sector march alongside each other. The same need is not recognised for training and development in the handling of public protest even though it is inherent in the workings of local democracy. It can be commonplace in local government for a relatively inexperienced officer to face unprepared the wrath of citizens at a public meeting. Public protest is encountered at many points in the work of authorities from a disputed planning case to the closing of a school or the location of residential facilities. Public protest is not an inherent condition of the private sector, where such protest will only arise in very special circumstances such as public concern about pollution, and even then much of the protest will be directed at the local authority's assumed failure to act against the firm concerned.

Management education and development for the public domain often has difficulties in coming to terms with the political process: a basic condition for management in local government. It is either treated as external to and separate from the process of management or as a hindrance to management, a view given expression in off-hand remarks such as 'it would be easy to manage in local government were it not for the political process'. That is almost the equivalent of saying 'it would be easy to manage in the private sector were it not for the need to make a profit'. The political process should not be treated as external to management, but as a basic condition of local government and the means by which its purposes are set. The political process should not be treated as a hindrance to management but as defining its role. Management approaches are required that both support and express an effective political process.

Private sector models applied to management in local government can distort the approach to topics like strategy and performance management, because they have no place for the distinctive purposes, conditions and tasks of the public domain. Local government is not a single-purpose organisation but a multi-purpose one. For that reason setting objectives is not the key task, but the need to balance different and differing objectives. In the budget different purposes compete for resources and the resulting budget expresses political judgement on the balance between those purposes. Even within services different public interests and objectives have to be balanced against each other. Yet balancing objectives is not often seen as the basis for the development of strategy in local government, because it does not have an equivalent role in the private sector.

Performance management has been discussed above. One additional point can be made. In the public domain, good performance can never be finally defined, because in the final resort it is a matter of public judgement. That judgement is mediated through the political process and can be the subject of genuine disagreement. If the Green Party took control of a local authority many existing performance indicators would be inadequate because good performance would be redefined to give much greater weight to environmental considerations. Performance measures in local government should provide the basis for political discussion and deliberation on the nature of good performance and management should support and express that process.

Recently under the influence of the private sector model, marketing approaches have been developed in some local authorities. But in many areas of local government activity, the marketing approaches developed in the private sector cannot be applied, since these approaches are designed to stimulate demand for goods or services, whereas in local government that is hardly the major problem. Demand for services can easily exceed the resources available. In local authorities, the management of rationing is more often the task than stimulating demand. The aim should be to identify significant need and even to discourage demand by those whose need is less. Yet the management of rationing is an unspoken topic in much discussion of management in local government.

The discussion has emphasised topics important for the management of local authorities, yet outside the private sector model and therefore relatively or totally neglected in the development of management:

- the management of public protest;
- supporting the political process;
- balancing objectives, interests and demands;
- managing performance when good performance can never be finally defined; and
- the management of rationing.

Local authorities require the development of management analysis as rigorous as in the private sector, but analysis grounded in the distinctive purpose, conditions and tasks of local government. Those purposes include promoting community, building citizenship, enabling democracy and achieving equity. The constitutive conditions include public accountability, the political process and the public right to be heard and to be involved. There are distinctive tasks in the management of coercion and more generally the balancing of objectives, interests and needs.

Conclusion

The approach of the modernisation programme to management has brought clear benefits, but has also brought problems. These can be resolved, provided they are recognised.

The first problem is a tendency to regard the favoured development as an end in itself rather than as a means to an end. This is illustrated by the almost indiscriminate use of performance measures as targets. The emphasis has been on having targets rather than on how they are to be used, with the result that the consequences of target-setting have rarely been adequately considered.

Second, the different management requirements of different services and different situations have not been sufficiently distinguished. This is illustrated by the use of the same word 'customer' to describe the very different relationships between the authority and its publics. The rhetoric of management proclaims universal remedies rather than fitness for purpose, based on analysis of service and situation.

The third problem requires more explanation. Most of the favoured management changes are directed at overcoming perceived weaknesses in the existing organisation. The danger is that in seeking to overcome the weaknesses, the organisation faces new problems because the change is carried too far. Thus an organisation that is regarded as overcentralised can become so decentralised that it ceases to be an organisation. An organisation that is seen as rigid and unchanging can become so flexible and continuously changing that it lacks the capacity to carry out necessary routines. An organisation that is overdepartmentalised can become so dominated by corporate working that necessary specialisms are devalued. In considering organisational change, it is wise to identify the strengths of existing organisations as well as their weaknesses. Overreaction should be guarded against and a balance sought between conflicting organisational characteristics. It is difficult to identify the right balance, but imbalance is more readily seen. When one approach becomes overdominant, countervailing forces need to be built into the workings of the organisation, as suggested throughout this chapter. An organisation can combine desirable decentralisation with necessary centralisation. An authority can build its capacity for continuing change within a framework that provides the required degree of stability.

The fourth problem is that developments in management in local government have been based more on the private sector model than on the distinctive purposes, conditions and tasks of local government and of the public domain. Whether those purposes, conditions and tasks have been correctly identified in this chapter can be disputed. They probably can never be finally defined as both the public domain and the scope of local government change in shape and size. Yet in so far as there are those purposes, conditions and tasks in the public domain, they should form the starting point for the full development of management, not eliminating relevant management approaches drawn from the private sector, but providing countervailing forces enabling the distinctive competence and values of local government and of the public domain to be realised.

The modernisation programme should have helped build an understanding of those values by its emphasis on community leadership, democratic renewal and improving performance. These themes are the strengths of the modernisation programme, but it is in their implementation that weaknesses lie, as this chapter has shown in the lack of balance in the approach to management encouraged by the programme. Management can only help to build effective local government if it is grounded in those values and gives expression to the purposes, conditions and tasks of local government.

10 Towards Regional Government?

The modernisation programme contained no proposals for reorganisation of the structure of local government tiers and boundaries – with one exception. The government was committed to the creation of an elected authority for Greater London and legislation was introduced early in its life. The lack of any immediate possibility of further structural change was a relief for most authorities, although some district councils still aspired to unitary status. The structural issue and reorganisation have not, however, gone away because of proposals for regional government, which have reopened the issue in the second term. It cannot therefore be neglected in this book, even though not seen as part of the original modernisation programme. The reopening of the issue and the possibility of regional government can create problems for effective local government and for the modernisation programme itself.

The unhappy story of local government reorganisation

Most local authorities looked back on the process of local government reorganisation that dominated much of the years from 1992 to 1996 as a wasted period. Counties and districts battled with each other in a struggle for survival, as each made their case for unitary status. The Local Government Commission's review often seemed to be the pursuit of structural change for its own sake, causing maximum disturbance in authorities and in relations between counties and districts.

The structure of local government in England outside London and in Wales had been established in 1974 and in Scotland in 1975. It was a two-tier structure (county and district in England and Wales; region and district in Scotland). A two-tier structure had been established in 1965 in London – the Greater London

Council and the London boroughs. There was a major difference between London and the six metropolitan counties and the rest of England, Scotland and Wales. Education and social services were at the upper tier in the latter, but were at the lower tier in London and the metropolitan counties with one exception – the Inner London Education Authority having responsibility for education in Inner London.

Those towns and cities that had previously been proud county boroughs deeply resented the new structure, seeing themselves reduced to the status of minor authorities in county areas. The new district councils outside the major towns and cities were normally amalgamations of previous authorities. They brought together a number of smaller towns and rural areas, often lacking any sense of shared identity. This change increased the differences between the structure of local government in the United Kingdom and that in Europe. After reorganisation the average population of shire districts was over ten times the average of the lower tier in Europe. Many district councils appeared artificial, bringing together in a single authority towns that in most countries in Europe would be authorities in their own right. The artificiality was virtually acknowledged in the names some selected – Wychavon, Vale Royal or Tendring – eschewing recognisable names from a town in the area because of opposition from other towns. Parish councils are based on similar areas to communes in some European countries, but have few responsibilities despite some recent changes and cannot be compared to European communes that have major responsibilities. The existence of parish councils does not, therefore, modify the conclusions about the relative size of UK authorities – a rarely acknowledged weakness of the local government structure, making authorities unnecessarily remote from local communities.

The scale of UK authorities reflected the dominant concept of local authorities as agencies for the provision of service and associated assumptions of sizeism dominant in government and public administration. It was widely assumed that size was associated with efficiency, despite the reality that investigations have failed to find any clear link between size and efficiency and/or effectiveness. Travers and his colleagues concluded, 'Having examined evidence from Britain and overseas, it does not appear possible to argue a conclusive case for a strong and one-directional link between population size and efficiency and effectiveness . . . It is not possible to say larger authorities perform, on the whole better than smaller, or smaller authorities better than larger' (Travers *et al.*, 1993, p. 4). In local government as in many spheres, small may be beautiful, but large-scale is too readily assumed to be efficient and effective. There are diseconomies as well as economies of scale.

The 1974–79 Labour government attempted to modify the structure by restoring some of the functions of major towns and cities in the name of 'organic change' (DoE, 1979; Stewart *et al.*, 1978), but the attempt proved abortive. The Conservative government made major changes. The government introduced legislation abolishing the Greater London Council and the metropolitan counties (and later the Inner London Education Authority), seeing them as an unnecessary and costly tier. The government argued the new structure would be both closer to and more understandable by local people (DoE, 1983). In reality, the structure became more complex because most of the functions – fire, police and public transport – remained at county level and were exercised by separate joint boards or in the case of some functions in London by central government.

The Conservative government justified the structural reorganisations of the early 1990s on much the same grounds of efficiency, comprehensibility and closeness to local communities. The consultation paper on *The Structure of Local government in England*, issued in 1991, set out the Government's intention to 'begin a process of change towards unitary authorities to achieve more efficient and more accountable local government that will also reflect people's own sense of identity with the community in which they live', although it was recognised that in some areas there could still be 'a case for two tiers' (DoE, 1991a, p. 6).

A new structure of unitary authorities was introduced in Scotland and Wales based on decisions made by the Secretaries of State without any investigation by an independent commission. In England, the Local Government Commission was set up to review local government structures in the shire areas. The Local Government Act of 1992 required the Commission to consider 'the identity and interests of local communities' and 'effective and convenient local government'. Recommendations were to be made to the Secretary of State, who could accept them with or without modification, reject them or ask for a further review. The Commission was directed to carry out the review county by county over a five-year period.

As Michael Chisholm, one of the commissioners, has pointed out, 'there appeared to be a general presumption on the part of Government that the task of the Commission was to find and recommend unitary structures' (Chisholm, 2000, p. 35). The original policy guidance, to which the commission was directed to have regard, stated that the Commission should examine each area 'to see whether a unitary structure would better reflect the identities and interests of local communities and secure effective and convenient local government' (DoE, 1992, p. 1).

The Commission's first recommendations were widely regarded as inconsistent and aroused considerable controversy. The controversy led the government to consider winding up the process. Instead it decided to carry it out as quickly as possible. The resulting speeding up of the process limited the capacity of the Commission to consider changes other than those based on existing boundaries, because of the greater workload involved in defining new boundaries.

The process was flawed from the outset. The structures that the Commission could consider were limited by the focus on unitary authorities. The weaknesses of the existing district structure were effectively outside the terms of reference implied by the policy guidance. The Commission was given a difficult task without adequate guidance on how to balance the very different considerations of community identity and of effective and convenient local government. The Commission itself made mistakes. Faced with inadequate guidance, the commissioners should have taken time to discuss how they would approach their task. They failed to do so: 'No time was allowed for the Commission to assess the nature of the problem and the extant evidence that was relevant; nor did it insist on being given this time' (Chisholm, 2000, p. 39).

Pairs of commissioners were sent out to particular counties to draw up recommendations without clear guidance on how they were to make their judgements. Their different conclusions led to suspicion that the recommendations reflected the particular views of the commissioners involved rather than the application of agreed principles to the evidence. As Michael Chisholm has pointed out, it quickly became apparent that Commissioners had divergent attitudes to their role. Some took the view that the task was to find and 'sell' a unitary structure for their area; some Commissioners engaged in attempts to broker deals for unitary solutions, either because that was what they believed was right or to ensure that in the event of a unitary solution being decided upon it would at least be a reasonable one. Others took a more judicial approach, regarding their role as being that of eliciting information and opinions as the basis on which to form a judgement on whether the two-tier arrangements could be bettered and if so with what structure. (Chisholm, 2000, pp. 40–1).

The basic problem lay with the task the Commission had been given. It was asked to devise a structure for local government without the government having made clear what the role of local government should be. It was as if an architect had been asked to design a building without a brief on the role of the building. While one expects that form should follow function, in the reorganisation process form preceded function and structure came before purpose. Unitary authorities had become an end in themselves. As suggested in Chapter 2, the phrase 'unitary authority' was and is misleading. All it means is that there is a single tier of local government, not that unitary authorities bring together all the powers of government exercised at local level or even those exercised through local organisations. The unitary authority was assumed by the government, almost without any serious consideration, to be a 'good thing'. Unitary authorities 'should reduce bureaucracy and improve the co-ordination of services, increasing quality and reducing costs . . . Such a structure is also important for financial accountability . . . people must know who is responsible' (DoE, 1991a, p. 6). No counter-arguments were given any weight. A moment's consideration of European local government might at least have caused reflection. Almost without exception there are two tiers of local government in European countries. In the larger countries there are three tiers of subnational government. The reason for the tiers is simple. Both the sense of community and the requirements of services are multilevelled and do not fit a single tier.

As the process of reorganisation developed, the difficulties in the general introduction of unitary authorities became clearer.

Whereas in the larger towns and cities the nature of community and the perceived requirements of services came closer together, this was not the case beyond their boundaries. If unitary authorities were to be created outside the larger urban areas, the Commission considered they would often have to be larger than many existing districts, themselves often too large to be based on any sense of community. The arguments of cost-effective service provision were seen as demanding larger authorities. The Commission expected that in most cases unitary authorities would have a population of 150,000 to 250,000 (LGCE, 1993, p. 41), reflecting the sizeism that so dominates British consideration of organisational structures.

Gradually many of those concerned with the review came to see that the case for unitary authorities was not so overwhelming as originally assumed. A two-tier system allowed different services to be delivered at different levels. The sense of community could be both local and multilevelled as in 'I come from Thirsk; that's in Yorkshire you know'. The work of the Commission was limited and constrained by the concentration on unitary status written into the policy guidance. The case for a two-tier system would have been even stronger if based on smaller districts, but that was effectively outside the Commission's terms of reference.

The search for unitary status inevitably created conflict between counties and districts, each making their own case and attacking the other's case. Local government reorganisation absorbed much of the energy of local authorities for three or four years, with the attention of leading councillors and officers focused on the issue. Reorganisation has costs and most of them are rarely accounted for, since they are opportunity costs in the time and effort taken from the main work of local government.

In the end after all the turmoil, the changes were limited. Far from the general introduction of unitary authorities, only 46 were created in England, while 238 districts and 34 counties remained. With a few exceptions the new structure was based on unitary status for the larger towns and cities and a two-tier system elsewhere. Only four counties were abolished, three being creations of the 1974 reorganisation: Avon, Cleveland and Humberside. The other county was Berkshire, the logic of which is difficult to understand and was possibly due to the approach of the county which had expected the general introduction of unitary authorities based largely on district authorities and given it early support. Most of the new structure, involving unitary status for a limited number of larger towns or cities, could have been introduced with a large measure of agreement without the drawn-out process of dispute and conflict.

There are now major differences between England on the one hand and Scotland and Wales on the other. There are unitary authorities throughout Scotland and Wales. Many of these unitary authorities are smaller in population than the population range considered necessary by the Commission in England, except in authorities such as Rutland, Herefordshire and the Isle of Wight, where history or geography determined the outcome.

The experience of reorganisation meant that with the exception of London the Labour government left the structure untouched in its first term. The process of reorganisation had left its mark, not merely on councillors and officers, but on national politicians who saw only unnecessary conflict as the likely outcome of raising the issue. This attitude prevailed, despite a traditional commitment by the Labour Party to what has been misleadingly called 'the unitary principle'. The government resisted pressure from some of the towns that had failed – in some cases narrowly – to achieve unitary status in the reorganisation process. It was doubtless realised that to concede unitary status even to a few would lead to increased pressure from others, reopening the whole issue.

The Greater London Authority

The Labour government was committed in its 1997 manifesto to an elected authority for London, where the loss of a London-wide authority had been widely resented, unlike the metropolitan counties where there was no pressure for their restoration, although there was some pressure for elected regional government. The government said it did not intend to bring back the Greater London Council, 'but to create a new model of government' that would be streamlined in terms of the size of the assembly and staffing (DETR, 1997, pp. 2–3).

In some quarters the creation of the Greater London Authority was regarded as a constitutional change along with the creation of the Scottish Parliament and the Welsh Assembly, rather than as an example of local government reorganisation.

The new authority differed significantly from other local authorities. The council is much smaller than most local authorities with
a mayor and only 25 councillors. The method of election of
assembly members differs from the method used for the election
of councillors elsewhere. Assembly members are elected by the
added member system – the form of proportional representation
used for the Scottish Parliament and the Welsh Assembly.
Electors have two votes – a constituency vote and a London-wide
vote. Fourteen of the assembly members are elected for constituencies on the first-past-the-post system. The remaining
eleven are elected by the London-wide votes, with seats allocated
to make the overall membership of the assembly (that is, including those elected for constituencies) as far as possible proportionate to the votes cast for different parties by these
London-wide votes. The mayor is elected by the supplementary
vote system used in mayoral elections elsewhere, already
described in Chapter 4.

Most of the main responsibilities of the GLA are exercised
through agencies: the London Fire and Emergency Planning
Authority, Transport for London and the London Development
Agency. The mayor appoints their membership. The mayor can
issue directions to Transport for London. He can issue directions to the London Development Agency and can revise its
strategy before publishing it. The mayor makes just over half
the appointments to the Metropolitan Police Authority.

The other main responsibility of the authority is to prepare
strategies or action plans. The most important is the strategy for
spatial development but other strategies and action plans cover
biodiversity, waste management, air quality, ambient noise and
culture. All these are issued by the mayor and do not need
assembly approval. The mayor has certain limited powers to
ensure compliance with the strategies and plans, although it
remains uncertain how effective these powers are in practice.
The mayor also has powers similar to the powers of community
well-being described in Chapter 2. The authority has a number
of other powers and responsibilities, all of which are exercised by
the mayor alone. These include promoting tourism, assisting
museums and art galleries and certain responsibilities for
Trafalgar and Parliament Squares.

Few of the GLA's responsibilities are exercised directly. The
government has taken powers of direction in relation to most of

the significant responsibilities and there is a general requirement that the authority's strategies 'must have regard to national policy' (Pimlott and Rao, 2002, p. 75). Taken together these factors make the GLA a relatively powerless authority, even compared with most local authorities, although it has used powers to introduce congestion charging. Its strength comes, if at all, from its scale and its ability to speak for London.

If the powers of the authority are limited, the powers of the assembly are even more limited. It has scrutiny powers, but no powers to enforce its conclusions. The assembly has no direct powers over the mayor's plans and policies, beyond the power to approve the budget. Even that power is limited, since the assembly can only reject or amend the budget by a two-thirds majority, although it has used that power in the first two years, since the mayor as an Independent cannot command automatic party support and can lack the support of even just over the third of the members that enables the mayors budget to prevail regardless of the views of the assembly.

The Greater London Authority differs both in its responsibilities and in its method of working from local authorities generally. The prospects for the GLA are uncertain. Its responsibilities are limited and constrained by central government's powers of direction. Pimlott and Rao concluded, 'The stumbling block is the limitation on the mayor's actual powers as defined by statute and his de facto subservience to central government' (2002, p. 170). Much turns on the ability of the mayor to use his position as an effective voice for London based on election by the whole electorate, although on a low turnout. Pimlott and Rao conclude that Livingstone as mayor 'has shown that the Authority, for all its lack of financial resources and legal weakness, is capable of providing a voice for London that previously did not exist' (2002, p. 176). Two issues are likely to be increasingly raised: the inadequacy of the Authority's powers and the weakness of the assembly as its members become frustrated by their ineffectiveness. It is difficult to believe that the present position can be maintained over the longer term.

The issue of reorganisation reopened by regional government

The issue of local government structure has been reopened by the White Paper on regional government – *Your Region, Your*

Choice (Cabinet Office and DTLR, 2002). This proposed the introduction of regional assemblies where they were approved in a referendum in the region. The Regional Assemblies (Preparation) Bill provides for referendums to be held in regions only when called by the Secretary of State after considering the level of interest in the region and it is expected that no more than two will be called in the first instance.

The Labour Party had often stressed that the introduction of regional government would require local government to be based on predominantly unitary authorities (For example, Labour Party, 1995b, 1997) and that view was reiterated in its 2001 manifesto (Labour Party, 2001). *Your Region, Your Choice* went further and stated that where regional authorities are introduced, 'there should be an associated move to a *wholly* unitary local government structure' (Cabinet Office and DTLR, 2002, p. 65; my italics) and the Regional Assemblies (Preparation) Bill provides that before a referendum is called in any region, the Boundary Committee for England should make recommendations for the introduction of unitary authorities in those parts of the region where there is a two-tier system.

Even though regional assemblies will only be introduced gradually, if at all – for the results cannot be assumed in advance – the issue of reorganisation is once again on the agenda for local government. This reopening of battles over unitary status was not inevitable. In major countries of the European Union (France, Germany, Italy, Spain), there remain two tiers of local government despite the presence or introduction of some form of regional government. The reason for the government's stance (apart from the possibility of it being a tactic of opponents of regional government within the government) is probably the difficulty of securing approval in the referendums on regional government promised by the government and provided for in the Regional Assemblies (Preparation) Bill. Opposition to regional government would campaign against 'over-government', if a regional tier were added to existing tiers. The government stressed concerns 'that this would be one tier too many' (Cabinet Office and DTLR, 2002, p. 65). It is, however, difficult to see the justification for reorganisation, given the government's assertion that the functions of the proposed regional assemblies are 'generally not being taken from local government' (ibid., p. 34). Why then reorganise local government?

The reopening of the structural issue will inevitably absorb much of the attention and much of the energy of counties and districts and harm attempts to build partnerships between them. The traumas of the early 1990s will be repeated. *Your Region, Your Choice* states, 'it is very important that the local authorities concerned continue to focus on service delivery' (Cabinet Office and DTLR, 2002, p. 65). The authorities will probably seek to do so, but it is naïve to believe there will be no time and attention lost in the distractions caused in making the authorities' cases, preparing for reorganisation and in building a new organisation. Structural change is easily decided upon nationally, but the costs are borne locally.

The government is proposing that regional authorities should be introduced gradually and argues that at any one time only a limited number of authorities will be involved. Optimistically the government asserts, 'Other local authorities certainly should not be distracted' (Cabinet Office and DTLR, 2002, p. 65). Yet every district and every county will see the issue of reorganisation being reopened. Cases will be made and counter-cases developed. The Pandora's box of structural change is being reopened and local government will have to live with the consequences. The Boundary Committee for England will draw up proposals for reorganisation before referendums are held. They will only be implemented if there is a 'yes' vote. If there is a 'no' vote and the proposed reorganisation is withdrawn (as the deputy prime minister stated in presenting the White Paper), it will lead to frustration for those seeking it and pressure for its implementation regardless of the referendum result.

The outcome of the Boundary Commission review is uncertain. In some cases the county may be proposed as the unitary authority, but it is probable that in the majority the abolition of the county will be proposed. Many existing districts are, however, unlikely to gain unitary status. Assumptions of sizeism mean that smaller district councils will not be thought capable of taking over such county council functions as education and social services. Districts will be merged into larger authorities, despite the fact that in other European countries local authorities are already much smaller than district councils in the United Kingdom and exercise a wide range of functions – including, in Scandinavia, most of and more than the functions of English county councils.

Instability in the present regional structures

Some see the introduction of regional government as necessary, because of instability in the present arrangements both in the United Kingdom as a whole and in the structures already developed in the English regions.

The role of the Scottish Parliament raises issues about the composition and procedures of the House of Commons. Scottish MPs have the right to vote on legislation that only applies to England and Wales. The position of a United Kingdom parliament in which the government was dependent on Scottish votes for all its English and Welsh legislation would be hard to justify. It has been suggested that the creation of regional government in England would overcome this difficulty, but that would only be the case if regional authorities were given equivalent powers to the Scottish Parliament, which few if any envisage.

The government has made important changes in the English regions. Regional development agencies (RDAs), with boards appointed by central government, were set up in 1999 in the eight English regions and in London. The RDAs prepare regional economic development strategies. They were financed by funds originally transferred from English Partnership, the Rural Development Commission and the Single Regeneration Budget, now combined in a single allocation. Membership of the RDAs is drawn mainly from industry and commerce with some membership from local government and other sources.

There is an issue of accountability, since with the possible exception of the London Development Agency, RDAs' accountability is not to people in the region, but to central government. In each region there are regional chambers, composed mainly of local authority representatives, but with representatives of the private and voluntary sectors. These chambers have been designated under the Regional Development Agencies Act to scrutinise the RDA. The RDAs are required to take account of, but not necessarily to accept, the views expressed by the chambers. This limited role falls short of ensuring regional accountability for the RDAs. The danger is that the regional chambers come to be seen as mere talking shops.

Government Offices of the Regions (GORs) were set up in 1994 to provide a central government presence in the regions. They brought together the regional functions of the transport, environment and trade and industry departments. These Government Offices play a leading role in the administration of certain government programmes within the region. The report by the Performance and Innovation Unit, *Reaching Out* (PIU, 2000), led to the role of the Government Offices being strengthened in 2001, by bringing together certain regional services from nine central government departments.

The issues raised by the interrelationships between RDAs, regional chambers and the GORs are unresolved, as are issues about the lack of regional accountability for other regional institutions. Regional government can be seen as a way of resolving the issues.

Arguments for regional government

The complexities of present regional structures do not provide positive arguments for regional government. Advocates normally put forward three main arguments for elected regional authorities. Regional government is advocated as decentralisation in an overcentralised system of government and as a more democratic system of government, bringing appointed boards within the region under democratic control. These two arguments can be linked together: 'The democratic arguments for regional government are closely linked with concern about centralisation, that decisions affecting people in the regions are taken remotely; and without proper regard to the diversity of conditions, needs and wishes between different parts of the country' (Sandford and MacQuail, 2001, p. 50). The third argument is economic, based on economic disparities and the need to build strong regional economies.

The White Paper reiterates these arguments. Elected regional assemblies will 'improve efficiency and deliver better regional outcomes' as 'a single streamlined body, focused on the region's priorities' and able 'to strengthen the region's economic capability'. They will provide greater accountability because decisions 'will be taken by people from the region' who will be 'directly elected by, and thus directly accountable to, people in the region' (Cabinet Office and DTLR, 2002, p. 32).

Whether elected regional authorities would fulfil the hopes implicit in these arguments should not be taken for granted. The arguments do, however, suggest criteria by which proposals and emerging practice can be judged. Will regional government lead to decentralisation? Will regional authorities have functions that lead to sufficient electoral interest to give them a strong democratic base? Will the assemblies ensure democratic control over the appointed boards in the region? Is the region an area in which strong economies can be built? Has the region sufficient powers to make an impact on regional disparities?

The responsibilities and powers of the regional assemblies

Both the Scottish Parliament and the Welsh Assembly have substantial legislative roles covering a wide range of domestic matters, although the powers of the Welsh Assembly only cover secondary legislation, important though that can be. In addition, they have taken over major administrative responsibilities and considerable budgets from the Scottish and Welsh Offices and other sources. The government's proposals for the responsibilities of the regional assemblies fall far very short of the responsibilities even of the Welsh Assembly. The regional assemblies will have no legislative powers even for secondary legislation, nor are they to take over any of the major administrative responsibilities of central government, beyond a few of those carried by the GORs.

Advocates of regional government have normally argued that the assemblies could take over the functions of the GORs and/or of quangos in the region (Marquand and Tomaney, 2000). Even if such changes took place, it might not be sufficient to give regional assemblies a role commanding public interest and attention. In one sense the Government Offices do not do anything. That is an over-simple statement, but it recognises that these offices provide few services. They are largely supervisory bodies, acting as intermediaries for central government in advising on and in some cases making decisions on grants, applications or proposals required by government procedures. For regional assemblies to take over these functions could make them merely intermediary bodies advising central government. If the change went further and the assemblies were to exercise these functions in their own right, they would become supervisory bodies over local authorities and other local public bodies rather than having their own direct responsibilities. The other source of functions proposed by advocates is from the regional quangos. The RDAs, health authorities and Learning and Skills Councils have most often been thought of as regional bodies to be made the responsibility of the assemblies, although the latter two operate at a sub-regional level.

The government is not proposing to give the regional assemblies the full powers of the Government Offices of the Region. The assemblies will appoint RDAs, which will, however, retain day-to-day operational independence. The assemblies will not take over the functions of other quangos and appointed boards such as health authorities or even have the right to appoint their members, other than two members of the Learning and Skills Councils and a few appointments on other bodies. The government is not ready to give the assemblies significant powers currently exercised by central departments. The conclusion must be that the changes proposed can hardly be regarded as a major step in decentralisation. They fall far short of the aspirations of the advocates.

The regional assemblies' main responsibilities would be the preparation of a wide range of regional strategies covering:

- sustainable development;
- economic development;
- skills and employment;
- spatial planning;
- transport;
- waste;
- housing;
- health improvement;
- culture including tourism; and
- biodiversity;

as well as being encouraged 'to produce an over-arching strategy to set out their vision for the region and their key priorities on the range of issues for which they have responsibility' (Cabinet Office and DTLR, 2002, p. 35). At first sight these appear to be substantial responsibilities. Two issues arise: whether regional assemblies will have sufficient freedom from central control to develop their own strategies; and whether they will have sufficient powers to ensure the strategies lead to action.

The government proposes to place constraints on the development of the regional strategies. The economic development strategy will continue to be prepared by the RDA, which will be subject to government guidance. The assembly will publish the strategy and can direct the RDA to make modifications. It will, however, have to consult the government, which will be able to require changes in the strategy. Although the assembly will draw up Frameworks for Regional Employment and Skills Action, to which local Learning and Skills Councils will have to have regard, these councils will still be subject to guidance from the National Learning and Skills Council. The regional assemblies will have to exercise their responsibilities for the arts and sports in 'a way which protects strategic national priorities' (Cabinet Office and DTLR, 2002, p. 41). While these and other constraints may seem reasonable to some, they reflect a pattern of reluctance by central government departments and national bodies to allow freedom for the assemblies to develop their own policies.

Once strategies have been prepared and approved, the issue becomes how the assemblies can ensure their implementation. The assemblies have few direct powers to take action. The scope for action remains with local authorities, central government departments, government agencies and local and national quangos. The powers proposed for the assemblies are rarely direct powers to act, but 'powers' to *advise* central government on the allocation of funds for local transport; to *make proposals* to the Highways Agency and the Strategic Rail Authority, to *be consulted* on bids to the Higher Education Innovation Funds and to *request* the Secretary of State to call in strategic planning applications. The main substantial powers that the assemblies will exercise directly are over capital allocations for housing and that funding for arts, sports and tourism that is regional in character. In addition the assemblies will have responsibilities for the regional development agencies, which will, however, have operational independence.

The proposals mean the assemblies will be constrained in drawing up their strategies and limited in their capacity to see them implemented. There is a real danger that with these limited responsibilities and powers, the regional assemblies would be regarded as talking shops that could be largely disregarded in practice. They can hardly be seen as a significant contribution to democratic vitality and electoral interest and turnout could be very low – lower probably than for local elections. Overall these proposed responsibilities hardly justify the creation of a new tier of elected government. It can be argued that these responsibilities are similar to (though less than) those of the Greater London Authority, but its effectiveness remains to be established. In addition, the GLA represents a clearly identifiable area and met a popular demand for a voice for London and that is not the case in most of the rest of England.

The limited functions proposed for regional assemblies raises the possibility of their assuming some of the functions of local authorities, even though the White Paper states that is not the government's intention. It may not be the intention at present, but the question is likely to be raised as any regional assemblies created realise how limited their role is. They might receive a ready response from the central government of the day. It is probably not unduly cynical to suggest that central government – both politicians and civil servants – would be more ready to see functions transferred from local authorities than from central government itself.

If the proposals for regional government involve the abolition of many of the counties, a reallocation of their functions is necessary. In that case, there could be pressure to transfer responsibilities for education, social services and fire to the new regional authorities rather than to relatively small unitary authorities. Such a change would not be limited to the counties and would eventually apply to metropolitan districts, existing unitary authorities and London boroughs. The introduction of regional government would then be largely the replacement of one two-tier system by another, with the upper tier being more remote from local communities than the present counties.

Overall the proposals cannot be regarded as in any way a significant move to decentralisation within the system of government. This conclusion is confirmed by the absence of any indication that the development of regional government will involve changes in the structure of central government. There is no sign that the radical restructuring of central government implied by a strong policy of decentralisation has even been considered. There has been no public discussion of the need for a reduction in the number or size of government departments or of a reduction in the number of ministers or of MPs as might have been expected from a strong policy of decentralisation. *Your Regions, Your Choice* sees the development of regional government as a gradual process, dependent on the views of people in each region. This gradual approach means that the issue of change in central government is effectively marginalised. Central government will continue unchanged because the proposal is for a gradual change with limited decentralisation, not the comprehensive process of decentralisation that could lead to a fundamental reconsideration of the system of government.

The lack of any powers even over secondary legislation shows the limits of what is proposed. If the regional assemblies were to be given the legislative powers and the related administrative responsibilities of the Welsh Assembly, it would, if comprehensive in scope, involve a reconsideration of the role of Parliament and of the structure of central government. Effective regional government in Europe is based on at least semi-legislative powers within framework legislation and in the case of Germany and Austria of certain powers of primary legislation. Such powers give regional bodies a role that distinguishes them from local authorities. The government is not even considering such a fundamental change.

Areas and boundaries

Your Region, Your Choice assumes that the regional authorities would be based, in the first instance, on the present boundaries of the Government Offices of the Region. Those regions differ in the extent to which they have a shared identity. A shared identity can be argued to exist in the North East, Yorkshire and the Humber and the North West, although even with the latter two there are questions to be asked. Cumbria sits uncomfortably in the North West, while Greater Manchester and Merseyside have their own separate identities. Similar issues arise in Yorkshire and the Humber with South Humberside and the differences between South Yorkshire and West Yorkshire.

There are even greater problems with some of the other regions. The problems are most acute in the South East region, which is best described as the area around London. It gains what little shared identity it has not from the region itself, but from the area it surrounds. The South West region may appear to have an identity, yet Cornwall is many miles away from Bristol which assumes it will be the regional centre, if the word 'centre' has any meaning in this context. Cornwall is likely to support regional government, but on condition that Cornwall is a region.

Sizeism has dominated the regional debate as it has dominated discussion of local government structures. It is assumed almost without any explicit justification that regions should normally have a population of at least five million, yet it is significant that the one region with the greatest visible public support is the North East, whose population is only a little above two million. The position in some European countries is very different. Regions differ in size because they reflect perceived regional identities. In Spain, while Catalonia has a population of six million, Rioja has a population of under 300,000 and Estramadura and Murcia of one million.

Regional government need not be built on the scale of the present regions. In many areas there is probably a stronger case for city-regions, based on major cities with the areas surrounding them. City-regions have an understood identity and often have a clearer economic base than the wider region. City-regions would separate Merseyside from Greater Manchester. The problem is that the geography does not fit the model in large parts of the country. Nor does such an approach necessarily command much popular support. Avon and Humberside were among the most criticised elements of the 1974 reorganisation, even though they covered city-regions built on and around Bristol and Hull respectively.

The argument suggests the possibility of smaller regions than those proposed. It is unlikely to happen. A combination of sizeism and inertia are likely to mean that, with the possible exception of the South East, existing boundaries will be maintained.

The implications for local government

The implications of a commitment to local government reorganisation have been discussed above, but there are also issues about the relationship between regional authorities and the local authorities that emerge from the process. The regional authorities can, in theory, be seen as a separate tier from local authorities whose main relationships remain with central government, and so the advocates often present them to avoid arousing antagonism from local authorities. That position is probably unsustainable in practice.

If the regional assemblies were to be given significant powers, they would have a major impact on local authorities. At one extreme, if the regions were to be given powers equivalent to those of the Welsh Assembly, they would take over the main responsibilities of central government departments in relation to local authorities. The regional assemblies would be responsible for the regulations governing local authorities including political structures and best value, as well as local government finance in the allocation of grants. The relationship with regional assemblies would be the main intergovernmental relationship for local authorities, greatly surpassing in importance any remaining relationship with central government. If, however, as the government proposes, regional authorities were given a much more limited role, their relationship with local authorities would still be important.

Much of the rhetoric surrounding regional government has minimised the impact on local authorities. It has been argued that the assemblies would not take powers from local authorities, although that is probably unrealistic if regional government is associated with the general introduction of unitary authorities. The regional assemblies will, in any event, assume certain planning functions previously held by counties. It is often suggested that the assemblies would not have a supervisory role over local authorities or be responsible for allocating resources. Yet the regional assemblies will be responsible for a range of strategies and if the strategies are to be more than paper documents, they would give the regional assemblies a supervisory role. Those strategies will be designed to have an impact on local authorities' policies and practices. If they do not have that impact it would be difficult to see any point in them and the regional assemblies would demand powers of enforcement. If the assemblies were given substantial powers to enforce their strategies, they would become supervisory bodies over local authorities. This can be illustrated by housing: the assemblies are to be given the power to allocate support for housing capital between councils and therefore, in effect, a supervisory role over them to enable the necessary judgements to be made.

The creation of regional assemblies is bound to have a major impact on local authorities. If it did not have such an impact, it is difficult to see the point of creating them. Over and above whether it involves a restructuring of local government, the removal of functions or the allocation of resources at the regional level, the work of the assemblies must overlap with that of local authorities. A regional authority is meant to have a significant

impact on the region, so it must have an impact on local authorities within the region.

There is another reason why the impact on local authorities is
likely to be significant. A new political institution is being
created. The regional assembly will attract leading figures from
local government. The members of the assembly will want to
establish its role as the major player in the region. They will not
be content for it to be a talking shop whose views can be disregarded. They will wish to speak and act with authority on issues
affecting the region or parts of the region. Members of the
assembly will feel close to the region and the areas within. They
will consider they have real local knowledge and are able to
speak out authoritatively on local issues. Ironically the fewer
powers that assemblies are given, the more assertive they are
likely to be in their use.

There is a potential conflict between regions and local authorities. Power is limited and there may not be room for two major
actors on the local/regional scene. European experience highlights this issue:

> Broadly speaking, regional powers, based on a high level of
> legislative power and finances tend to make local authorities
> dependent on the region both functionally and financially.
> The determination of the Spanish Autonomous Communities
> and the Belgian regions (or communities) to affirm their
> autonomy from the central authorities leads them to a particu-
> lar stress on their power over local authorities, which are
> sometimes advised to seek the support of the central govern-
> ment in certain fields.
>
> The proximity-based approach plays against the local
> authorities: the regional authority can exercise more detailed
> supervision than the state supervisor. The regional legislator is
> a subordinate legislator as he is bound by national legislation,
> and so he is tempted to legislate in more detail, which reduces
> the area in which municipal or local autonomy can be
> exercised. (Council of Europe, 1998, p. 41)

Where the regional authority has significant powers over local
authorities it can become dominant. In the absence of such powers
it is likely that local authorities and in particular large urban
authorities will dominate in the relationship with the regional

authorities. Le Galès suggests that this is a common position in Europe. Despite notable exceptions, 'regions as a level of elected government have generally remained relatively weak. They have weak autonomy, weak resources, weak political capacity and weak legitimacy' (Le Galès, 1998, p. 244). This is because there are only limited regional interests when compared with long-established city interests. He points out that in many countries, 'real or potential regions have to face a whole group of institutions, that generally have no desire to find themselves under the tutelage of a level rather close to government and they are hostile to any kind of regional centralisation' (1998, p. 249). These regions have only two possibilities: 'They are either a level of co-ordination which is accepted and defined as such by the much older local authorities, especially by cities, or they are condemned to remain a relatively undeveloped level of government' (ibid.).

Le Galès sees France as illustrating these conclusions. He argues more generally that competition is inherent in the relationship between regional and local authorities, although the outcome varies from country to country. It is uncertain how this issue would be resolved in England. Regions could remain relatively weak or local authorities could become weaker. If the creation of unitary authorities means an eventual loss of local authority powers to the regions, then the regions are likely to become dominant.

Other issues are raised by the introduction of regional government. There are issues about how they would be financed, the method of election, the number of members and the form of government. How some of these issues are resolved could have an impact on local authorities. If, as is proposed, regional assemblies were elected by proportional representation, it would strengthen the argument for a similar system of election in local government. If, as is also proposed, regional authorities were required to precept on local authorities for some of their funds, it would increase the pressure on local government finance. The overall conclusion must be that regional government would have a major impact on local government and in certain forms would significantly weaken it.

The criteria applied

Earlier in this chapter criteria were suggested as the basis for judgement on the effectiveness of regional government in the light of its stated aims. The present proposals do not meet those criteria. Substantial decentralisation is not proposed and there is a danger that far from decentralisation downwards, there will be regionalisation upwards. It remains uncertain whether regional assemblies will be given sufficient powers and responsibilities to arouse electoral interest and provide the basis for a strong democratic institution. The proposals do little to provide regional accountability for quangos in the region or to provide them with a democratic base. The economic role depends in part upon the powers and if the role of the regional assemblies focuses on regional economic strategies, whether they can be made effective in action. Regional disparities cannot necessarily be resolved at the regional level and may still require national action. There are issues about whether the likely regional areas are the appropriate areas for economic development, since sub-regions often have a greater shared economic identity.

The effectiveness of the proposals for regional government is, at best, uncertain.

Conclusion

Following the traumatic experience of local government reorganisation in the early 1990s, the government wisely left the structural issue untouched in its first term, with the exception of the creation of the Greater London Authority. To have raised the issue of reorganisation would have reopened the conflicts between counties and districts and would have been a major distraction from the modernisation programme.

It could not be assumed, however, that the structural issue would remain off the political agenda. Certain former county boroughs are still far from reconciled to district status. Authorities such as Norwich, Exeter and Northampton maintain their pressure for the restoration of what they see as their lost status. Arguments could also be mounted against a structure that brings together very different local communities within the artificial boundaries of some present districts, but the case for smaller districts lacks advocates, although it is possible to envisage further extensions of the powers of parish and town councils.

Further significant change would be unlikely in the immediate future, were it not for proposals for regional government. The introduction of regional government would have a direct effect on the structure of local government. Even without that, regional government in whatever form would have a significant impact on local authorities; yet it is often discussed as if the creation of regional assemblies would have no effect on local government. Inevitably whatever is said before their actual creation, there will an impact, as there will be an impact of local authorities on the working of regional government. In the limited policy space of the region, significant actors are bound to have an effect on each other.

There are problems in central–local relations as the next chapter shows. Regional government will raise issues of central–regional and regional–local relations to add to the continuing issues of central–local relations. If past experience of central–local relations is any guide, regional government will bring new and even more complex problems of intergovernmental relations. These issues and the many other issues raised in this chapter need to be thought through before regional government is introduced, rather than being faced unexpectedly in the actual working of the new system of government.

The prospect of regional government can be regarded as weakening the drive to effective local government, by unnecessarily turning attention away from its main tasks and from the modernisation programme to new struggles over local government reorganisation. In addition the possible development of regional government raises issues too rarely discussed about the future of local government and the possibility of a reduction in its role.

11 Have Central–Local Relations Been Modernised?

There was a significant omission in *Modern Local Government*. The nature of central–local relations is critical to building effective local government, yet there were no proposals to modernise central–local relations alongside the proposals for modernising local government. Some of the problems in central–local relations were recognised in *Strong Local Leadership*, but central–local relations still await modernisation. While that paper identifies problems, it fails to analyse how they have arisen and therefore how they can be avoided in the future, and other problems have yet to be acknowledged by the government.

Research on Scotland and Wales has suggested that while there are inevitably some problems in central–local relations, they are better than in England or than the previous relations with the Scottish and Welsh Offices (Bennett *et al.*, 2002; Laffin *et al.*, 2002). More consideration has been given to central–local relations in Scotland and Wales, in part as a necessary response to the creation of the Scottish Parliament and the Welsh Assembly, with the report of the Commission on *Local Government and the Scottish Parliament* (McIntosh, 1999) and the work of the Partnership Council provided for in the Welsh devolution legislation.

This chapter focuses on relations between central government and individual local authorities, rather than on the relationship between central government and the Local Government Association, which is often the focus for commentators on central–local relations. The government has sought to put its relations with the LGA on a new basis. The Consultative Council on Local Government Finance had been set up by the 1974–79 Labour government as a forum bringing together the local authority associations and central government to discuss financial issues. Its role had diminished under the Conservative government, and the Labour government replaced it with the Central Local Partnership, given new weight by the government and covering not merely finance, but all major issues affecting local government in England. Representatives of the government and the LGA signed a Framework for Partnership in November 1997. The Framework set out principles to govern consultation between central government and the LGA. While from time to time the LGA has seen problems in the relationship, it considers that access to ministers has been strengthened and consultation deepened.

The principle of selectivity

The period of the Labour government has seen the emergence of the principle of selectivity in its relations with local authorities. Rather than applying the same approach to all authorities, the government has been increasingly selective, distinguishing between how it treats authorities according to judgements on their performance or on how far they have modernised themselves. This principle has not been developed to anything like the same extent in Scotland or Wales.

The reason for this approach lay in the government's analysis of the state of local government and its belief in the dominance of the traditional culture. The challenge to local authorities was to modernise. The prime minister set out the challenge in the extract quoted in Chapter 1:

> A changing role is part of your heritage. The people's needs require you to change again so that you can play your part in helping to modernise Britain and in partnership with others, deliver the policies on which this government was elected.
>
> If you accept this challenge, you will not find us wanting. You can look forward to an enhanced role and new powers. Your contribution will be recognised. Your status enhanced.
>
> If you are unwilling or unable to work to the modern agenda then the government will have to look to other partners to take on your role. (Blair, 1998, p. 22)

This statement was a message both to local government generally and to individual authorities. If a local authority modernised all would be well, but if not beware! At its simplest the principle of selectivity can be described as 'reward the good authorities and punish the bad ones', although the government would prefer to say earning freedoms and flexibilities for the highly performing authorities and dealing with the weaknesses in the poorly performing. The principle of selectivity had begun to emerge under the Conservative government with the powers of intervention taken both on capping described in the next chapter and on compulsory competitive tendering. Under the Labour government, the principle of selectivity has been applied to the whole range of local authority activities.

The government took new powers to intervene in the workings of individual authorities. It has not been generally appreciated by the public or by the media that even after the Conservative government's legislation, central government had no general power to intervene in the workings of particular authorities. Talk in the press of sending in a commissioner to take over an authority at the time of conflicts over the budgets in Lambeth and Liverpool ignored the reality that the government had no such general powers. There were certain specific, but limited, powers to send in a commissioner in relation to a particular function. This was done in the case of civil defence in Coventry and in St Pancras in the 1950s and in connection with housing rents in Clay Cross in the 1980s. The threat was used against Norwich over the sale of council houses and was sufficient to ensure compliance. There were powers of direction for certain functions, although they were so little used that Tameside became a cause célèbre when in the 1970s the recently elected Conservative council successfully challenged in the courts the use of those powers against its withdrawal of the previous Labour council's scheme for comprehensive education.

The Secretary of State was given general powers of intervention by the Local Government Act 1999. Section 15 provides that, normally after following certain specified procedures, the Secretary of State may take action against an authority 'failing to comply with the requirements' of the Act. These include the general requirement on local authorities 'to make arrangements to secure continuous improvement in the way in which its functions are exercised, having regard to a combination of economy, efficiency and effectiveness' (s. 3). It would be hard to draft a wider power to intervene in an authority. The Secretary of State can direct:

(a) that a specified function of the authority shall be exercised by the Secretary of State or a person nominated by him for a period specified in the direction or for so long as the Secretary of State considers appropriate, and

(b) that the authority shall comply with any instruction of the Secretary of State or his nominee in relation to the exercise of that function and shall provide such assistance as the Secretary of State or his nominee may require for the purpose of exercising the function. (s. 15.6)

For the first time central government has general powers of intervention in particular authorities.

These powers or threats of their use have been employed in giving directions to Hackney and in requiring the appointment of a new management team in Walsall. They are being increasingly used or threatened for authorities judged to be poor or weak in comprehensive performance assessments (CPAs). The powers remain important even when not used, because the threat of their use can have much the same effect as their actual use. Similar powers in relation to education have induced local authorities to involve external organisations in their education functions, even though the powers have not actually been used. The threat to use the powers can ensure that authorities accept central government's proposals for action.

The basis for rewarding high-performing authorities developed gradually. The government extended the number and amount of funds awarded on the basis of its evaluation of proposals from different authorities. Such processes can be used to reward authorities with the justification that funds are being awarded to authorities able to use them effectively. In its proposals for the reform of local government finance the government considered allocating part of the grant according to judgements on the performance or the plans of the authority. While this proposal has not been directly pursued, the introduction of public service agreements has a similar effect, since individual authorities will be rewarded on the basis of their achievement in relation to agreed targets. New freedoms and flexibilities described in this and the next chapter are available to authorities categorised as excellent and good in the comprehensive performance assessment.

The comprehensive performance assessment firmly embeds the principle of selectivity in central–local relations, involving different approaches by central government according to the category in which an authority is placed.

Arguments on selectivity

It has been argued that whereas under the Conservative government the problems with particular authorities were used as an argument for legislation affecting all authorities, the principle of selectivity relates action by the government to the problem authorities. The most important argument is that action necessary for low-performing authorities should not hold back high-performing authorities that should be free from at least some of the centrally imposed constraints. It is also argued that these freedoms would not be justified for low-performing authorities, where intervention should be used to overcome the problems in their performance. This argument assumes that intervention would be effective. It may be, but intervention brings its own problems. Intervention is likely to be intervention in a situation imperfectly understood, for central government is both geographically and organisationally remote from the situation being intervened in, even with the appointment by central government of the relationship managers described in Chapter 8.

The government's own study of the literature on intervention pointed out that:

> Interventions are likely to be triggered by problems in a particular service – in an era of corporate cross service working, direct interventions in any one service will impact on others with unforeseen effects. There is no inherent reason that such interventions will have positive outcomes . . . It is quite possible that direct interventions may solve the problems in a failing council, but whilst doing so create other problems. (DETR, 1999d, p. 40)

The report identified four problems for intervention in the best value regime:

- exploitation or opportunistic behaviour threatening or undermining the intervention;

- displacement or intervention becoming an end in itself, leading to failing councils being focused on rather than successful ones;
- provocation or stirring up antagonisms locally leading to a lack of co-operation; and
- over-commitment of resources in pursuit of unrealistic targets. (Based on DETR, 1999d, pp. 40–1)

The report recognised that these problems could be dealt with if faced. The report must, however, be regarded as a warning that external intervention in poorly performing authorities cannot be assumed to be an automatic success and can make the situation worse.

The major problem with the principle of selectivity is the basis on which the judgement is made about the authority. That judgment results in an authority being treated as a successful or a failing authority or being fitted into one of the five categories into which authorities are classified under the comprehensive performance assessment. The principle of selectivity substitutes that external judgement for the judgment made by the authority and by the local electors and raises the issue of how that judgement is made and the validity that can be attached to it. In making those judgements in the comprehensive performance assessments used to categorise authorities, the views of inspectors and assessors are the main determinants of the outcomes.

The growth in the inspectorates

The growth in both the number and the importance of inspectors is a major development in central–local relations, begun under the Conservative government, but intensified by the Labour government. The responsibilities of Ofsted have been extended beyond schools to cover the work of education authorities. The Social Services Inspectorate has been strengthened. A Housing Inspectorate and a Benefits Fraud Inspectorate have been established. The most significant development has been the extension of the role of the Audit Commission in auditing the best value performance plans, in inspections of best value reviews, and in corporate and comprehensive performance assessments.

External inspection including external assessment plays an ever-increasing role in the work of authorities, occupying the time and attention of both councillors and officers. It has been estimated that the direct cost of inspection in local government is £600 million per annum (IPPR, 2000). This estimate takes no account of the time taken by officers and councillors, who have to prepare for the inspections, deal with the inspectors and respond to their reports. Sandra Taylor, the Director of Social Services of Birmingham, described preparation alone as a 'four to five month process' which is 'incredibly resource intensive' (*Local Government Chronicle*, 20 October 2000, p. 20). As Hood and his colleagues have pointed out, estimates of the cost of inspections neglect compliance costs (Hood *et al.*, 1999, p. 101).

External inspections can have a value in bringing fresh insights to the work of the authority, but Byatt and Lyons have pointed out that 'Evidence of the effects of inspection is limited' (Byatt and Lyons, 2001, p. 10). They point out a series of risks:

- failure to get the most from the system, by not looking at the whole of the overall picture;
- duplication of effort;
- excessive cumulative burdens;
- creation of a compliance (rather than performance) culture;
- inconsistency. (Ibid., p. 8)

There can be too much inspection as well as too little. There has been little consideration until recently of what is the optimum level of inspection. It has now been recognised by the government that the level of inspection needs consideration (DLTR, 2001a, p. 29), although the government has at the same time introduced new forms of external assessment.

The assumption of inspectoral infallibility

Even more important than the number of inspections are the attitudes towards inspections. Inspections can be regarded as providing a set of views meriting serious consideration by authorities, but with no more and probably less weight than the views of officers, councillors and the public locally. Alternatively they can be and apparently are regarded by the government as inherently correct and therefore to be accepted as an authoritative judgement on the local authority and its services, providing a firm basis for action in relation to individual authorities. This latter view is dangerous, reflecting an apparent doctrine of inspectoral infallibility.

The assumption of inspectoral infallibility is strange, since inspectors form their views on the basis of limited time and limited local knowledge. The inspectors have no responsibility to local people or for the consequences of their recommendations. They do not have to implement proposals based on their views. It is difficult to see why their views should have more weight than those of councillors and officers, who have deep local knowledge and much practical experience, have spent time and effort considering the issues faced locally and have a direct responsibility to local people. It is even more difficult to understand why inspectors' views should be regarded as infallible. The issues on which inspectors are expected to form judgements illustrate the problem. Thus in environmental services, it is expected that inspectors will judge 'the quality of results achieved through the implementation of the Development Plan' and the 'quality of decision-making in development control' (Audit Commission, 2002a, p. 26). It is not clear why inspectors' judgements on such issues should be regarded as more reliable than those made by councillors and officers. None of these arguments mean that external views have no value. Such views can challenge possible organisational inertia, but should not be treated as necessarily correct.

Judgements are made by inspectors about the leadership of both officers and councillors. The corporate assessments 'judge an authority's capacity to improve through an analysis of the leadership and management of the council' (Audit Commission, 2002a, p. 72). The quality of leadership is not easily assessed, for it involves judgement of the style of leadership required as well as of the leadership itself. Different authorities at different times require different styles of leadership, best judged by those at local level who understand the local situation. Reports by inspectors have tended to assume the need for a directive style of leadership as opposed to a consensus-building style. Inspectors need to appreciate there is no single model of leadership, but that effective leadership should be grounded in local conditions, which are much more likely to be understood by local councillors than by external inspectors.

There is growing evidence, admittedly based on the views of interested parties – local authority chief executives – that inspectors are far from infallible. The Society of Chief Executives collected a range of views. 'No one on the inspection team had any knowledge or experience of tourism. This showed.' 'From the first day of inspection, staff were complaining about the "prejudice" of the inspectors who appeared to conclude quite early on that our service was unlikely to improve.' 'The results as presented at the "interim challenge" session were grossly inaccurate, based on flawed or insufficient (or no) evidence and delivered in a confrontational, aggressive manner; and overall demonstrated a lack of professionalism, on the part of the review team.' Such views were balanced by other favourable views, but these and other examples suggest, at the very least, that there are as many or possibly more failing inspectors as there are failing authorities and certainly as many 'coasting' inspectors, as some authorities were to have been called.

The dangers of necessarily fallible inspection processes are greater the more weight is attached to the views of inspectors and asssessors, as is happening with the categorisation of authorities by the comprehensive performance assessment. It is becoming more important to satisfy the inspectors than to meet the concerns of local people. *Lessons Learnt from Intervention* cautiously suggested 'There seems to be at least a slight contradiction in emphasising the public's role in defining Best Value and then jettisoning them when compliance is assessed' (DETR, 1999d, p. 20) and the same surely applies to the CPA.

The growth of the inspectorates and the importance of their views in forming the central government's judgements on particular authorities – and indeed on local government generally – makes it important to understand more about the role of inspectors, their background and how they form their views. There has been no systematic study of the inspectors as opposed to the process of inspection (Hood *et al.*, 1999; Byatt and Lyons, 2001). When, as in the establishment of the best value inspectorate, large number of appointments have to be made in a short period of time, one suspects some of those appointed may not have been able to obtain promotion in local government or have become frustrated with the requirements of actually managing services and for whom inspection seemed an easier option. The Best Value Inspectorate aimed to have 400 inspectors. Inevitably while 'the new inspectorates . . . have gone to considerable lengths to establish the credentials of their inspectors' it has been 'difficult to recruit suitably qualified staff' (Davis *et al.*, 2001, p. 20). It seems inevitable that some, and maybe many, inspectors have less experience and less ability than those being inspected. The danger is if the inspectors themselves do not appreciate it.

Little is known about how inspectors form their views. If the inspectors have a model of good practice to guide them, then corporate arrangements, services or best value reviews that do not conform to the model will be judged to be of a lower standard than those that do. In that event, the role of inspectors can be to impose or seek to impose uniformity on the diversity that is the strength of local government. Inspection can then lead to a reluctance to take the risk of innovation for fear of the inspector's views. 'Authorities may be wary of appearing to be different and, faced with inspectorates that already have a clear view of "what works", many could be disinclined to risk new approaches' (Davis *et al.*, 2001, p. 21). The alternative danger is a lack of consistency with the results of the inspection depending on who the inspectors or the members of the assessment teams happen to be. If inspectors have no model to guide them everything depends on their own personal judgements. There is a difficult balance to be struck between inspections that seek to impose uniformity and inspections that vary in their conclusions according to inspectors' personal judgements. That balance will be achieved not by a diversity of inspections but by inspections that recognise the diversity of local government as a strength to be nurtured, and balance can best be achieved by inspections that assume until proved otherwise that the local authority knows best.

Inspection has long been recognised by authorities to be a costly and disruptive process involving much more than direct costs in time, effort and stress. Over-inspection is now being recognised as a problem by the government. The three-year inspection holiday has been introduced for authorities categorised as excellent and light-touch inspections based on risk assessments are being introduced for others. The Audit Commission has identified 40 pathfinder councils to pilot a new approach to inspection. The pathfinder authorities have an integrated work programme and a single manager to liaise with the council. These developments are to be welcomed, but may be cancelled out for many authorities by the new burdens of comprehensive performance assessments and of the follow-up action described in Chapter 8. In any event, these changes do not meet the key problems.

While the accountability of authorities is clear, it is not clear what is the accountability of the inspectors. To whom are the inspectors accountable? Who inspects the inspectors? Who assesses the assessors? Or even who audits the auditors? Most inspectorates have internal control procedures, but that is only to transfer the problem. To whom are chief inspectors accountable? Who inspects the chief inspectors? The inspectorates, it can be argued, are accountable to ministers, but at the same time their independence is asserted. The conclusion must be that there is a critical lack of clarity about the accountability of the whole of the inspection system, and yet it is directed at institutions with a clear basis of accountability. The issue of accountability becomes more important the greater the role inspectors play in applying the principle of selectivity with its consequences for authorities.

The underlying issue is the role that inspectors are expected to play. There is a continuum between two extremes. At one extreme is the commissar sent to ensure that what happens in an authority conforms to predetermined requirements. The commissar knows what is required, being the guardian of nationally prescribed policies, procedures and practice. The infallibility of the inspector both supports and expresses the commissar role. At the other extreme is the partner in shared learning, for whom the role is that of a partner – albeit a junior partner – working with authorities in learning how performance can be improved. As partners in shared learning, inspectors recognise their own need to learn. They start from the assumption that local authorities have good reasons for their policies and practice and that it is important to learn those reasons. Such inspectors welcome diversity and the learning that it brings. They see an inspection as an opportunity to learn. Listening and discussion are their important tools. Humility is a quality valued in a partner in shared learning.

The reality is that there will be occasions when the inspectors will have to operate nearer to the commissar mode, but those should be the exceptions. Inspectors should normally operate in the partnership mode, which means that they can speak with more authority and more impact when they have to move towards the commissar model. The effective inspector recognises the value of the partnership model, but some inspectors may be incapable of doing so. It has been said above that there are probably more failing inspectors than failing authorities and those inspectors are those who 'know' the right answer – they are commissars through and through, yet judgement upon authority performance and action taken by the government can rest upon such inspectors.

The dangers of the principle of selectivity embedded in the comprehensive performance assessment are that the assessment is based on the assumption of inspectoral infallibility and on the commissar role and that accountability to inspectors can supplant local accountability to the electorate.

The other policies

Policies and practices in central–local relations developed outside the modernisation programme as different central departments followed their own separate approaches. There have been two important developments: the development of area-based initiatives with related ring-fenced grants and the growth of planning procedures.

Area-based initiatives

The Performance and Innovation Unit of the Cabinet Office mapped the development of area-based initiatives in *Reaching Out: The Role of Central Government at Regional and Local Level*. Area-based initiatives were listed in an annex to the report, most, although not all, dating from the election of the Labour government. Thirty-two initiatives are listed, including Burglary Initiatives, New Deal for Communities, Education Action Zones, the Healthy Schools Initiative and Lifelong Learning Partnerships (PIU, 2000, Annex F).

In an area-based initiative, the government allocates funds to selected authorities, normally ring-fenced so that they can only be used for the specified purposes. Bids may be required from authorities or authorities may be chosen directly by the government. Matched funding is normally required from authorities and the bids may have to be made by partnerships, rather than by the local authority alone. If a bid is successful, monitoring procedures will require reports from authorities at regular intervals. These initiatives are time-limited, leaving local authorities, their partners and local communities to find funds to continue activities begun under the initiative.

The proliferation of initiatives reflected the imperatives of ministers in power after long years in opposition and wanting to take action. Each of the initiatives has its own rationale and justification. The problems created lie not in each single initiative, but in the cumulative impact of many initiatives. Although each initiative can be justified on its merits considered in isolation, the cumulative impact has consequences that were not seriously considered by the government, at least until the publication of *Reaching Out*. *Reaching Out* sets out concerns expressed not merely by local authorities but by other public bodies at local level:

- While area-based initiatives to tackle problems are very welcome, they are often poorly coordinated and waste local capacity and effort.
- Area-based initiatives and mainstream programmes do not complement each other.
- Government concentrates too much on short-term outputs rather than longer-term outcomes.
- It is difficult to have a dialogue with central government which takes account of local circumstances; often it is not clear who within central government is in the best position to help tackle complex social problems. (PIU, 2000, p. 31)

Area-based initiatives are not clearly related to each other. The areas covered by particular initiatives can create a patchwork quilt of initiatives to be managed by the authority. The guidance on one initiative rarely explains how it relates to other initiatives. The information required by central government for monitoring can vary from initiative to initiative, even on closely related topics. Even if the variation is only slight, it can add significantly to the problems for authorities. The overall impact of initiatives fragments the work of the authority and its partners. The resources allocated by the government are normally ring-fenced and requirements for matched funding effectively ring-fence part of the authority's own resources. The growth of these initiatives creates barriers to joined-up government at local level, even though the emphasis on partnership is meant to encourage it. These initiatives separate off the activities covered by the initiative from the main work of the authority and its partners.

Area-based initiatives impose additional work on local authorities. The time taken in forming partnerships, making applications, negotiating over the arrangements and dealing with the
monitoring procedures is all time taken from mainstream
programmes and the task of maintaining and improving services.
They impose national priorities on local conditions. If a local
authority had a choice on how all the funds allocated by initiatives should be used to meet local needs, it is likely they would be
used in very different ways. Of course a local authority need not
apply for an initiative or if it was allocated one could, in theory,
refuse it. That is never likely to happen on any scale. Additional
resources are not going to be refused at any time and certainly
not at a time of felt financial constraint. Resources will, if refused,
not be added to the authority's general grant, but merely be
allocated to another authority. There have been no adequate
mechanisms for discussion with authorities of whether the area-
based initiative is the best way to use the resources made available. The development of community planning and to a lesser
extent of PSAs provides the opportunity for such a dialogue, but
it is not clear how central government intends to respond to community planning, if it intends to respond at all.

The lack of any mechanism to consider the overall impact of
area-based initiatives was recognised by the government following the *Reaching Out* report. *Strong Local Leadership* stated the
government was reviewing these initiatives 'with a view to amal-
gamation, integration or mainstreaming' (DTLR, 2001a, p. 45).
A 'Gateway' has been set up 'to stop unnecessary bureaucracy',
including ring-fenced grants and area-based initiatives, and to
'review the need for existing regulatory requirements' (ODPM,
2002e, para. 22). The outcome remains to be seen. The drive to
initiatives by the separate departments of central government
may prove too strong to be restrained by these procedures.

Plans, plans and yet more plans

Reaching Out also dealt with the proliferation of plans required
by central government from local authorities. It listed 45 plans
required from local authorities or other local bodies (PIU,
2000, Annex G). Research by DTLR has now found 66 such
plans (DTLR, 2002c) and that is not a complete list, with other
plans discovered since. Nor does the number take account of

plans required from particular authorities in connection with specific schemes. Some of the plans predate the election of the Labour government, but there has been a marked growth since 1997.

The problems with the growth of plans are similar to the problem with the growth of area-based initiatives. The procedures involve considerable staff time and effort that is not necessarily directed at local priorities. The DTLR research study concluded, 'The interviews with government officials indicated there had been, to date, little overt consideration of the issue of the cost of producing the plans' (DTLR, 2002c, p. 49). There had been no attempt by the government to evaluate the overall impact of planning requirements on local authorities even to the extent of assessing the workload imposed. So little attention was paid to the overall impact that it took the research project to find out how many separate plans were required from authorities. As with area-based initiatives, each new plan was considered on its own merits without regard to the overall impact on authorities of the number of plans required.

The planning procedures reflect the separate requirements of central departments of central government or of divisions within them. *Reaching Out* pointed out that 'many local authorities of different types said that the mainstream planning requirements placed upon them by central Government within mainstream policy were overwhelming and unhelpful because they specified detailed action in accordance with the separately conceived interests of central Government Departments' (PIU, 2000, p. 40). There has until recently been little consideration of how the plans produced relate to community strategies or to best value performance plans. Indeed it has not always been made clear how different plans required by the same department relate to each other.

The lack of joined-up government at the centre makes more difficult its achievement at local level. The emphasis on separate plans encourages a fragmentation of local authorities' internal planning procedures, which authorities either had to accept, or find ways of overcoming by developing an integrating framework. The latter was made difficult 'by the current level of duplication or inconsistency between existing planning requirements' (DTLR, 2002c, p. 49). Over-prescription of how the plans should be prepared was also seen as hindering a joined-up response by local authorities and inhibiting innovation (ibid., p. 52).

Strong Local Leadership recognised the need to reduce the burdens imposed by the multiplication of planning procedures and to clarify the relationship between different planning procedures. It described reviews of and changes in procedures through local public service agreements, including the rolling together of a number of plans into a single education plan. There is a commitment to reduce the number of plans to a maximum of 16 (ODPM, 2002e, para. 48) and to ensure that the 'remaining requirements should work, as far as possible, with the grain of councils' own activities' (DTLR, 2001a, p. 45). The new Gateway will vet any proposals for new plans put forward by departments. Again the proof of the intention lies in the action taken and whether the reduction is followed later by a gradual increase in the number of plans.

The overall impact and the response

The three developments described in this chapter – the growth of the role of inspectors, the explosion of area-based initiatives and the proliferation of plans – place heavy demands upon local authorities involving senior and other staff in considerable work. *Strong Local Leadership* also identified 'consent regimes' requiring prior consent by government to action by authorities and other procedures imposing unnecessary 'red tape' as adding to the burden on local authorities (DTLR, 2001a, p. 46). All these requirements can be obstacles to be overcome by authorities developing their own initiatives and seeking to improve their performance. There is an opportunity cost. Time taken in meeting these requirements is time not given to improving services and meeting local priorities. It may well be that more than half the time of many managers is devoted to dealing with inspections, area-based initiatives and centrally imposed planning ptrocedures. Whether this is correct is uncertain. What is certain is that central government did not and probably still does not know the impact of all these requirements on local authorities or perhaps even on central government's own workload.

Strong Local Leadership recognised implicitly, if not always explicitly, that the Government's own actions had placed these obstacles in the way of improving performance and of effective local government. The government now proposes, as set out above, to reduce the burdens on local authorities. As well as the introduction of lighter inspectoral regimes for some, the reduction in the number of plans and the streamlining of area-based initiatives, 84 consent regimes have been abolished along with many items of red tape (ODPM, 2001e, para. 36). These proposals are seen as elements in the general policy of increasing freedoms and flexibilities to 'give councils more space to innovate, to respond in ways that are appropriate to local circumstances and to provide more effective leadership' (DTLR, 2001a, p. 41).

Some freedoms and flexibilities are to be given to all authorities. Authorities judged to be 'excellent' under the comprehensive performance assessment are to be given much greater freedoms and flexibilities, as well as the three-year inspection holiday. All service plan requirements will be removed, except the community plan and the best value performance plan (ODPM, 2002e, para. 2). Financial freedom and flexibilities for the excellent and in some cases the good authorities will be described in the next chapter, along with those more generally available.

The general freedoms and flexibilities make a contribution to building effective local government. The problem is that there is no guarantee that over the next few years all this good work will not be undone as new plans, new area-based initiatives and new controls creep back. There are indications that the separate departments of central government are considering new initiatives and have been reluctant to abandon past practices. The Conservative government announced a bonfire of 300 controls shortly after the 1979 election, but over the life of that government they were more than replaced both in number and significance. The same could easily happen again; what has been abolished could gradually be replaced.

Strong Local Leadership recognised the need for 'effective means'to be 'in place to minimise the imposition of new requirements'. The government was piloting 'a new policy evaluation tool – the Policy Effects Framework – which will seek to prevent the imposition of unnecessary burdens' (DTLR, 2001a, p. 46), which will presumably be used by the new Gateway, although there is no indication of the nature of the Framework and what authority the Gateway carries and how its conclusions will be imposed. The proposal for the Policy Effects Framework received less than half a page in a paper covering 139 pages, which hardly indicates that it was being given the importance required for effective action.

The Policy Effects Framework and the Gateway are unlikely to be sufficient to overcome the departmental forces that have led to the problems identified in *Strong Local Leadership*, unless given much more weight than in that document. *Strong Local Leadership* does not discuss how it was that what are now seen as obstacles to improving performance were instituted by central government. Until the problems that led to these obstacles are identified and dealt with, it is hard to believe the same factors will not be at play in the future or that the Policy Effects Framework and the Gateway will be sufficient to overcome them. The danger has been recognised by the government. It plans to put pressure on departments by creating local management centres in the Government Offices of the Region 'to focus on removing bureaucracy and challenging departments to improve local discretion over delivery' (ODPM, 2002e, para. 36). But pressure from the Government Offices is unlikely to be sufficient by itself to overcome the entrenched attitudes of central departments that are a major factor in creating the problems identified in *Strong Local Leadership*.

Command and control

There is a general problem in the government's approach to local government and to the modernisation programme. There has been little understanding of the problems of managing with and through other organisations and in particular of the management of change in an inter-organisational setting.

At times, it seems that the government knows no way to bring about change other than through a command and control approach that assumes only central government understands not merely what changes are required, but how they should be carried out. Central government legislates and regulates, expecting its requirements to be carried out, although it also develops mechanisms such as inspection and targets to enforce those requirements. The command and control approach leads to a problem not identified in *Strong Local Leadership* – over-prescription. There could be no clearer example of over-prescription than the government's approach to new political structures.

As pointed out in Chapter 4, the government legislated through the Local Government Act 2000, but in addition to the primary legislation it has issued over twenty regulations and directions, and guidance running to over 180 pages. There is something ludicrous in such detailed prescription drawn up largely by central government where there is still only limited practical experience of the workings of local authorities, despite recent steps to widen that experience. It may be that so much of the work of central government involves legislation and regulation that prescription, command and control are seen as the way to effect change.

The command and control approach is reinforced by what I have described as elite contempt for local authorities (Stewart, 2000a). Jones and Travers illustrate this attitude from interviews in central government: 'A number of ministers and civil servants appear to believe the quality of local government members is not as good as it used to be and not good enough by any standards. The mundane nature of many local government services appears to encourage (at least some) civil servants to believe that they possess "Rolls Royce minds, while local government officers have motor cyclists' minds"' (Jones and Travers, 1996, p. 101). Such views are based not on knowledge, but on distance from local authorities. Although not universal, those attitudes, reinforced by ministers' suspicions about the dominance of the traditional culture in many authorities, lead to both the over-prescription and the growth of inspection. It is feared that unless there is detailed prescription and inspection, authorities will find ways of evading the requirements of legislation or be incapable of implementing it without detailed guidance enforced by regulation. For too many in central government, command and control appears the only way to proceed in the management of change.

Dependence on a command and control approach can be self-defeating in the management of change. It assumes a degree of understanding of the circumstances in which change is to be carried through. That understanding does not often exist in departments at the centre. Command and control rarely allows for the diversity of local government that should be regarded as a strength to be nurtured. It gives little recognition to the scope for initiative and innovation at local level or even to the need to motivate those who have to carry through the changes sought by the centre. The need for effective organisational learning in central government departments is not acknowledged or is channelled into the necessarily limited perspective of inspectors rather than drawing fully on the learning of local authorities. The scope for learning from both the experience and ideas within local author-ities is limited by top-down approaches. Attempts to prescribe not merely the outcome but the detail of the means are likely to be counterproductive when tested by the reality of local circum-stances.

There are lessons to be learnt by central government on the management of change. The first is the need for involvement of those who have to carry out the change. Bottom-up should complement top-down. The second is to leave as much freedom as possible for innovation and initiative at local level. The third is that there are more effective instruments for the management of change than command and control. Government has valuable instruments through its ability to command attention and influ-ence in discourse. Social exclusion has received increasing atten-tion in many local authorities, not through command and control, but through the impact government reports and minis-terial speeches have had on public discourse. The fourth lesson is the need for a process of learning between authorities and the centre, drawing upon the diversity of local government.

Conclusion

The failure to consider the need for change in central–local relations was a severe weakness in the original modernisation programme. However the additional freedoms and flexibilities following *Strong Local Leadership* are a strength for that programme. Some of those freedoms and flexibilities are, how-ever, limited by the application of the principle of selectivity. That principle makes the approach of central government to individual authorities dependent on judgements about their performance, made largely by inspectors and assessors. Their judgements cannot be regarded as infallible and yet are treated as necessarily correct and on that basis the government rewards and penalises individual authorities, although it would not describe the process in that way. As already stressed in the con-clusion of Chapter 8, the consequences are that it can be more important for authorities to satisfy inspectors and assessors than their own electorate and that authorities' readiness to take initiatives in meeting local needs can be constrained, lest they meet with inspectoral disapproval. Second-guessing what an inspector might say is hardly a basis for innovation by authorities or for the local accountability necessary for effective local government.

Although the freedoms and flexibilities are useful as far as they go, the modernisation programme is still limited in dealing with the weaknesses in central–local relations and in the workings of central government. The lack of understanding of the management of change both generally and in the special circumstance of central–local relations is a basic weakness in the working of central government, reflected in the dominance of command and control in its approach to local government. The lack of joined-up government is another weakness, illustrated throughout this chapter by the failure to relate initiative to initiative or plan to plan, and the lack of any adequate overview or mapping of the impact of central government actions a further weakness. There has been no capacity to consider the overall impact on local authorities of a series of separate initiatives. Even where problems have been identified there is a lack of a clear point of authority to ensure action is taken to overcome them, hence the problems faced by the Office of the Deputy Prime Minister in securing action by departments on the limited proposals of *Strong Local Leadership*. A closely related weakness is the failure to consider the potential of changes in local government for the working of central government. The clearest example has been the failure to consider the full implications of the development of community planning for the various departments of central government. Community strategies could enable joined-up working in central government and provide a stimulus for organisational learning at the centre.

There has not been sufficient analysis as to why the government has made even those mistakes in central–local relations that were recognised in *Strong Local Leadership*. Analysis was not carried back from the problems of too many plans and initiatives or of unnecessary controls into the culture and structure of central government that generated these developments. As a result, little has fundamentally changed. This is shown by the failure to identify overdetailed prescription as a problem to be faced. Overdetailed prescription reflects attitudes that local authorities are not able of or cannot be trusted to work out for themselves the consequences when the general direction is given by legislation. Modernisation still has to have a full impact on central–local relations and on central government's understanding of the management of change. The stress on command and control limits local choice and reduces the capacity for diversity through innovation and initiative that should be one of the strengths of effective local government. The failure to recognise the need for fundamental change in central–local relations remains a major weakness in the modernisation programme.

The Conclusion of the book returns to the need for change in central–local relations. For the moment four points are sufficient. Local authorities know better than central government or inspectors and assessors how to achieve desired outcomes in their area. New means of learning are required by central government and by local authorities in dialogue with each other. Central government needs an overview of the cumulative impact of its measures on local authorities, with a capacity for action to overcome problems so highlighted. The most difficult and yet the most important change is for central government to recognise the limits of its understanding of the problems faced by local authorities and of their initiatives and successes as well as of their failures. It requires recognition that the centre does not necessarily know best and that about the actual workings of local authorities it barely knows anything at all.

12 Modernisation and Local Government Finance

The main themes of the modernisation programme raise critical issues for local government finance. Community leadership should focus attention on the mobilisation of resources for community needs; democratic renewal highlights the need for strong local financial accountability; and improving performance through best value requires the effective and efficient use of resources. Effective local government needs the support of a system of local government finance geared to its requirements. Local government finance should have been an integral part of the modernisation programme, guided by its principles of community leadership, democratic renewal and improving performance and by the need to build effective local government.

The Labour government rightly regarded local government finance as part of the modernisation programme but has not given it any priority. Although three of the original consultation papers and three chapters of *Modern Local Government* were devoted to the topic, legislation in the first term was limited to the renewal and modification of the capping powers described below. While legislation in the first term covered most other topics in *Modern Local Government*, the main legislation on local government finance was delayed, being subject to a further review with a Green Paper issued in 2000 (DETR, 2000e), leading in 2001 to *Strong Local Leadership* and the Local Government Bill introduced in December 2002, with the hope of enactment in 2003. Even that legislation is limited in scope, not covering the balance of funding available to local government. The failure to give priority to legislation on local government finance follows the neglect of central–local relations in the modernisation programme.

Local financial accountability and the balance of funding

Although legislation on local government finance has been introduced in the Local Government Bill, the government's approach remains limited because of failure to accept the need to strengthen local financial accountability by enhancing the tax base of local authorities.

The Layfield Report, *Local Government Finance*, argued that the then balance of funding between local taxation and government grant confused where responsibility lay for decisions on local government expenditure (Layfield Report, 1976), and without clarity on responsibility accountability is hard to enforce. At that time 66 per cent of relevant expenditure, net of fees and charges, was financed by government grant. By 1997, when the Labour government was elected, the percentage financed by grant had increased, due to changes brought about by the Conservative government. The domestic rates (a form of property tax on householders) had been replaced by the poll tax (a flat rate tax on each adult) which had then been replaced by the council tax (a modified form of property tax). During this period the non-domestic rates (a tax on other property) had been turned into a national tax, the proceeds of which were distributed as a grant to local authorities according to their population, making them more dependent on central government grant than ever before, weakening local financial accountability.

The present balance of funding distorts budgetary decisions and gives misleading signals to the electorate. In 1999/2000 about 74 per cent of relevant expenditure derived from the revenue support grant and the national non-domestic rate, both outside the control of local authorities. The only revenue (apart from fees and charges) under the control of the authority was the 26 per cent raised by the council tax. This causes the gearing effect, which, as the government itself pointed out, means that a 1 per cent increase in expenditure requires a 4 per cent increase in taxation. The gearing effect distorts budgetary decisions by magnifying the impact of increases or decreases in expenditure. Local financial accountability is weakened because misleading messages are given to the electorate who naturally believe that a 4 per cent increase in taxation means an equivalent increase in expenditure even though it has only increased by 1 per cent. Yet in *Modern Local Government*, it was said, 'Strengthening local financial accountability is vital. It is as important as creating new political structures and improving local democracy, if councils everywhere are to put their local communities and people first' (DETR, 1998a, p. 44). Transparency is a necessary condition of accountability and that condition is not met because of the distortion caused by the present balance of funding.

The balance of funding has an impact on central government too. It is commonplace for ministers and civil servants to argue that central government must inevitably be interested in control over local government expenditure when the majority of that expenditure is financed by central government. 'So long as central government remains the primary source of funding, it is inevitable the centre will exercise control' or 'Central government cannot stand aside when it supplies nearly 50 billion pounds and 74 per cent of local government expenditure' is the commonplace of discourse in central government.

The government has never accepted that there is any need to change the balance of funding, although a high-level working group has been announced to consider the issue implies that it is not completely ruled out. Representatives of the Department stated to a Select Committee of the House of Commons, 'The Government . . . cannot see that in terms of strengthening or weakening local accountability to local electors or the autonomy of local government is [*sic*] in spending its money it [the balance of funding] makes an enormous difference' (Select Committee on the Environment, Transport and Regional Affairs, 1998, Q28). That position has been reiterated on a number of occasions. In *Strong Local Leadership* the government stated that all its previous investigations had concluded that 'the balance of funding and the balance of control are separate issues'. Yet in the same section of the paper, the government argues that the gearing effect means that authorities are encouraged 'to look for ways of increasing their spending power by driving down costs, rather than pushing up taxes' (DTLR, 2001a, pp. 69–70). Surely that is an argument that the gearing effect caused by 'the balance of funding' affects the 'balance of control'.

Strong Local Leadership claimed there is little hard evidence for or against the view that the current balance of funding 'has an adverse impact on local authorities' autonomy' (DTLR, 2001a, p. 69). But the argument about the balance of funding is not necessarily about autonomy but about local accountability. Despite its views, but avowedly impressed by the weight of representations on the issue, the government is setting up the 'high-level working group involving Ministers and senior figures from local government, to look at all aspects of the balance of funding' (DTLR, 2001a, p. 70). The government does not, however, appear to be giving any priority to the issue.

A significant change in the balance of funding would require new sources of local taxation. At present the government has not made any proposals for a significant increase in local authority powers of taxation, although it has made powers available for road charging and parking levies by authorities as an element in its transport policies. The Layfield Report put forward proposals for a local income tax as well as a property tax. Many in local government have felt the Treasury would always oppose a local income tax. It is not, however, impossible that an imaginative chancellor of the exchequer might be attracted by the prospects of a reduction in the national level of income tax made possible by an equivalent reduction in grant, with much of the cost of current and increasing expenditure on local services borne by the local income tax. Local authorities might not all welcome the responsibility being placed on them, but that is what local financial accountability is all about.

The Local Government Association has pressed for the restoration of the non-domestic rate as a local tax rather than a national tax redistributed to local authorities on the basis of population. *Modern Local Government* contained proposals for local authorities to set a supplementary non-domestic rate (or to grant a rebate), albeit within strict limits. This arrangement was to be subject to broad agreement with the local business community on the process and on how the income was to be used. The government has not pursued these proposals because of opposition by business. The Local Government Bill does, however, include arrangements (based on experience in the United States) for a limited supplementary business rate to support schemes for business improvement districts (BIDs), if supported by a majority of relevant businesses in the area and agreed by the authority.

The government has maintained the council tax in its previous form, but has recognised criticism of its fairness. The council tax is a property tax based on the assessed capital value of domestic property. The council tax is levied at set rates on broad bands of property value. Unlike the previous domestic rates, the tax, while increasing with the value of the property bands, does not increase proportionately. A greater relative burden is imposed on lower-valued property and a lesser burden on higher-valued property. The upper band includes properties of very high value, which have thereby a relatively light burden. In so far as the value of property is related to the income of the household (as it is broadly, but not perfectly), the council tax in its present form discriminates against poorer families in favour of more affluent families. The government is to examine and consult on options for improving the fairness of the tax. The Local Government Bill allows for additional bands for higher-valued property, if and when it is decided to introduce them.

Capping

The government inherited the system of capping local authorities' expenditure introduced by the Conservative government. Legislation allowed the government to limit the expenditure of individual authorities if that expenditure or the increase in that expenditure was considered 'excessive' by the Secretary of State. The power had to be used in accordance with principles applicable to all authorities or to a specified class of authority.

The Secretary of State did not have to set out in advance the principles covering capping levels, but could determine the levels after considering the budgetary decisions made by authorities, creating uncertainty in authorities as to what they would be. Because of the uncertainty and the disruption caused by decisions made by the Secretary of State after the financial year had begun and council tax demands sent out, the local government associations successfully pressed the Secretary of State to announce the principles in advance. The associations probably failed to appreciate the full consequences of this change. The result was that after the Secretary of State announced the principles, most authorities effectively capped themselves to avoid the uncertainty and disruption of the capping process. The government did not have to face the political difficulty of capping, since authorities capped themselves. It is probable that capping was more severe than it would have been if the principles had continued to be set after authorities' budgetary decisions. If authorities could generally be relied upon to cap themselves, there were few political costs in setting severe capping levels – a very different situation from government imposing capping on agreed budgets and therefore cuts in budgeted expenditure.

The Labour government was committed in its 1997 manifesto to end 'crude and universal tax capping' (Labour Party, 1997, p. 34). If the alternative to crude capping were to be sophisticated capping, it was not clear authorities would welcome the change, since it could involve detailed investigation of an authority's finances. The reference to the abolition of universal capping has meant that the principles are no longer announced in advance. The government legislated to amend the capping powers by the Local Government Act 1999, enabling the Secretary of State to take account of the pattern of expenditure over a number of years in determining whether the level of or increases in expenditure were excessive.

Strong Local Leadership pointed out that the government had not used its capping powers for the last three years. It stated, 'Ideally our long-term goal is to dispense with the power to cap local authority budgets altogether' (DTLR, 2001a, p. 104). The government continues, however, to treat those powers as a threat, sometimes calling in for discussions authorities whose expenditure increases are considered to be verging on the excessive, as a warning for the future. Stephen Byers, the then Secretary of State, gave a general warning to authorities: 'There was no capping last year or the year before. But that doesn't mean that the Government is not taking very seriously our responsibility to local taxpayers. Hilary Armstrong said back in March that some of this year's council tax increases are disappointing. We are taking a very hard look at the steeper increases. I do have a range of powers which I can use' (Byers, 2001, p. 9). The government has, however, indicated that it will not use those powers against authorities categorised as excellent or good in the comprehensive performance assessment.

It has always been difficult to see the justification for capping. These powers have normally been described as powers to cap local authorities, but in reality they are powers to limit the choices open to local people. Local people cannot then decide through local elections that expenditure on services should be increased, even if they are willing to pay the taxation involved. Capping appears particularly inappropriate given the emphasis on the local authority's role in community leadership. Community leadership should mean that a local authority is able to raise resources from local taxation to meet community needs. Capping distorts the electoral process, limiting choice on budgetary policy.

A number of writers have argued there is no economic case for control over local authority expenditure covered by local taxation (Chisholm, 2001; Fender and Watt, 2002). Under the Conservative government the reasons for capping were not so much economic, but derived from a political commitment to reduce public expenditure generally. Stephen Byers stressed the government's responsibility to local taxpayers. Yet it is the local authority, not the government, that is directly responsible to local taxpayers for decisions on expenditure and on taxation. The Byers argument if acted upon would weaken that local financial accountability the government has said it wishes to strengthen. If central government intervenes to prevent a local authority from pursuing the expenditure policies for which it has been elected, it undermines the link between the local authority and the electorate that constitutes local accountability.

Defenders of capping argue that electoral accountability is weak because of low turnouts, but that is not an argument for weakening further the need to vote in local elections. It is also argued that there is no evidence that decisions on local taxation influence local election results. Research has shown the reverse is the case. Gibson summarised the evidence about the domestic rates and concluded that changes in the level of the rates had 'an important role in local elections' (Gibson, 1990, p. 163).

Although the Labour government has not used its capping powers recently, it introduced a measure which bore upon local authority budgetary decisions, making it more difficult to increase expenditure beyond a certain point. At that point the amount of council tax benefit subsidy paid by the government gradually reduced, throwing an increasing burden on local authorities. The gearing effect meant that any loss of grant had a disproportionate impact, making the point at which the reduction started to bite a quasi-cap on local authorities' expenditure decisions. This arrangement had a short life as the government has decided to abolish it, because of widespread opposition.

The government's insistence on maintaining its capping powers reflects a continuing concern for control over local government finance. That concern is reflected in the Local Government

Bill, which contains a new power to specify the minimum financial reserves that authorities would have to maintain in their budgets to cover contingencies (ODPM, 2002d). The government has not indicated any problems requiring such a power and, indeed, states, 'Our preference would be not to make use of these powers' (DTLR, 2001a, p. 134). The Select Committee's report on the draft bill pointed out, 'Some local councils may choose to operate with low levels of reserves – provided that they are prepared to take appropriate action as and when necessary', and therefore saw no need for the new power, recommending it should be removed from the bill (Select Committee on Transport, Local Government and the Regions, 2002b, pp. 13–14), although that has not been acted upon.

'Reforming' government grant

Modern Local Government identified the need for greater stability in government funding as necessary for local accountability:

> Stronger local financial accountability also depends on people understanding better the link between their council's spending decisions and the council tax bills which they have to face. People need to know easily where responsibility lies for council tax changes. It will be easier for them to see the effect of their council's decisions on their local tax bills, if there is stability year on year in the funding which government gives to councils. (DETR, 1998a, p. 46)

The government announced overall grant totals for the next three years and that the formulae used to calculate the grant would remain stable for that period, although not necessarily the data to which the formulae were applied. The government set up an investigation in partnership with local government into whether 'there is a better way of determining the distribution of revenue support grant which is simpler, more stable, more robust and fairer than the present arrangements' (ibid., p. 47).

The Labour government is not the first to seek a simpler, more stable, more robust and fairer system of distributing grant. It was never likely to be easy, given the nature of grant distribution. The system depended upon calculating for each authority its

standard spending assessment (SSA) – the government's calculation of its relative need for expenditure based on a set of formulae. After deducting from the SSA the money distributed from
the non-domestic rate, the amount of specific grants and the
amount that would be raised by a nationally assumed level of
council tax, the grant was then calculated for each authority. The
nature of the formulae for calculating SSAs was therefore critical
for each and every authority. The government inherited a system for calculating SSAs based on complex formulae, making it
difficult for authorities, never mind the public, to understand the
rationale for their grant.

Strong Local Government stated that the government regarded
the reform of the grant system as a priority. A consultation paper
was issued in 2002 setting out a range of options (ODPM, 2002b)
and the new grant system was introduced for 2003/4. The consultation paper restated the need for 'formulae that are fairer,
simpler; more intelligible and more stable' (ibid., p. 4). It pointed
out that the search for simplicity and intelligibility must 'be balanced against other pressures, including the technical merits of
particular options. So it may be the case that following consultation, the government decides that relatively complex formulae
give the most appropriate grant distribution' (ibid, p. 195) The
government argued that a distinction 'can be drawn between the
complexity of the formulae and the way it is presented' (ibid).

The 2003/4 settlement contains a new presentation, incorpo-
rating a new terminology with formula spending share (FSS)
replacing standard spending assessment (SSA). The grant presentation includes:

- a basic amount;
- a deprivation top-up;
- an area cost top-up; and
- other top-ups which can be up to six in number

for each of up to seven service blocks. The results are then added
together to arrive at an authority's FSS (ODPM, 2002b, p. 195).
Whether this would be seen as more intelligible must be doubted!
Nor would it satisfy anyone who wanted to know how the basic
allocation and top-ups were arrived at, which the grant settlement papers take over fifty pages to describe – hardly the simpler
formulae sought.

Stability can be achieved for a time by freezing changes in the formulae, as was done for the three years up to 2001/2. This has been extended by a further year and will be done again for the future. Freezing the formulae can mean that instead of gradual change a major change occurs at the end of the period. Complexity is then increased because transitional safety nets and ceilings on grant changes have to be introduced to prevent sudden major changes for individual authorities.

The problem of achieving simpler grants is increased by the degree of dependence on grants. The effect on an authority of getting the 'wrong' grant is multiplied by the gearing. If an authority loses grant because the formula is 2 per cent 'wrong' from its point of view, the authority has to increase its rate of tax by 8 per cent to cover a given level of expenditure. If the grant is 'wrong' (although the authority would never recognise it) in its favour by 2 per cent, then the authority can reduce its level of tax by the same 8 per cent. In practice errors are likely to be greater than 2 per cent, given the necessary imperfections of the process. The search for the Holy Grail of grant simplicity, combined with fairness, is never likely to be attained so long as local authorities remain so dependent on government grant.

There is a conflict between the search for a simple grant and the search for a fairer grant. Local authorities, while calling for simplicity and stability, still press for the inclusion of factors in the formulae that recognise their special needs. The complexity of the grant formula is not because anyone sought complexity, but because the government has felt under pressure to get 'better' and more refined ways of measuring need. The search for perfection in need assessment is the search for complexity and yet perfection is unattainable, because need can be and is contested, as illustrated by the different pressures from authorities and groups of authorities. There can be no totally objective assessment of the need for expenditure. Thus it is rightly assumed that the need for certain services is related to the extent of deprivation, but deprivation is a contested concept and the factors used to assess deprivation are inevitably subject to dispute.

The government's consultation paper on the grant system recognises these difficulties. 'Any system based on formulae cannot reflect all possible circumstances, so there will inevitably be an element of rough justice. This tends to increase as formulae are made simpler . . . Clearly the extremely technical nature of the issues means that there is frequently no clear-cut optimum solution. The government recognises that pragmatic decisions will be needed to produce a workable system' (ODPM, 2002b, p. 5). It is not just the 'extremely technical nature of the issues' that prevents an optimum solution being found. There cannot be an optimum solution when one is trying to assess need to spend. The government has made clear that it is not seeking 'absolute measurements of the need to spend', but 'since the system can only distribute the resources available' it must be based on comparisons between authorities (ibid.). That presumably rests on assessment of the comparative need to spend, which still depends on subjective judgement, since different values can always be placed on different needs and on factors affecting those needs. This is well illustrated by the wide range of options put forward in the consultation paper and by the differing responses of authorities.

The government has effectively abandoned the search for simplicity and with it what most would regard as intelligibility. Whether it will be seen as fairer will vary from authority to authority and hence in the long run stability is unlikely to be achieved. So long as authorities are still dependent on grant for so much of their income, too much is at stake for stability to be easily achieved as the pressures for change in any grant system will remain strong.

Ring-fencing and specific grants

The strength of the revenue support grant is as a general grant. Local authorities are largely free to determine how they allocate their revenue from the grant to different services, giving expression to their own assessment of local needs and aspirations. But not all the revenue support grant is allocated as a general grant, some being allocated as specific grants ring-fenced for particular purposes. The percentage of the total grant allocated in this way has grown from 5 per cent when the government was elected to 12 per cent in 2001/2 and was planned to increase to 15 per cent in 2003/4 (DTLR, 2001a, p. 71). The growth in ring-fenced specific grants was largely the result of the growth of the area-based initiatives described in the last chapter.

The more ring-fencing reduces the amount of general grant, the more restricted is the ability of the local authority to make its own decisions on the allocation of resources and the more the resource allocation process is fragmented. Fragmentation is increased when as is often the case specific grants require matching funding, which has either to be taken out of the general grant or met by local taxation.

Strong Local Leadership recognised the problems caused by the growth of ring-fenced specific grants and proposed to reverse the upward trend in their number and amount. It stated that in future they would be restricted to major government priorities and even then only introduced when the government's aims cannot be attained by other means. Any new such grants introduced were to be time-limited and would normally not require matched funding (DTLR, 2001a, p. 71). Whether good intentions will be sufficient to withstand the departmental pressures that led to the increase in specific grants remains uncertain. Indeed good intentions have already been undermined by the government taking reserve powers in the Education Act 2002 to direct a local authority to set a budget for expenditure on education at no less than a level determined by the Secretary of State, which would effectively ring-fence not merely part of the revenue support, but also the allocation of revenue from local taxation. It is now stated that ring-fenced grants will be reduced to below 10 per cent of the total grant by 2005/6 – a rather slow and limited reduction, although authorities categorised as excellent will have all ring-fencing removed, except for grants passed to schools.

While arguing for a reduction in specific ring-fenced grants, the government stated it saw a case for targeted grants. The distinction is not entirely clear. A targeted grant may be paid to particular authorities and 'will be a named grant intended for a specific purpose' (DTLR, 2001a, p. 78). It will not, however, be ring-fenced so that it has to be spent in a defined way. The neighbourhood renewal grant and grants paid as rewards for achieving the targets set in public service agreements were given as examples. The distinction appears to be that while targeted grants remain specific grants having a defined purpose, they are not required to be spent in a specific way.

The government rejected a form of targeted grants put forward for consideration in the Green Paper on *Local Government*

Finance (DETR, 2000e). That paper suggested part of the revenue support grant should be awarded according to the government's judgement on policy plans prepared by authorities. If implemented it would have been another application of the principle of selectivity. The danger of this proposal was that it could have made it seem more important to local authorities to satisfy central government on their plans than to satisfy the local electorate. Even if only 5 per cent of the grant had been allocated on this basis, the gearing effect would have meant it had a 20 per cent impact on local taxation, almost overwhelming other factors in the budgetary process.

The government concluded in *Strong Local Leadership* that although it could still see arguments for plan-based grants this 'level of central government's judgement over local budgets is incompatible with our vision of local government rather than local administration' (DTLR, 2001a, p. 78). The arguments that persuaded the government could be used against other developments. Thus PSAs could equally be regarded as turning local authorities into 'local administration' of government policies, local authorities receiving rewards in grants when they meet certain targets for central government priorities.

As well as ring-fencing through specific grants, there has been a growth of informal ring-fencing which has been practised to a greater or lesser extent by ministers who claim that resources allocated in the general grant because of the needs of a specific service should all be used for that service. These views are backed by implied threats that the authority will suffer in the future if it does not heed the minister's views. This tendency has been carried furthest in education with demands under both the previous Conservative government and the Labour government that the whole of any increase in SSAs (now FSSs) be 'passported' to the schools by the local authority. Many authorities were spending above their SSA for education and did not see why they should necessarily passport the whole of the government's additional amount to education rather than to other services regarded as relatively underfunded. In 2003 the Government threatened it could use its powers to enforce passporting on Westminster and Croydon even though they have been categorised under the comprehensive performance assessment as respectively excellent and good authorities and promised new freedoms and flexibilities.

Service SSAs became known to councillors and officers, as FSSs will now also become known, and to groups in the community who put pressure on any authority spending less than SSAs on the services with which they are concerned. This tendency to regard SSAs or FSSs as measuring rods gives them a status not justified by their uncertain methodology and threatens the ability of local authorities to make their own judgements. In presenting the proposed 2003/4 grant settlement, the minister said:

> One of the problems with the old SSA system was that it attempted to take a view on what authorities needed to spend. That was unrealistic, and inconsistent with the approach to devolving responsibilities, so we will not continue the arrangements. Notional spending allocations do not imply anything about the budget or spending choices that will need to be made. Councils in consultation with their council tax payers should properly take those decisions. (House of Commons, 5 December 2002, col. 1065/6)

Whether everybody, including the government and especially departmental ministers, accepts that reality for the new FSSs remains to be seen. The government certainly continues to make an exception to this principle in respect of education where they continue to expect authorities to 'pass on increases to schools' (Col. 1066), irrespective of how much they are already spending.

Fees and charges

Although the government is not committed to an extension of the taxation powers of local authorities, it is introducing changes 'not aimed at shifting the balance of funding, but at broadening the sources of revenue available to authorities from fees and charges and from penalties, and giving them greater freedom to decide how these revenues are spent' (DTLR, 2001a, p. 120). The Local Government Bill allows local authorities to charge for a discretionary service including those provided under the powers of community well-being, provided the amount raised does not exceed the cost of the service. The government will also allow all local authorities to retain and use for environmental purposes the revenue from fines for litter and for dog fouling as well as extending the possible use of parking fines for environmental work. It will give wider powers of this type to excellent and good authorities.

The government is extending local authority powers to trade, although the principle of selectivity limits the extent of that freedom. 'Councils should be able to trade in any service in which they have a strong performance on delivery. High-performers should be able to trade across the full range of their services' (DTLR, 2001a, p. 121). Previously the power to trade was restricted by the Local Authorities (Goods and Services Act) 1970 to trade with other local authorities and specified public bodies. Where the power is extended it will cover trade with the private and voluntary sectors as well as the public sector generally. The powers to trade are included in the Local Government Bill, which requires that authorities exercise them through a company.

These changes will not have a significant impact on an authority's financial position, but will significantly extend its scope for action – particularly the power to charge for discretionary services, and thus cover all or part of their costs.

Changes in capital finance

The most significant change in local government finance is in capital finance. *Modern Local Government* proposed the creation of 'a single capital pot' for the allocation of capital grants to authorities:

> At present a number of service-specific funding arrangements are used to allocate capital resources to councils. The trend over recent years has been on increasing use of allocation for restricted purposes and a consequent reduction in block allocations that can be used flexibly to meet a range of spending priorities.
>
> The Government will introduce a cross-service allocation for the bulk of central government capital support to councils – a single capital pot. (DETR, 1998a, p. 85)

The government argued that this capital pot would give authorities greater flexibility to make their own decisions and thereby increase 'local accountability and autonomy'. However, a single capital pot 'could not be implemented overnight' (ibid.) partly because it required a means of assessing need as a basis for allocating the pot between authorities and it was not introduced until 2002/3. It was inevitable that central government departments would be reluctant to see 'their' allocations disappear into a single pot and in the first year just under half the capital resources were distributed through the single capital pot, although the amount so distributed will increase to at least 60 per cent in 2003/4, and will cover all capital grants in authorities categorised as excellent or good.

Modern Local Government emphasised that the government's overall priorities should not be jeopardised by this change. Reference was made to the New Deal for Schools as an example of such a priority. These were, however, not arguments for delay, but arguments against a single capital pot. If it is the New Deal this year, it will be something else next year. This argument assumes a command and control model. It is thought that unless compelled to do so, authorities will have no regard to central government priorities. The reverse is probably true as central government priorities provide a powerful argument in authority discussions on resource allocation and can command attention without the paraphernalia of detailed controls and allocations. Influence is an underestimated instrument in central–local relations, although it is an instrument stressed by the government in discussing local authorities' own role in community leadership.

The government originally proposed that while some of the capital pot would be allocated according to a needs-based formula, some of it would be allocated by a 'competitive assessment of councils' services and corporate capital strategies and their performance in delivering them' (DETR, 1998a, p. 80). The principle of selectivity would have been at work, raising again issues about the basis of central government's judgements and the weakening of local accountability, but these proposals have not been implemented to any significant extent. In the first year only 5 per cent of the pot has been allocated in this way with the remainder distributed through a needs-based formula, but the selective element could grow in future years.

Much capital expenditure by local authorities is not financed by government grants, but by borrowing, which has been controlled by central government. The most significant change proposed in *Strong Local Leadership* was the replacement of that control by a new 'prudential system'. That system is introduced by the Local Government Bill and is intended to give local authorities freedom to borrow subject to 'prudential limits' on the extent of that borrowing. Authorities will set these limits after taking account of existing borrowing and future revenue. They will have a duty to determine and keep under review the amount of their affordable borrowing limit.

The change could mean an important increase in local financial accountability, although the government is taking reserve powers in the Local Government Bill to set a limit on the level of borrowing 'for national economic reasons', and to ensure that a particular authority 'does not borrow more than it can afford'. The bill allows the government to prescribe in detail how authorities should set the limits based on the Prudential Code produced by the Chartered Institute of Public Finance and Accountancy (ODPM, 2002d). The powers proposed for regulations covering these and other issues mean that the suggested freedoms could prove limited in practice.

A search for resources

One feature of local government finance, inherited in part from the Conservative government, has been the growing importance of sources of funds that are outside the main central government allocation processes. These are not merely the area-based initiatives and ring-fenced grants or the PFIs and PPPs discussed earlier in the book but include lottery funds and European funds. These are normally time-limited, require matching funds, can involve partnerships and are likely to have monitoring procedures associated with them. At a time when authorities feel themselves heavily constrained by a lack of resources, these funds assume an importance not otherwise justified by the amounts involved. The projects for which funds are available are not necessarily the authorities' own priorities, yet they have often involved authorities finding matching funds and funds to replace the external funding when the project comes to an official end.

There are skills involved in seeking these funds. Some authorities have gained considerable expertise in grantmanship or the art of preparing and negotiating proposals to maximise the chance of success. Time and effort are required. Bids have to be prepared, negotiations undertaken, partnerships formed and maintained, monitoring procedures observed and preparations made for any follow-through. Considerable work is involved for projects that may be of less importance to the authority than other projects that are not able to attract funds.

PFIs and PPPs were discussed in Chapter 8. Their importance to local authorities is that they often appear to be the only way that necessary capital expenditure can be undertaken, given the limitations on borrowing. Both share with the other sources of funds the extent of time and effort required and the importance of expertise; indeed these are probably greater with these approaches. PFIs and PPPs also commit the authority to continuing financial obligations, replacing the interest or more than the interest the authority would have had to meet if it had financed the project itself, and in some cases continuing operational expenditure. Flexibility for the future is limited by such commitments.

All these developments occupy much of the time of senior staff, with the result that the projects may receive more attention than work directly financed by the authority. These projects can constrain authorities for the future, committing funds over time. The cumulative impact of these developments has often been too little appreciated in central government, although the stated intention to control the growth of area-based initiatives and ring-fenced grants shows it is now beginning to be realised in some, but, one suspects, not in all departments.

Conclusion

Whereas legislation has been introduced to implement most of the modernisation programme, the proposals on local government finance still await implementation, although the Local Government Bill brings this nearer. Some of the proposals on local government finance required detailed investigation, although the same point could and probably should have been made about the new political structures. The delay has meant the separation of financial issues from the main modernisation programme, implying they did not have the same urgency and that the programme could apparently be implemented without major change in local government finance. Even after the introduction of the Local Government Bill many of the proposals are unlikely to be implemented until 2004, six years after the publication of *Modern Local Government* and seven years after the election of the Labour government. The failure to modernise local government finance has limited the achievement of the potential of the modernisation programme. Yet *Modern Local Government* stated that 'modern councils fit for the 21st century . . . are built on a culture of openness and accountability' (DETR, 1998a, p. 12) and stressed the importance of local financial accountability.

The recognition of the importance of local financial accountability was the strength of the modernisation programme; the weakness lies in the limited nature of the measures taken as well as in the delay in introducing them. The Local Government Bill makes a contribution to strengthening local financial accountability through the changes in relation to capital expenditure, but the bill reflects the tension between that avowed aim and engrained attitudes of command and control, accompanying as it does the new arrangements with new powers of government intervention.

The most serious weakness in the government's changes in local government finance is that there are no significant proposals for strengthening local financial accountability for revenue expenditure. The government has not faced up to the problems for accountability caused by the extreme dependence of authorities on central government grant. This chapter has shown how the gearing effect distorts the messages to the electorate conveyed by authorities' budgetary decisions. *Strong Local Leadership* signalled at least a new willingness to review the balance of funding, but does not connect the issue to local financial accountability, recognised as being at the heart of the modernisation programme when it was first outlined. So long as this issue is not faced there is a major gap in the modernisation programme and a limitation on building effective local government.

13 Conclusion

Strengths and weaknesses of the modernisation programme

As stressed in Chapter 1, the book is based on recognition of the importance of effective local government in the government of a complex and changing society. Local government has a value in its own right but also has a value within the whole system of government, building learning within that system through its capacity for diversity. The system of government, to be effective, has to maintain a balance between uniformity and diversity. There will always be arguments about where the balance should properly be struck, but local government had become more an agency for local administration of national services than the local government of the community. Even in that role as agency, continuing processes of centralisation had weakened local government and strengthened the forces for uniformity, reducing critically the scope for local choice on which the capacity for diversity depends. The challenge for the modernisation programme was to build effective local government with the capacity to respond to the diversity of communities, to relate policy to local circumstance and for innovation and initiative.

The main themes assessed

Judged by the requirements of effective local government, as set out in Chapter 1, the modernisation programme has strengths but also weaknesses and both are reflected in the three main themes. Community leadership strengthens local government. The powers of community well-being and the duty of community planning enhance the capacity to recognise diversity and to develop initiatives. There remain doubts whether central government has recognised the implication of the development of community planning for its own workings. Democratic renewal strengthens local government, based as it is on local democracy. It can build an active relationship between authorities and their citizens, strengthening the basis of local government and its role in community leadership. The stress on democratic renewal was a clear strength of the modernisation programme, but its weakness is its focus on new political structures, whose contribution to democratic renewal is at best uncertain. The emphasis on improving performance given by best value is a strength, enhancing local authorities' capacity to meet community needs effectively. The weaknesses have been the focus on who delivers rather on how needs are best met and the emphasis on targets and performance measures as ends in themselves both in best value and in local public service agreements, rather than as a means of understanding performance.

The limitations of the modernisation programme

The most striking gap in the modernisation programme and a significant weakness was the failure to recognise the need to modernise central–local relations, or even to consider them in the original programme. As the modernisation programme has developed over time, the principle of selectivity has emerged as a defining principle in central–local relations, distinguishing through the comprehensive performance assessment the relationship between local authorities and individual authorities according to categories based on their performance. The application of the principle depends upon external assessment of each authority and that assessment inevitably depends upon judgement. Central government does not have sufficient knowledge to make that judgement itself and has to base its approach mainly on the judgements of inspectors and assessors, relying on the suspect assumption of inspectoral infallibility. That judgement can weaken local accountability by substituting external judgements for judgement by local citizens, while the basis for those judgements can be and has been challenged. The comprehensive performance assessment can lead on to intervention by central government in some authorities and a wider involvement in authorities by central government relationship managers, representing an emphasis on external action rather than action by effective local government based on strong local democracy.

The modernisation programme has also been limited because of the failure to accept that radical change was required in local government finance. Not only was change in local government finance not seen as a priority, being left largely to the second term, but even then the importance of strengthening the local authority base of local taxation has not been recognised, important though it is in strengthening local accountability.

Although the modernisation programme as originally set out did not directly cover central–local relations, those relations have been affected by other measures taken by central government departments outside the programme and often without regard to it. The commitment to reorganisation of local government associated with proposals for regional assemblies could distract attention from the modernisation programme and improving performance. There has been a proliferation of area-based initiatives tied to ring-fenced grants and a growth in centrally required plans, which with the parallel growth in the number of inspectors and inspections can absorb the time of councillors and officers as well as weakening local authorities' capacity for joined-up government through the fragmentation of resource allocation and planning processes. The government recognises the need to reduce these burdens, but it remains to be seen how strongly that commitment is maintained over time under the pressure of central departments.

Strong Local Leadership contains the statement on central–local relations that was missing from earlier presentations of the modernisation programme. 'Central and local government have a common interest: improving people's quality of life. The ability of local government to play its part in this joint endeavour is affected, in part, by the way in which central government seeks to influence its action. In the past, too little importance has been attached to the relationship, and how well it works' (DTLR, 2001a, p. 56). The recognition of the need for change is welcome, but the paper does not recognise that change in the relationship requires change in the workings and attitudes of central government and its departments. If there is a single lesson to be drawn from this book, it is that the modernisation programme will not achieve its full potential unless there is a change in the central–local relations and in the workings of central government.

The management of change

Throughout the book, issues have been raised about the way the modernisation programme has been implemented. The government's approach to the management of change has been curiously old-fashioned, being based more on command and control, and marked out by over-prescription, a narrow focus on targets and the use of inspection, rather than on approaches that involve central and local government together in shared learning as one would expect from a modernisation programme. The dependence on command and control is a major limitation on the effectiveness of the programme.

Different analyses lead to different approaches to the management of change. There is clearly a difference between an approach that encourages change by holding up a few authorities as examples to be followed and an approach that, while encouraging authorities to learn from others, encourages all authorities to build on their own good practice. The latter approach will normally be more effective than the former; yet it is the former that the government has preferred to follow.

Because of its assumption about the dominant culture and about the excellent few set apart from the general mass of authorities, the government failed to recognise the extent to which the themes of the modernisation programme were already of concern to many in local government. Far from past cultures being unchanged, local government had been and is a significantly changing institution. Some of the changes were imposed on local authorities by, for example, the legislation on compulsory competitive tendering. Even those authorities opposed to the legislation had to review their ways of working. Financial constraints and cut-backs meant that authorities had to consider 'how to get more out of available resources'. The extent to which local authorities changed under the impact of the Conservative government's policies meant that assumptions about an unchanging culture were seriously misleading. More significant, however, are the changes brought about by local authorities themselves. *The Nature of British Local Government* (Stewart, 2000a) sets out the extent of that change. There had been a major change in management ideas as the New Public Management began to influence local authorities. Local authorities developed strategic plans within which management responsibilities were devolved based on performance targets. A new emphasis was placed on customer care. Local authorities had faced directly the challenges of a changing society.

The impact of legislation, developing approaches to public management and changes in society had already led authorities to pursue the themes that were to be given expression in the modernisation programme. Local authorities saw the need for community leadership in facing the problems of both urban and rural society within the fragmented structure of governance at local level. Ideas about best value had developed in local government as an alternative to the rigidities of compulsory competitive tendering. Local authorities recognised the need for democratic renewal to establish positive relations with the public as citizens as well as recognising the relationship with the public as customers.

The government's enunciation of the themes of the modernisation programme provided a new opportunity in central–local relations, because they reflected a shared perspective between local and central government which could have been built on. Yet, because of its suspicions of local authorities and its views about the dominant culture, the government pursued approaches to the management of change that worked against the grain of effective change. What was required was legislation to enable the development of those themes by local authorities, and a strategy for implementation based upon recognition of a shared sense of direction within which local authorities could develop their own initiatives.

The government's approach to implementation assumed change had to be imposed on reluctant local authorities. Ministers adopted a style of advocacy that was often counterproductive. Instead of grounding the modernisation programme in the existing direction of change in local government, the emphasis was placed on the perceived weaknesses of the dominant culture without any recognition that it also had strengths. Ministers appeared to see themselves as missionaries preaching to the heathen, failing to appreciate that their themes were widely accepted in authorities. It was remarkable to hear a minister advocating as a new approach that councillors should play a representative role meeting their constituents and contacting community groups. Councillors in the audience could hardly believe their ears, as even within the so-called traditional culture that was hardly a new approach.

The overall position

None of this analysis means that the modernisation programme in England should be condemned. That would be to treat the programme in the same way as its advocates treated the dominant culture, seeing only weaknesses and ignoring strengths. It has already been argued that the key themes are welcome. Much of the legislation through which it is expressed is helpful in principle, if not always in detail or in practice. Its limitations and weaknesses must be recognised if effective local government is to be built, as must the need for change in central–local relations and in the government's approach to the management of change.

There are lessons to be learnt from Scotland and Wales. There has been greater flexibility in the application of best value, much less emphasis on the principle of selectivity and in Scotland the avoidance of prescription on political structures and in Wales wider opportunities for alternative arrangements. The management of change in Scotland and Wales is less dependent on command and control. In Wales research suggests 'there is a striking contrast with English central–local relations where central government is more remote from local authorities and Labour Ministers do not see local authorities as an important constituency' (Laffin *et al.*, 2002, p. vii). Similar research in Scotland found that the Scottish Executive was perceived as more open and ready to listen than the Scottish Office had been before devolution (Bennett *et al.*, 2002, p. vi), while the relationship with the Scottish Parliament was viewed even more favourably (ibid., p. 19). In both countries there remain problems of central–local relations, but a greater recognition that effective management change must involve centre and locality working together–a recognition needed in England.

A changing local government

Change is required in central–local relations and in the workings of central government, but change is also required in local government to realise the strengths of the modernisation programme, to overcome its weaknesses and to build effective local government. Authorities need to give a greater emphasis to the role of community leadership and to make greater use of the powers of community well-being, as these represent major advances in the role of local government and in its ability to meet community needs. Democratic renewal must move beyond the focus on political structures towards a focus on the involvement of citizens in the workings of the authority when acting both by itself and with its partners. Political structures must be reviewed to ensure an effective role for all councillors and to maximise the opportunities for innovation. On best value what has been in danger of becoming a burdensome routine could become a continuing focus on service improvement. There is a need to develop management approaches that sustain the distinctive purposes, conditions and tasks of the public domain and of local government in particular.

Most of these changes are within the scope of local authorities and their present powers. There remains the issue of whether there is a need for further legislation and further developments in government policy. There is a good argument for no further changes in legislation or regulation and for no new initiatives in government policy towards local government. There are times when it is better to do nothing and let past changes develop through experience. There is a restlessness in the modernisation programme that can make past changes out of date before they have had a chance to achieve their potential.

While it is right to pose the possibility of no change, there are areas where the modernisation programme is incomplete. The proposals in the Local Government Bill to extend the right of local authorities to charge and to trade are necessary if the powers of community well-being are to be fully used. The powers of well-being should be matched by a relaxation of central government control over by-laws as a further means of realising community well-being. Freedoms and flexibilities should be extended beyond the selected few.

A major remaining gap in the modernisation programme is in local government finance where legislation was delayed. Effective local government grounded in local accountability requires a system in which changes in expenditure level match to a much greater extent changes in local taxation. The government should accept the need to widen the tax base of local government, recognising that excessive grant dependence weakens local accountability. The Local Government Association has urged the government to restore the non-domestic rate as a local tax, with decisions on its level tied to decisions on the level of the council tax. There are issues, however, about whether the restoration of the non-domestic rate would enhance local financial accountability, since the incidence does not necessarily fall on the local electorate, although failing any alternative it would go far to overcome the gearing effect.

One alternative would be to allow local authorities to levy a series of minor taxes such as the tourist taxes commonly found in Europe. Local government in the United Kingdom is almost unique in Europe in having only one local tax, with the result that it will always seem unfair to those on whom the tax bears. The issue is whether minor taxes would make sufficient difference to the gearing effect. If there were a real commitment to strengthening local accountability and responsibility, then there is a strong case – as recommended by the Layfield Report – for a system of local government finance based on a property tax (the council tax) and a local income tax. The modernisation programme strengthens the case for such a change. If community leadership is to be meaningful, then local authorities must be given greater freedom to raise the financial resources to meet community needs and to be accountable locally for their decisions. Without radical legislation on local government finance, the modernisation programme remains incomplete.

A further gap in the modernisation programme is the need to make the electoral system more representative of the diversity of political views through the introduction of a system based on proportional representation. While arguments for the introduction of proportional representation at national level are contested, the case at local level needs separate consideration. The relative social and economic homogeneity of many local authority areas can lead to the creation of what are virtually one-party states, sometimes without that party even obtaining a majority of the votes. There are authorities in which the opposition parties have only one or two seats, or even at times no seats at all. It is hard to see how effective community leadership can be built on such an unrepresentative base. If proportional representation were to be introduced, it would be important to retain ward representatives as a strong link between the authority and local communities. This could be achieved by the added member system used for elections to the Scottish Parliament, the Welsh Assembly and the London Assembly, and proposed for regional assemblies. In Scotland such an approach has been suggested by the Scottish Executive.

Ideally, although not, I fear, realistically, the comprehensive performance assessment and related developments should be recognised as fundamentally flawed and withdrawn. The new political structures should become discretionary rather than prescriptive. Once established and past patterns broken, the new structures should stand on their merits and much greater change and innovation made possible. There is a need to confront the lack of a clear relationship between local appointed boards and local communities. The local authority could play a role in introducing a degree of local accountability, giving a new emphasis within community leadership. All local appointed boards should be under a statutory requirement to have regard to the community strategy. The overview and scrutiny role, building on the responsibilities for health, could help appointed boards and local authorities explore together the implications of the strategy. Local authorities could be given rights of appointment on local boards. Local boards could be required to submit their policies and budgets for appraisal or even approval by the local authority. These new powers would recognise the significance of the community leadership role, not merely for local authorities, but for all public bodies at local level.

Earlier I suggested the need for a no-change approach to be considered. It will be seen from what followed that I am an advocate of limited or no change except for the changes I favour!

Changing central–local relations and a changing central government

The key issue remains change in the central–local relationship with its implications for the working of central government. The problems that have to be overcome are

- the model of command and control leading to over-prescription, over-inspection and over-regulation;
- the lack of joined-up government leading to a failure to consider the full impact of the modernisation programme for departments or the interrelationship between different initiatives;
- the absence of any adequate overview of developments in central–local relations, so that there has been little consideration of the overall impact of central government action upon local authorities; and

- attitudes in the culture of central government that prevent a recognition of the strengths of local government and of its councillors and officers.

These problems reflect negatives to be overcome. There are positives to be realised in a new basis for central–local relations. The argument for change in central government and in central–local relations is not merely to strengthen local government, but to strengthen the overall system of government. Effective local government can be the means of learning in government. Its capacity for diversity, which its basis in local elections legitimates, can be an important source of initiative and innovation. Its myriad of contacts in the locality can build understanding at national level if there is an effective means of learning at local level and of learning from local government at national level. If means were sought for the too little recognised need for democratic renewal at national level, the role of local government as an arena for citizen involvement could become more important if central government can learn to draw upon it. Some of the principles on which such a relationship could be built can be outlined, both overcoming the negatives and realising the positives of central–local relations.

There is a need for the centre to step back from detailed prescription. Nothing is more ridiculous than the almost endless pages in which central government seeks to prescribe every detail of the new political structures. Legislation and regulation should wherever possible be based on stating key directions, but should not set out the detailed route. Of course, realism suggests there will be exceptions, but that is what they should be – exceptions.

Central government should seek new means of dialogue with individual authorities: a very different dialogue from the necessary and important dialogue with the Local Government Association. Public Service Agreements offer one possibility, but are restricted by the narrow focus on targets. The relationship managers associated with the follow-up to comprehensive performance assessments may appear to provide a basis for dialogue, but it is a one-sided dialogue so long as it is set in the context of central government oversight. Much more valuable would be dialogue focused on community strategies, so that central government could both learn from and respond to the policies, priorities and directions seen as important at local level, not merely by local authorities but also by their partners. Such dialogue would raise issues that cannot be dealt with on a narrow departmental basis, since the strategies reflect views grounded in a community perspective. Consideration of the implications of community strategies within central government should be on a similar cross-service and community basis to that on which they will have been prepared locally. Community strategies can be a means for building joined-up government, not merely locally but at national level.

The government has recognised the need to restrain the proliferation of plans and of area-based initiatives. The stated intention is not enough, unless the factors that led to this proliferation are faced. Unless that is done, good intentions will not last long as new pressures for plans and initiatives grow in departments. It is necessary to ensure there is a continuing overview of the impact of central government actions upon authorities. Proposals for new initiatives should be evaluated not merely on their own merits but against that background, and their cumulative impact assessed and considered. Such evaluation will not easily be achieved and enforced in a system of central government grounded in departmentalism. There is a need to ensure that there is authority within central government to enforce conclusions from that evaluation. Change is required in the relationship between the departments concerned with the services provided by local authorities. There have already been indications of resistance by departments to the policies set out in *Strong Local Leadership* for new freedoms and flexibilities for authorities. One department needs clear responsibility and authority for the relationship between central government and local authorities: a responsibility and an authority beyond that currently held by the Office of the Deputy Prime Minister or that seems likely to be achieved by the new Gateway.

The role of the inspectorates should be reviewed to ensure a reduction in the burden of time and effort imposed upon local authorities and much greater clarity as to the basis on which judgements are made. The main change required, however, is a change in what is expected of inspectors. Their main role should be as partners in shared learning rather than as commissars. The doctrine of inspectoral infallibility must be challenged.

There is a need for improved training and development of inspectors to inculcate an attitude of learning, rather than of knowing. Some of the precepts that should underlie these processes are:

- There is no one right approach.
- A deviation from accepted good practice may represent better practice and is to be welcomed, rather than condemned.
- There will always be reasons why an authority acts in a certain way and   the inspector must gain understanding of those reasons.
- The inspector is likely to learn more from the inspection than the authority.
- A degree of humility is better than an assumed authority in the inspector.
- Inspectoral failure is always a possibility.

The process of inspection should itself be subject to inspection – with inspectors drawn from the ranks of the inspected. That process of inspection of inspections should not be seen as any more infallible than inspections themselves. Humility is again better than assumed authority.

Change in the attitudes of civil servants is required and will not be easily achieved. There is a need for them to appreciate the limitations of their experience and understanding of community issues and to learn the value of the experience and understanding of those in local authorities who confront those problems directly both in urban and in rural areas. Dialogue on community strategies could contribute to that appreciation. Deepening the experience of civil servants dealing with local government and its services would enhance their understanding. It should be the normal rule that nobody holds such a position without working experience in local government, either in their normal career development or on secondment for periods of at least two or more years. Career movement and secondments from local authorities into central government should match this development so that on both sides there is shared experience. Such movement is developing but at too slow a rate, so that it remains the exception rather than the normal pattern. The need is for both central and local government to learn from and about each other and that applies to ministers and MPs as much as the civil service, involving much-needed changes in attitude.

The government has to recognise the importance for its own effectiveness of the development of community strategies. If fully developed, these strategies can provide the basis for work between partners at local level and local communities, and give expression to citizen involvement. These strategies can then provide a rich resource for learning in central government. On that basis central government can develop holistic government and can build on local community involvement, leading to a new style of governing and a new basis for central–local relations reflecting that style.

In the final resort the modernisation programme for local government will only be successful when it is appreciated that it is as much about change in central government as in local government. The key change required is the recognition that the diversity made possible by effective local government is necessary for the effectiveness of the overall system of government. On that basis a learning government can be built for the learning society required to meet the challenges of the present and the future.

Bibliography

Audit Commission (1990) *We Can't Go On Meeting Like This* (London: Audit Commission).

—— (1997) *Representing the People: The Role of Councillors* (London: Audit Commission).

—— (2001a) *Changing Gear: Best Value Annual Statement 2001* (London: Audit Commission).

—— (2001b) *Waste Management: The Strategic Challenge* (London: Audit Commission).

—— (2002a) *Delivering Comprehensive Performance Assessments: Consultation Draft* (London: Audit Commission).

—— (2002b) *The Comprehensive Performance Assessment Framework for Single Tier and County Councils* (London: Audit Commission).

—— (2002c) *Guidance for Authorities on the Corporate Assessment Process: Consultation Draft* (London: Audit Commission).

—— (2002d) *Self-assessment: The Guidance* (London: Audit Commission).

—— (2002e) *Guidance for Single Tier and County Councils on the Corporate Assessment Process* (London: Audit Commission).

—— (2003) *PFIs in Schools* (London: The Audit Commission).

Bains Report (1972) *The New Local Authorities: Management and Structure* (London: HMSO).

Baldersheim, H. and Stahlberg, K. (1994) *Towards the Self-Regulating Municipality* (Aldershot: Dartmouth).

Barron, J., Crawley, G. and Wood, T. (1991) *Councillors in Crisis: the political and Private Worlds of Local Councillors* (London: Macmillan – now Palgrave Macmillan).

Bennett, M., Fairley, J. and McAteer, M. (2002) *Devolution in Scotland* (York: York Publishing Services).

Blair, P. (1991) 'Trends in Local Autonomy and Democracy: Reflections from a European Perspective', in R. Batley and G. Stoker (eds), *Local Government in Europe* (London: Macmillan – now Palgrave Macmillan).

Blair, T. (1998) *Leading the Way: A New Vision for Local Government* (London: Institute of Public Policy Research).

Bloch, A. (1992) *The Turnover of Councillors* (York: Joseph Rowntree Foundation).

Brown, A., Jones, A. and Mackay, F. (1999) *The Representativeness of Councillors* (York: Joseph Rowntree Foundation).

Bullman, H. and Page, E. (1994) 'Executive Leadership in German Local Government', in Joseph Rowntree Foundation, *Local Leadership and Decision-Making* (York: Joseph Rowntree Foundation).

Byatt, Sir Ian and Lyons, Sir Michael (2001) *Role of External Review in Improving Performance* (London: Public Service Productivity Panel).

Byers, S. (2001) *Speech to the Local Government Association Annual General Meeting* (London: DTLR Press Release).

Cabinet Office (1999) *Modernising Government* (Norwich: The Stationery Office).

—— (2001) *A New Commitment to Neighbourhood Renewal* (Norwich: The Stationery Office).

Cabinet Office and DTLR (Department of Transport, Local Government and the Regions) (2002) *Your Region, Your Choice* (Norwich: The Stationery Office).

Chisholm, M. (2000) *Structural Reform of British Local Government: Rhetoric and Reality* (Manchester: Manchester University Press).

—— (2001) 'Economic Doctrines, Politics and Local Government Finance', *Journal of Local Government Law*, 4: 18–23.

Cirell, S. and Bennett, J. (2002) 'Welsh Lessons', *Public Finance*, June: 30.

Clarke, M., Davis, H., Hall, D. and Stewart, J. (1996) *Elected Mayors for Britain?* (Birmingham: School of Public Policy).

Copus, C. (2001) *It's my Party: The Role of the Group in Executive Arrangements* (London: LGA).

Corrigan, P. (2001) *The Case for the Public Interest Company: A New Form of Enterprise for Service Delivery* (London: Public Management Forum).

Council of Europe (1995) *The Size of Municipalities, Efficiency and Citizen Participation* (Strasbourg: Council of Europe).

—— (1998) *Regionalisation and its Effects on Local Self-Government* (Strasbourg: Council of Europe).

Cronin, T. (1989) *Direct Democracy* (Cambridge, Mass.: Harvard University Press).

Davis, H. Downe, J. and Martin, S. (2001) *External Inspection of Local Government: Driving Improvement or Drowning in Detail* (York: Joseph Rowntree Foundation).

Day, K. (n. d.) *What a Difference a Mayor Makes* (London: New Local Government Network).

DETR (Department of the Environment, Transport and the Regions) (1997) *New Leadership for London* (Norwich: The Stationery Office).

—— (1998a) *Modern Local Government: In Touch with the People* (London: DETR).

—— (1998b) *Modernising Local Government: Local Democracy and Community Leadership* (London: DETR).

—— (1998c) *Modernising Local Government: Improving Service through Best Value* (London: DETR).

—— (1999a) *Circular 10/99 Local Government Act 1999: Part 1 Best Value* (London: DETR).

—— (1999b) *The Beacon Scheme: How it will Work* (London: DETR).

—— (1999c) *First Report of the Advisory Panel on Beacon Councils* (London: DETR).

—— (1999d) *Lessons Learnt from Intervention: The Literature Review* (London: DETR).

—— (1999e) *Local Leadership: Local Choice* (London: DETR).

—— (2000a) *Preparing Community Strategies* (London: DETR).

—— (2000b) *Joining It up Locally* (London: DETR).

—— (2000c) *Best Value Indicators for 2001/2* (London: DETR).
—— (2000d) *Protocol on US. of Intervention Powers* (London: DETR).
—— (2000e) *Modernising Local Government Finance* (London: DETR).
—— (2000–2) *New Council Constitutions: Guidance Pack, Volume 1* (London: DETR).
—— (2001a) *Power to Promote or Improve Economic, Social or Environmental Well-Being* (London: DETR).
—— (2001b) *Local Strategic Partnerships* (London: DETR).
—— (2001c) *Pensions for Elected Member [sic] of Local Authorities* (London: DETR).
DOE (Department of the Environment) (1979) *Organic Change in Local Government* (London: DOE).
—— (1983) *Streamlining the Cities* (London: HMSO).
—— (1991a) *The Structure of Local Government in England* (London: DOE).
—— (1991b) *The Internal Management of Local Authorities in England* (London: DOE).
—— (1992) *Policy Guidance to the Local Government Commission for England* (London: DOE).
DOH (Department of Health) (2001) *On Tackling Health Inequalities* (London: DOH).
DTLR (Department of Transport, Local Government and the Regions) (2001a) *Strong Local Leadership: Quality Public Services* (London: DTLR).
DTLR (2001b) *Working with Others to Achieve Best Value* (London: DTLR).
—— (2001c) *Best Value Inspectorate Forum for England: Joint Statement on Better Local Inspection* (London: DTLR).
—— (2001d) *Supporting Strategic Delivery Partnerships in Local Government: A Research and Development Programme* (London: DTLR).
—— (2001e) *Local Public Service Agreements: New Challenges* (London: DTLR).
—— (2002a) *Guidance on Best Value Performance Indicators 2002/3* (London: DTLR).
—— (2002b) *Guidance Note: Best Value Performance Plans and Reviews* (London: DTLR).
—— (2002c) *A Review of Local Authority Statutory and Non-Statutory Service and Policy Planning Requirements* (London: DTLR).
—— (2002d) *Conduct of Councillors: Local Investigation and Determination of Misconduct Allegations: A Consultation Paper* (London: DTLR).
DTLR/LGA (Department of Transport, Local Government and the Regions and the Local Government Association) (2002) *E-Government Local: Towards a National Strategy of Local E-Gov* (London: DTLR).
Electoral Commission (2002) *Modernising Elections: A Strategic Evaluation of the 2002 Electoral Pilot Schemes* (London: Electoral Commission).
Fender, J. and Watt, P. (2002) 'Should Central Government Seek to Control the Level of Local Authority Expenditures', *Fiscal Studies*, June: 265–85.
Filkin, G., Allen, E. and Williams, J. (2001a) *Strategic Partnership for Service Delivery* (London: New Local Government Network).

Filkin, G., Stoker, G., Wilkinson, G. and Williams, J. (2001b) *Towards a New Localism* (London: New Local Government Network).

Fishkin, J. (1991) *Democracy and Deliberation* (New Haven, Conn: Yale University Press).

Game, C. and Leach, S. (1993) *Councillor Recruitment and Turnover: An Emerging Precipice* (Luton: Local Government Management Board).

Gibson, J. (1990) *The Politics and Economics of the Poll Tax: Mrs Thatcher's Downfall* (Warley: EMAS).

Hall, D., Dunstan, E. and Hobson, M. (1998) *Democratic Practice: A Guide* (London: Democratic Network).

Hall, D. and Stewart, J. (1996) *Citizens Juries in Local Government* (London: Local Government Management Board).

Hamsell, W. (1993) 'Council–Manager Government: A Form Whose Time has Come Again', *Quality Cities*, June: 6–7.

Hennock, E. (1973) *Fit and Proper Persons* (London: Edward Arnold).

Hetherington, P. (2000) *Back to the Future* (London: LGA).

Hood, C., Scott, C., James, O., Jones, G. and Travers, T. (1999) *Regulation Inside Government: Waste-Watchers, Quality Police, and Sleaze Busters* (Oxford: Oxford University Press).

ICMA (International City Management Association) (1989) *Service Delivery in the 1990s: Alternative Approaches for Local Government* (Washington, DC: ICMA).

IDeA (Improvement and Development Agency) (2000) *The Local Government Improvement Programme: A Year in Focus 1999–2000* (London: IDeA).

—— (2002) *National Census of Local Authority Councillors in England and Wales 2001* (London: IDeA).

INLOGOV (Institute of Local Government Studies) (2001) *Refurbishing Councillors' Worth to their Communities* (Birmingham: INLOGOV).

IPPR (Institute of Public Policy Research) (2000) *Delivering Change, Supporting Change* (London: IPPR).

—— (2001) *Building Better Partnerships: The Final Report of the Commission on Public Private Partnerships* (London: IPPR).

Jones, G. and Travers, T. (1996) 'Central Government Perceptions of Local Government', in L. Pratchett and D. Wilson (eds), *Local Democracy and Local Government* (London: Macmillan – now Palgrave Macmillan).

Kerley Report (2000) *Renewing Local Democracy* (Edinburgh: Scottish Executive).

Labour Party (1995a) *Renewing Democracy, Rebuilding Communities* (London: Labour Party).

Labour Party (1995b) *A Choice for England* (London: Labour Party).

Labour Party (1997) *New Labour because Britain Deserves Better* (London: Labour Party).

Labour Party (2001) *Ambitions for Britain* (London: Labour Party).

Laffin, M. Taylor, G. and Thomas, A. (2002) *A New Partnership?* (York: York Publishing Services).

Laski, H. (1935) 'The Committee System in Local Government', in H. Laski, I. Jennings and W. Robson (eds), *A Century of Municipal Progress* (London: Allen & Unwin).

Layfield Report (1976) *Committee on Local Government Finance: Report* (London: HMSO).

Le Galès, P. (1998) 'Conclusion – Government and Governance of Regions: Structural Weaknesses and New Mobilisations', in P. Le Galès and C. Lequesne (eds), *Regions in Europe* (London: Routledge).

Le Galès, P. and Mawson, J. (1995) *Management Innovations in Urban Policy: Lessons from France* (Luton: Local Government Management Board).

LGA (Local Government Association) (1999) *Futures Work: The Local Challenge* (London: LGA).

—— (2000a) *Powerpack: Using the New Power to Promote Well-Being* (London: LGA).

—— (2000b) *Elections – the 21st* Century Model: An Evaluation of May 2000 Local Elections Pilots (London: LGA).

—— (2000c) *Joining up the Local Jigsaw: Taking Forward the Local Challenge* (London: LGA).

—— (2001a) *Representing the People* (London: LGA).

—— (2001b) *Examples of Local Strategic Partnerships in Development* (London: LGA).

—— (2001c) *Improving Public Services: Local Public Service Agreements* (London: LGA).

LGA/LGMB (Local Government Association and Local Government Management Board) (1998) *The Local Government Improvement Model* (London: LGMB).

LGCE (Local Government Commission for England) (1993) *Renewing Local Government in the English Shires* (London: HMSO).

Lowndes, V., Pratchett, L. and Stoker, G. (2001a) 'Trends in Public Participation: Part 1, Local Government Perspective'; *Public Administration*, 79, 1: 205–22.

Lowndes, V., Pratchett, L. and Stoker, G. (2001b) 'Trends in Public Participation: Part 2, Citizens' Perspective', *Public Administration*, 79, 2: 445–56.

Lowndes, V., Stoker, G., Pratchett, L., Wilson, D. and Leach, S. (1998a) *Enhancing Public Participation in Local Government* (London: DETR).

Lowndes, V., Stoker, G., Pratchett, L., Wilson, D. and Leach, S. (1998b) *Guidance on Enhancing Public Participation in Local Government* (London: DETR).

Luke, J. (1998) *Leadership: Strategies for an Interconnected World* (San Francisco: Jossey-Bass).

Marquand, D. and Tomaney, J. (2000) *Democratising England* (London: Regional Policy Forum).

Martin, S., Davis, H., Bovaird, T., Downe, J., Geddes, H., Hartley, J., Lewis, M., Sanderson, I. and Sapwell, P. (2001) *Improving Public Services: Evaluation of the Pilot Projects: Final Report* (London: DETR).

Maud Report (1967a) *Committee on the Management of Local Government: Volume 1, Report* (London: HMSO).

Maud Report (1967b) *Committee on the Management of Local Government: Volume 2, The Local Government Councillor* (London: HMSO).

McIntosh Report (1999) *Moving Forward: Local Government and the Scottish Parliament* (Edinburgh: The Stationery Office).

Mill, J. S. (1904) *Considerations on Representative Government* (London: Routledge).

Miller, D. (1992) 'Deliberative Democracy and Social Choice', *Political Studies*, XL (Special Issue): 74–90.

NAO (National Audit Office) (2001) *Managing the Relationship to Secure a Successful Partnership in PFI Projects* (London: The Stationery Office).

—— (2003) *PFI: Construction Performance* (London: The Stationery Office).

National Civic League (1992) *Model City Charter*, 7th edn (Denver, Colo: National Civic League).

New Economic Foundation (2000) *Participation Works* (London: NEF).

Newman, J. (2001) *Modernising Government* (London: Sage).

Nolan Report (1997) *Standards of Conduct in Public Life: Report on Local Government* (London: HMSO).

Norton, A. (1994) *International Handbook of Local and Regional Government* (Aldershot: Edward Elgar).

ODPM (Office of the Deputy Prime Minister) (2002a) *Draft Circular on Best Value and Performance Improvement* (London: ODPM).

—— (2002b) *Consultation on the Local Government Formula Grant Distribution* (London: ODPM).

—— (2002c) *Tackling Poor Performance in Local Government* (London: ODPM).

—— (2002d) *Local Government Bill: Consultation on Draft Legislation* (London: ODPM).

—— (2002e) *Government Action following the Comprehensive Performance Assessment* (London: ODPM).

—— (2002f) *The Government's Response to the Transport, Local Government and Regional Affairs Sub-Committees Fourteenth Report on How the Local Government Act 2000 is Working* (Norwich: The Stationery Office).

ODPM/LGA (Office of the Deputy Prime Minister and the Local Government Association) (2002a) *Delivering our Priorities* (London: ODPM).

—— (2002b) *National Priorities* (London: ODPM).

OPM (Office for Public Management) (2002) *Process Evaluation of the Negotiation of Pilot Public Service Agreements* (London: OPM).

Osborne, S. (2000) 'Reformulating Wolfenden? The Roles and Impact of Local Development Agencies in Supporting Voluntary and Community Action in the UK', *Local Government Studies*, 26, 4: 23–48.

PIU (Performance and Innovation Unit, Cabinet Office) (2000) *Reaching Out: The Role of Central Government at Regional and Local Level* (Norwich: The Stationery Office).

Philpot, T. (2001) 'What a Performance', *Community Care*, October: 34–5.

Pimlott, B. and Rao, N. (2002) *Governing London* (Oxford: Oxford University Press).

Pollock, A., Shaoul, J., Rowland, D. and Player, S. (2001) *Public Services and the Private Sector* (London: Catalyst).

Prime Minister and Chancellor of the Duchy of Lancaster (1992) *The Citizen's Charter: First Report* (London: HMSO).

Rallings, C. and Thrasher, M. (1997) *Local Elections in Britain* (London: Routledge).

Rallings, C. and Thrasher, M. (1999–2001) *Local Elections Handbook* (Plymouth: University of Plymouth).

Rallings, C., Thrasher, M. and Downes, J. (1996) *Enhancing Local Electoral Turnout* (York: Joseph Rowntree Foundation).

Rao, N. (1992) *Managing Change: Councillors and the New Local Government* (York: Joseph Rowntree Foundation).

Rashman, L. and Hartley, J. (2002) 'Leading and Learning: Knowledge Transfer in the Beacon Council Scheme', *Public Administration*, 80, 3: 523–42.

Renner, T. and De Santis, V. (1998) 'Municipal Forms of Government: Issues and Trends', in International City/County Management Association, *Municipal Yearbook, 1998* (Washington, DC: ICMA).

Rittel, H. and Webber, M. (1973) 'Dilemmas in a General Theory of Planning', *Policy Sciences*, 4, 3: 155–69.

Rogers, S. (1998) 'Community Planning – a Report on the Pilot Projects', in *Community Planning and Engagement* (Birmingham: School of Public Policy, University of Birmingham).

Sandford, M. and MacQuail, P. (2001) *Unexplored Territory: Elected Regional Assemblies in England* (London: Constitution Unit, University College London).

Schumpeter, J. (1950) *Capitalism, Socialism and Democracy* (New York: Harper & Row).

Select Committee on the Environment, Transport and Regional Affairs: Environment Sub-Committee (1998) *Local Government Finance, Memorandum of Evidence 39* (London: The Stationery Office).

Select Committee on Public Administration (2001) *Public Participation: Issues and Innovations* (London: The Stationery Office).

Select Committee on Transport, Local Government and the Regions (2002a) *How the Local Government Act 2000 is Working* (London: The Stationery Office).

Select Committee on Transport, Local Government and the Regions (2002b) *Draft Local Government Bill* (London: The Stationery Office).

Snape, S., Leach, S. and Copus, C. (2002) *The Development of Overview and Scrutiny in Local Government* (London: ODPM).

SOLACE (Society of Local Authority Chief Executives) (2001) *Sing When You're Winning* (London: SOLACE).

Stewart, J. (1995) *Innovation in Democratic Practice* (Birmingham: INLOGOV).

—— (1996) *Further Innovation in Democratic Practice* (Birmingham: School of Public Policy, University of Birmingham).

—— (1997) *More Innovation in Democratic Practice* (Birmingham: School of Public Policy, University of Birmingham).

—— (1999) *From Innovation in Democratic Practice towards a Deliberative Democracy* (Birmingham: School of Public Policy, University of Birmingham).

—— (2000a) *The Nature of British Local Government* (Basingstoke: Palgrave Macmillan).

—— (2000b) *A Role for All Members: The Council Meeting* (London: LGA)

Stewart, J. and Stoker, G. (eds) (1995) *Local Government in the 1990s* (London: Macmillan – now Palgrave Macmillan).

Stewart, J., Leach, S. and Skelcher, C. (1978) *Organic Change* (Birmingham: Institute of Local Government Studies).

Stewart, M., Goss, S., Gillander, G., Clarke, R., Rowe, J. and Shaftoe, M. (1999) *Cross-cutting Issues Affecting Local Government* (London: DETR).

Stoker, G., John, P., Gains, F., Rao, N. and Harding, A. (2002) *The Implementation of New Council Constitutions and the New Ethical Framework: Report of ELG Survey Findings for ODPM Advisory Group* (London: ODPM).

Travers, T., Jones, G. and Burnham, J. (1993) *Impact of Population Size on Local Authority Costs and Effectiveness* (York: Joseph Rowntree Foundation).

Vickers, Sir Geoffrey (1972) *Freedom in a Rocking Boat* (Harmondsworth: Penguin).

Weisbrod, H. and Janoff, S. (1995) *Future Search* (San Francisco: Barrett Koehler).

Welsh Assembly (2002) *Freedom and Responsibility in Local Government* (Cardiff: The Welsh Assembly).

Widdicombe Report (1986) *Committee on the Conduct of Local Authority Business: Report* (London: HMSO).

Wilson, D. and Game, C. (2002) *Local Government in the United Kingdom*, 3rd edn (Basingstoke: Palgrave Macmillan).

Working Party on the Internal Management of Local Authorities in England (1993) *Community Leadership and Representation: Unlocking the Potential* (London: HMSO).

Yankelovich, D. (1991) *Coming to Public Judgment: Making Democracy Work in a Complex World* (Syracus, NY: Syracuse University Press).

Young, K. and Rao, N. (1994) *Coming to Terms with Change? The Local Government Councillor in 1993* (London: LGC Communications).

Index